Banyan Tree Adventures

Travels in India

Banyan Tree Adventures

Travels in India

Keith Forrester

BOOKS

Winchester, UK
Washington, USA

First published by O-Books, 2018
O-Books is an imprint of John Hunt Publishing Ltd., 3 East St., Alresford,
Hampshire SO24 9EE, UK
office1@jhpbooks.net
www.johnhuntpublishing.com

For distributor details and how to order please visit the 'Ordering' section on our website.

Text copyright: Keith Forrester 2017

ISBN: 978 1 78535 808 1
978 1 78535 809 8 (ebook)
Library of Congress Control Number: 2017960373

A CIP catalogue record for this book is available from the British Library.

Design: Stuart Davies

Printed and bound by CPI Group (UK) Ltd, Croydon, CR0 4YY, UK

We operate a distinctive and ethical publishing philosophy in
all areas of our business, from our global network of authors to
production and worldwide distribution.

Contents

Map of India   x

Chapter 1. An Introduction   **1**
An unusual month?   1
Doing tourism   12
The Raj   17
Travel writing   19
Powering ahead?   21
A vignette: a Colaba walk   24

Chapter 2. India for the first time   **33**
A working knowledge   33
India for the first time   37
So where do tourists go?   42
The Tourist business in India   57
Being a tourist   64

Chapter 3. Fighting over the past   **67**
Navigating history; Akbar and the Mughals   67
The 'Indic civilisation'   73
The Indus Valley civilisation   77
The Ashoka discoveries   80
Ajanta and Ellora Caves   82
Down south – the temple trail and their dynasties   84
History in the crossfire   90

Chapter 4. Konkani blues   **99**
Magical Goa   99
Portugal, Goa and India   104
Those beaches   108
Green Goa   113

Goa and tourism – dark clouds in the blue sky? 118
And the Goans themselves – being a Goan 126
A vignette: the Great India Roadtrip 130

Chapter 5. That Empire – then and now **139**
Calcutta delights 139
Post-colonial understandings 144
So what were the British doing in India? 148
Has India always been poor? The economic debate 154
Some good, some bad 159
Partition and Britain's secrets 164
Post-colonial dilemmas 168

**Chapter 6. The 'Uncertain Glory': poverty
   and riches** **172**
Searching for that key 172
The shock of the everyday 176
"Tolerance of the intolerable" 185
Abolishing hunger? 188
Working, India style 194
"The monster that crosses your path" 198
Women and the 'new' India 206

Chapter 7. "The nearest thing to another planet" **211**
Contradictory tourists 211
"Clothes, ganeshas and bangles" back home 215
Bollywood and the land of the mad hatter 218
The imperial game 225
Why cricket and why India? 232

Chapter 8. Getting richer and its problems **237**
On the move 237
'India Shining' 240
Rural desperation 247

The new middle class. "We are coming, we
    are developing."   250
Looking out for the environment   256
Shit everywhere   260
'So, how is India?'   265

Chapter 9. The "good days are ahead"   **270**
The great experiment   270
Modi and the India of 2014   275
India's democratic 'top dressing'   286
Secular India   291

Chapter 10. Of Tigers and Elephants   **299**
The Sri Lanka nightmare   299
An overbusy military   302
That background noise   309

To Susan, Jack, Jim and Alice in memory of that first visit to India in December 2003.

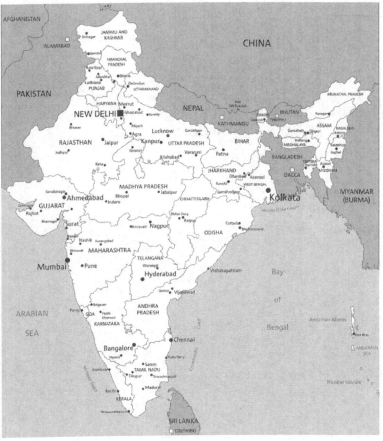

Map of India

Chapter 1

An Introduction

An unusual month?

One of my favourite venues in Bombay (now renamed Mumbai) is the Oval Maidan in the southern business district of the city. Like most Indian cities, Mumbai does not have too many open public spaces but the Oval Maidan (or 'ground') together with the Cross Maidan across the road is one such space. Renovated and run by volunteers since 1997, the Maidan is 750 metres long and usually features half a dozen overlapping cricket games involving teams in matching outfits – sometimes white. This important recreational space in the centre of busy Bombay is surrounded by palm trees and today is protected by the newly-painted steel fencing. Entrance to the Maidan is limited to two gates halfway along the park which join the always busy pathway across the park. Seating within the Oval Maidan amounts to a few benches, invariably occupied. At the end of the day with all the matches completed, out comes the elaborately decorated watering lorries pulling trailers loaded with six-foot nets to fence off the cricket squares and a team of groundsman to attend to the pitches – all very professional. Grass seed and soil are scattered across the cricket squares, carefully watched by waiting groups of pigeons.

In the midst of the noisy crazy bustle of the Colaba district in this most southern stretch of Bombay, the Maidans provide a rare oasis of relative calm and orderly activity. I have spent many an hour usually in the cooler late afternoons sitting on the red dusty ground with my back resting against one of the palm trees watching simultaneously three or four cricket games and even, to the amazement of myself and bewilderment of local Mumbaikars, a game of touch rugby. As it is usually in the months of January through to April that I visit India, all that I need for my Oval Maidan trips is water and shade. It helps of course if you enjoy cricket which I do, even though the experience is a little different to that of Headingley in Leeds, Yorkshire.

However, it is not only sporting goings-on within the Oval Maidan that is of interest; it is also the surrounds of the park. These seem to encapsulate important aspects of the city's recent history. Immediately to the east for example, and halfway down is the Big Ben-like Rajabai Clock Tower rising from the Mumbai University Library. Built in 1874, the university looks very much like one of the older British universities. To the left of the university is the imposing Bombay High Court, still very much in business as the numerous black-gowned employees congregating outside the tea and coffee stands testify. The Old Secretariat housing the offices of the Maharashtra State's chief minister and other top officials adjoins the university and is similarly built in the same Gothic-style buff-coloured stone brought in from Gujarat. Walking along the street – Mayo Road, now renamed Baburao Patel Marg – is a little intimidating with the towering Gothic architecture all protected by heavily armed military police personnel at every entrance. Across on the opposite, western, side of the Oval Maidan is Queen's Road. It is the Queen's Road residents who are today responsible for the maintenance and upkeep of the Oval Maidan. Back in the 1920s the British reclaimed this part of the southern Bombay peninsula from the sea and extended the land some 700 metres through to the famous Marine Drive. The Maidan was established as a recreational ground and was used as a dog and horse showground (naturally!) in the late nineteenth, early twentieth century before falling into disrepair. So today, it is to the Queen's Road residents that I owe a debt of gratitude for my many hours of pleasure and indolence spent at 'their' park. Walking along Queen's Road underneath the magnificent row of sprawling Banyan trees that line the middle of the dual carriageway, the Victorian art deco buildings provide an arresting political footnote to the pretentiousness of the occupying powers' architectural tastes and styles when contrasted with the dark Gothic monuments on the opposite side of the Oval Maidan. The matching Victorian art deco housing alongside Queen's Road, and built by the local Parsi community, still retain their rather wistful colonial names such as Fairlawn, Palm Court, Belvedere Court and, of course, Empress Court.

Wandering around the Oval Maidan looking for something to eat or on my way back to my nearby hotel, I pass a number of other favourite landmarks – the cubist inspired 1940 Parsi community's church (the Bhikha Behram Well), the 1889 colonial Western Railway Headquarters with its mix of Gothic and Indian design, the art deco Eros cinema and, of course, Churchgate station. Although not so grand and dramatic as the nearby Victoria Terminus – now renamed Chhatrapati Shivaji Terminus (CST), Churchgate has a more local city feel despite being one of the busiest stations in the world. There is a coffee bar opposite Churchgate which I often visit in the evening rush hour to watch the hundreds of thousands of commuters rushing to catch their trains out to the suburbs. The other attraction at this time of the evening is the beginnings of the night market on the pavements around the station – out of nowhere, hundreds of traders appear spreading their blankets or sheets of plastic on the pavements and selling everything that the passers-by never really wanted until they saw the cheap prices. Indians must be amongst the most impulsive consumers anywhere gauging by the crowds that quickly gather around each patch of blanket or plastic. On some of the smaller backstreets around the station are numerous street families with their tidy bit of pavement fenced off with pots and pans and with the barefooted children running around, immune to the traffic or walkers attempting to share the pavement.

I have often wondered why it is that I enjoy so much this little corner of India. It helps obviously that I enjoy watching cricket (and even managed to catch the opening games of the one-day Women's World Cup cricket championship in February 2013 at the nearby Brabourne Stadium). It might also be due to a certain smugness on my behalf arising from the hot dry weather of Mumbai while the rest of Europe struggles with the cold and the snow. There are possibly more serious reasons. Sitting there in the Oval Maidan, there are the sounds and the sights of the 'new' India, of a country and economy on the move, and at the centre of this movement is Mumbai (or Bombay as the city is still commonly known). Modern skyscrapers with prominent advertising displays are visible from most vantage points in the Oval park. And of course, there are the traffic, noise, smells and sheer mass of people moving around the Maidan that suggest everywhere energy, activity and purpose. It is not without reason that Bombay, and more generally India, welcomes politely a steady trek of European political leaders with their eager crowd of business personnel in tow. A certain weariness but national pride characterises the press reports of the visits. This picture of modernity, however, contrasts somewhat with the very visible images of the recent imperial colonial history; the British were here, expected to be here forever and constructed buildings, industries and infrastructure that were designed to make this an economic and political reality and, also just as important, to remind the local population of this fact. Perhaps for me, it is the cricket in the Maidan together with the surrounding British Gothic architecture that keep the historical imperial past a continuing part of the modern. On the other hand, it might be my own colonial childhood in central Africa that foregrounds this past with the present. Whatever the reasons, few countries that have experienced the colonial domination and oppression inflicted on India by the British have, it seems to me, managed to encompass this history with the contemporary in a way that is the case in India.

This is a book about the historical and the contemporary in

India but also it is about visiting tourists' experiences and views of this India. When I first visited India in late December 2003 with Susan and our three young children – Jack, Jim and Alice – it was on a short ten-day visit that was the beginning of a longer three-month adventure to a variety of countries in Southeast Asia and South America. It was India, however, that for me had the greatest impact. I don't think that any of us, like most first-time visitors, will ever forget those first few days wandering around the Colaba district in southern Bombay. The noise, the sheer volume of people everywhere, the traffic and tuc-tucs, the colours and the heat limited our walking to around an hour or so: rest and appraisal was necessary. It was exhilarating if a little scary. Urban understandings and expectations were challenged, often collapsed and then had to be revised.

Talking to other tourists in Mumbai and later in Goa, another unexpected feature became apparent. Most of these overseas tourists had visited India many times and were very knowledgeable and enthused about particular parts of India and different aspects of Indian culture, history and politics. I was staggered. While we pored slavishly over our guides to the country, these tourists appeared to be visiting encyclopaedias. They had been all over the place in this huge country, were knowledgeable about particular peoples and places, and seemed well versed in making sense of the stories from the daily newspapers. Since that first visit in 2003–4, Susan and I have returned to India some five or six times visiting different parts of the country on the wonderful train network and, always, seeking guidance from local people as well as these overseas tourists. Slowly, we are becoming more familiar with little bits of this complex, contradictory but absorbing country. Slowly we are acquiring friends from different cities that we have visited and, slowly, we are getting more familiar with the newspapers, journals and more popular authors. It is always 'slowly' because we are never in a rush and, anyway, India can't be rushed but is best enjoyed at a snail's pace.

This book then is about India. It is not a guidebook; there are many such books already available. They are invariably all good and are excellent for getting you about on a restricted timescale with different places and sites to cover. It is not a sightseeing book; again, numerous such books are available, nor is it a diary or travelogue-type of book. Not only are there many such popular travelogues but there is an enormous amount of popular literature about historical and contemporary India written by local authors, journalists and scholars. Any perusal at the literature available on the plastic sheets spread out on the pavements in the great Indian cities (and especially, Bombay) suggests a culture that takes the printed word seriously. Many of my most enjoyable reads about India have come from the recommendations of these street sellers. They know their stuff.

For foreign visitors to India or those simply interested in understanding more about the country, it's not only books. The 'serious' journals and magazines that are available dwarf the equivalent output in most European countries, and certainly Britain. Sometimes it seems that India has bookshops like we have banks or estate agents on our high streets. Some of the journals I have noticed over the years are getting more difficult to get hold of. The excellent monthly journal of politics and culture *The Caravan*, for example, used to be available literally 'on the streets' but is now more difficult to spot. Of course the street vendors will get it for you on a regular basis if they trust that you will be back next month. Similarly, the sparky, opinionated, polemical but always readable *Economic and Political Weekly* (*EPW*) is a favourite search for me when in India. Most good bookshops usually stocked the magazine but today it is more difficult to find. I suspect that the *EPW* was always poorly circulated and instead depended on its readers seeking out the current edition – an unusual business model. On the other hand, perhaps it is a case of the digital format slowly replacing the hard copy text.

The numerous weekly or biweekly news commentary magazines by contrast still remain available everywhere – a wonderful variety reflecting different perspectives and content. For anyone from abroad interested in keeping abreast of developments in India, there are no excuses beyond the problem of time.

So this is not a guidebook or a travelogue on India. It is a 'tourist' book in that it uses and discusses the Indian experiences and views of non-domestic travellers in their explorations and adventures around this huge country. As mentioned above, when we arrived in India for the first time in 2003–4, I was surprised to meet other tourists who had visited the country many times, had visited different parts of the country over the years and who were pretty knowledgeable about aspects of culture, politics or the country's geography. Eventually in 2013, I decided to record a number of informal discussions with this group. I was becoming more interested in India, was reading more about the country and had visited a number of areas and cities in the country. What, I wondered, did these tourists find interesting in the country, why did they keep returning and where had they been? These questions interested me and, I assumed, would be of interest to a wider audience. They would open up issues and parts of the country that we didn't know about or hadn't visited. The people I talked to were not a particular sample, carefully selected to represent certain characteristics. Instead they were the opposite – eight or nine people who happened, in the main, to reside in the same homestay in Goa as me and who had visited India a number of times. I had met most of them before but not everyone. In Sany's case for example I hadn't met her before, but over breakfast one morning heard her talking to some local workmen in Konkani, the local language of the western coast – fluent, flowing and confident Konkani. I was most impressed. Where, I wondered, did a person from just outside Paris, France pick up this language and what were her experiences of India? So I asked if she would mind if we had a discussion around her times in India and that I recorded it. Thankfully, she agreed. Listening back to the tapes reminded me it was less a 'discussion' and more a case of me listening to her in an apprehensive silence. She seemed to enjoy the excuse to sound off on all the frustrations that had accumulated over a few years. In the main though I had met with the interviewees before 2013 when I did the interviews.

So it was very much a 'non-scientific' series of discussions with these foreign tourists. I have used their observations and experiences throughout the book but especially in the next two chapters. Their comments and observations have provided a springboard as it were for me to bounce off and to add my own commentary and experiences. Above all though I learned from them a lot about India. They had done things that I hadn't or had been to places I wouldn't be visiting. The discussions broadened my understandings, introduced me to new topics and, sometimes, forced me rethink my own experiences. Very briefly the people I interviewed were:

- Gina (with her partner Mick in the background) who has visited India some 24 times. She first came to India in 1991 because of the Gulf War. It was either going to Africa or India – India won. Gina is from Britain and works part-time in a post office.
- Steven is a chartered accountant and works in the City of London. Like Gina, it was in the early 1990s when he first came to India. Since then he has returned to the country many times.
- Andy has been to India 8 or 9 times, usually for quite long stays of 2–3 months. Andy works as a care assistant in Britain but likes to get away from the British winters as often as possible.
- Janet and Mike have been to India about 8 times and usually stay for about 6 months at a time. They own a caravan park

in Colorado in the USA, probably "like a Hill Station here in India". Their park is high in the mountains at around 3,000 metres and during winter is closed due to the depth of the snow.

- Sheila and Tony who first arrived in India in 1986 have returned 20–30 times. They have been elsewhere but "nowhere else filled the gap". Sheila and Tony live near us in Yorkshire, UK and it was they who first suggested we visit India and them, on our trip with the children in 2003–4. Both Sheila and Tony have traditionally worked on a part-time basis (in education and landscape gardening) back in England.

- Helle Ryslinge is from Copenhagen, Denmark. She is an actress and filmmaker who has been to India "many, many times". I didn't know Helle before I interviewed her. I met her as she was staying next door to me in the homestay.

- Sany from Paris, France has been coming to India for 10 years and occasionally spent considerable time on particular visits – up to two and half years on one trip.

- Pauline and Sjoerd first came to India in 1997 and have visited India about 13 times. Pauline is from Britain and Sjoerd from the Netherlands.

- Jeff is from Britain but lives and works in Munich, Germany. He first visited India in 1997 and has returned about 12 times. Jeff works as a tour guide in Munich and is able to take time off from his work during European winters.

As is clear from these notes, this is a very eclectic but experienced group of visitors to India. As already mentioned, they were not a selected group but simply, in the main, stayed at the same homestay as myself. The only criteria used in their selection was that they had visited India a number of times. I had never come across groups of 'frequent travellers' to the same place before. I was staggered. And as I have come to realise, there are hundreds and probably thousands of other frequent visitors I could have interviewed. Each of them would have very interesting, absorbing but different stories to tell about their times in India. I am most grateful to my small group for agreeing to discuss with me their experiences and for their patience and insights.

The issues and questions that I discussed with these frequent returners to India will become clearer in subsequent chapters, especially in the next chapter. Why India for example, and why not some other country? What is it and where is it in India that attracts them, and how do they choose to spend their time while in India? Where have they been and what aspects of Indian culture, policy and history interest them and why? So, while the Taj Mahal or the magnificent medieval Meenakshi Temple in southern Tamil Nadu do not prominently figure in the following chapters (see the numerous guide and sightseeing books), there is instead a focus on trying to understand and interpret the 'everyday' sensitivities of being-in and travelling-around India. Given that trains are the preferred mode of travel for these Indian tourists, for example, what I wondered is the financial health of the network, how was it shaped by the colonial powers and what part does it play in the lives of Indians? Or take one of the most infamous features of India today – poverty; how widespread are the poor and what are some of the reforms and political initiatives that have attempted to address this problem? How does caste, religion and gender contribute towards resolving or strengthening poverty in India? How do these overseas tourists cope, understand and explain the shocking evidence of poverty while travelling around the country? Their 'understandings' and mine as well to these and other complicated questions and issues don't take the form of dissertations. Instead, they are the result of an interest and enthusiasm to people and things around them, a working knowledge developed through reading and conversations with other interested parties while in India, and also on their return home. Regularly reading some of the numerous English daily newspapers available in India as is done by many long-stay visitors develops a growing awareness of macro and micro Indian agendas that informs discussion and analysis in the local community as well as at the national level. There is, in other words, an everyday working knowledge of aspects of India that contextualises this tourist group's experiences of 'being a tourist' and which, in my interviews with them, I was keen to explore.

It is this 'context' that is a major consideration for me as will be seen in the discussions within this book. I remember one morning in February 2013 sitting down after breakfast, having finished the morning's newspapers, and jotting some notes on these 'wider happenings' that were around at that time. Some of the 'contextual headlines' during this period, for example, included:

- Continuing mass demonstrations in Delhi and elsewhere in India against the rape by a group of six men of a 23-year-old physiotherapist student in Delhi on 16th December 2012.
- On 8th February 2013, Mohammed Guru from Kashmir was secretly executed in New Delhi. According to the Supreme Court, Guru was one of those responsible for the attack on Parliament House and which resulted in the death of nine people. Against a background of widespread protest in Kashmir, the region was placed under indefinite curfew. A number of Indian journals were busy examining the "mockery of the constitutional principles of the rule of law and due process".
- On 9th and 10th February, over 120 million devotees attended the Maha Kumbh Mela (religious festival held every 12 years) near Allahabad in North India where the sacred rivers of the Ganges and Yamuna meet.
- On the 12th February, another major corruption scandal

was outlined in the national press involving several major politicians and military officers allegedly receiving bribes from the European helicopter manufacturer AgustaWestland. India purchased twelve helicopters at a cost of 560 million Euros in 2010 from AgustaWestland.

- On 20th and 21st February, a national strike organised by all eleven national trade unions closed down most urban centres throughout India. This was the first time ever that all trade union confederations had worked together.
- On 21st February two 'terrorist bombs' exploded in Hyderabad in Andhra Pradesh, killing 17 people and injuring at least 119 other people.
- On 21st February, India played Australia in the first of four cricket Test Matches. India won all four matches.
- Throughout February, there was a relentless push within the State and national media promoting Narendra Modi from the BJP political party as a Prime Ministerial candidate in the 2014 general elections. Modi is a controversial and divisive politician in a controversial and divisive party.

Doing tourism

Was this an unusual month? Would any other month have been different to this February in 2013? Of course, I don't know but I doubt it. Corruption scandals, the fortunes of the Indian cricket team, military activity in Kashmir, religious festivals, trade union activity and even 'bombings' are not rare events in India. However, what these February headlines do illustrate is the day-to-day 'background noise' within which touristic activities are situated and experienced. Visiting Jodhpur in Rajasthan or trekking in the mountains around Darjeeling in West Bengal does not occur in a vacuum – there is always 'background noise'. Most of the 'tourists' interviewed for this book were aware to a greater or lesser extent of these February news items. These episodes helped shape and influence their understandings and narratives about where they had been and what they had seen. Despite being 'outsiders', there was this engagement with aspects of Indian everyday reality as portrayed in the newspapers and as discussed with local people. In a small number of cases, this engagement resulted in extended periods of professional practice being undertaken in India over a number of years. For most people, their visits to India had resulted in the discovery and practice of new interests and of a deeper historical awareness not only about India but also their own country. None of this of course is particularly unusual or surprising although it is rarely documented. Instead the overwhelming emphasis in the media and in the written word on visits to India is on 'touristic' descriptions and itineraries, many of them very valuable and illuminating. In my own case, it was this unusual, I think, encounter between the 'outsider tourist' experience with the routine contextual circumstances in India that was of interest and that I missed when reading some of the popularly-available travel literature. Do most people go to school, how much does it cost and is it any good? What is that film that is drawing crowds every day outside that cinema? What do people do when they are ill, how do they earn a living, and have things changed that much over the years? None of these questions are particular to India – indeed, they might be very similar to Indian tourists visiting Europe or some other unfamiliar country. The interesting thing though – for me, anyway – is that for this particular group of 'tourists', it was tourism or 'being a tourist' that opened up these areas of interest and inquiry. Tourism as a way of engagement or agency is not usually coupled together.

If these 'contextual features' of February 2013 listed above and the subsequent questions that arise from the list suggest the sort of things that interest me as a traveller, they also hint or suggest why this is not a guidebook or a travel diary or a holiday memoir. Most of the things that interest me while in different or new countries are not the focus of guidebooks although you often find brief historical or cultural outlines in the Appendix sections.

The notions of 'tourist' or of 'tourism', however, carries a variety of connotations – passive, consuming, escapism, arrogance, affluence, for example. This is especially the case when talking about 'foreign' tourists which is invariably the case in this book. These implications are often negative and mainly embedded within a marketing or business model. The 'tourists' in this book who discuss their experiences of India are of a particular group (of which I am a member) in that they are white, from rich parts of the world, include both females and males and have visited India many times but, apart from Sany, don't speak any of India's indigenous languages. These characteristics will shape obviously their perceptions and understandings of India as is explored in later chapters – as they shape mine. In one sense, the entire book can be read as a discussion of 'tourism', albeit a particular variety of tourism. It is perhaps more a tourism of 'everyday life' in India set against a varying background of geography, history, politics and culture. In fact, 'tourism' – its nature, its consequences, its relation to other sectors and developments in society – emerged as an interest for me while thinking about India and this book. How could this not be the case when I was one of these 'tourists'? It was quite an eye-opener. I didn't realise for example how large and popular a subject 'tourism' or 'hospitality studies' is within British higher education – very large and growing. This probably reflects the heightened emphasis on jobs, employment and vocationalism that seems to define increasingly university learning in Britain today. But there were also more interesting perspectives to some of these studies; a more sociological influence that treats the nature of 'the tourist' or of 'tourism' as problematic and not something straightforward. By adopting a view that tourism is not understood similarly by everyone provides a more critical discussion of people like me and what we do when we travel to other countries. In contrast to these more critical discussions, there are numerous government and multi-agency reports and studies on tourism that reflect the economic importance of tourism to local and national development from around the world. In fact, this perspective seems to be the dominant narrative within these types of studies and generally to have a simple, causal and operational focus. There appears to be a large quantity of literature discussing how best to measure this growth and significance. More interesting though for me are the former, more conceptual and critical explorations of trying to understand the nature of the tourist experience. In such discussions for example, there is analysis of tourism as expressions of power, of seeing tourism in poorer countries as incorporating existing exploitations, inequalities and social divisions, of ignoring the displacement (of people, of traditional jobs such as fishing, of lands, of forests) and of ignoring other aspects such as the climate change consequences of the industry. The 'tourist industry' in any country and not just India doesn't exist in a vacuum. Instead it is a part of wider economic and social relationships. Even 'socially responsible tourism' manages often to hide the implications of these wider concerns and relationships. From a post-colonial perspective there is talk of a modern tourism characterised by the servant of yesteryear becoming the host of today, often in partnership with the local or national state. Other more theoretical studies concentrate on understanding the nature of 'being a tourist' where attention focuses on a detachment from one's natural environment, the importance of 'play' as part of being a tourist and the importance of 'being away' (language, infrastructure, ethnicity, values) from one's normal environment. These are important considerations and are worth the effort of trying to get to grips with the issues they raise. Some of these issues will be returned to in subsequent chapters. Difficult as are some of these issues, they certainly go way beyond the rather bland, uncritical definition of tourism by the World Tourism Organization (WTO): namely, that "tourism comprises the activities of persons traveling to and staying in places outside their usual environment for not more than one consecutive year for leisure..."

So yes, I did get more interested in all things 'tourist' when thinking, discussing and reading about Indian travels, and also, thinking about my own experiences. I understood along with the people I interviewed that 'understanding' India would always be a very partial and incomplete process, irrespective of how much time and attention we spent on this effort. We would always be 'like fish out of water', different, materially and culturally set apart. Our arguments and analysis with each other deep into the warm Indian nights would and will always display gross misunderstandings and cultural prejudices despite our best efforts and ignorance on a grand scale. But and here is the strange thing, it doesn't matter. What we and me in this book are doing is trying to better understand and engage with this country that fascinates most of us and which we return to periodically. Yes, we might go elsewhere away from home on visits but India somehow retains this special affection and interest that has developed over many years. India is *so* different and mind-boggling. Everyone soon realises that after their first few hours in the country. The ride from the airport to the city centre remains an abiding memory for most first-time foreign visitors. Regular returners have realised this but enjoy the emotional, aesthetic and intellectual experience of trying to make sense of the country. It is an 'enjoyment' characterised by frustration, self-satisfaction, cul-de-sacs, contradictions and achievement, as my interviews demonstrated. It's all very strange. I'm sure that within the vast annals of 'tourist studies', there will be some studies of the 'psychological deficits' of these types of visitors but I won't be bothering to track them down.

The Raj

So yes, my own visits to India and thinking about this book led to a general interest in tourism and being a tourist. The other unexpected 'discovery' that emerged in visits to different parts of India and in my reading and explorations of various issues was the Raj connection. The Imperial connection between India and Britain is hard to ignore for Western visitors. It depends obviously on where you go, but in most areas and regions of this vast country, there is seemingly this British connection. For me coming from Britain, these connections might be more pertinent, raw and immediate than for visitors from other Western countries. Irrespective of where these foreign visitors come from, however, they will be aware to some extent of this colonial relationship. Some of the seminal and globally important historical episodes of the twentieth century revolved around the breaking of this relationship. The Independence of India in August 1947 for example was not only the culmination of many decades of struggle by Indians through the subcontinent but also heralded the beginning of the end for the mightiest Empire the world had ever seen. Africa and especially South Africa together with Vietnam recognised what was possible and drew inspiration from India's struggles. For Britain in the end, it all unravelled so quickly that the country today continues to adjust to this loss of imperial legacy and understand itself as a small insignificant island situated offshore from continental Europe. It is finding this new role difficult as assumptions of 'what once were' continue to inform its present-day practices, assumptions and policies, especially in the area of foreign policy. A key to any understanding of Britain over the last six or seven decades is India – not the only key, but one of the master keys. It might have been 'in the past' but it continues today to haunt and shape who we are as British and, possibly, the slow break-up of the 'United Kingdom'.

The subsequent relationships of the coloniser with its former colonies are always complicated and confusing. Where power, exploitation and oppression are involved, there will always be tears during and after the ending of the relationship. The problem is that the 'ending' is not always that clear cut. It often continues but in ways that are different. So in the second decade of the twenty-first century, we have here in Britain a lively debate supported by major television series and publications around the benefits or otherwise of the country's past imperial adventures. India – 'the jewel in the crown' – figures largely in these discussions. Although the debates have been unsurprisingly not too critical of the Empire enterprise they have reinforced a number of features in this history. To take a few examples: firstly they have demonstrated the continuing fascination for India within British history and culture. Secondly various painful but important historical episodes of Britain's time in India remain hidden or ignored. The Bengal Famine of 1943 where some three million people died of starvation and disease is an obvious case in point. Other 'mysterious' examples include the disappearance of almost any recognition and memorial to arguably the world's first multinational company – the East India Company.

The reasons for these omissions might be controversial but there is that saying that histories of the dominant tend to reflect the views and perspectives of the dominant. Britain's time in India in general does not disprove this saying, unfortunately. For the tourist in India especially in the great cities, however, Britain is a part of the tourist experience. So prevalent was the British presence that it is difficult to ignore its legacies.

Similar to most other foreign tourists in India then I rekindled an interest in the British Empire and its time in India. This theme forms an important focus in Chapter 5 where I suggest that one cannot understand either India or Britain today without revisiting their time together.

Travel writing

This then is a travel book about travelling around India. Travel books have formed an important genre in English writing and publications. Their popularity has varied over time but today in most bookshops in the West, there is a 'travel writing' section next to the 'country guides' section. I have always enjoyed reading travel writing, although as usual it takes time to identify publications that satisfy what you are looking for – the variations within 'travel writing' are huge. At the time of the British Empire, many of these publications were little more than apologies for the imperial enterprise – and were very popular. For some modern scholars such as Edward Said, travelogues figured prominently in his critique of 'Orientalism' – the patronising process whereby Western writers or painters or designers appropriate or claim ownership (intellectually, culturally) of distinct, different ('oriental') processes or products from non-Western countries. The hidden or explicit agenda was usually to legitimate further the dominance of the West. Other commentators have talked of the 'imperialist travelogue'. Perhaps the most famous examples of this category of travel writers and explorers were the national heroes David Livingstone or Richard Burton, who were seen as bringing British civilisation (and Christianity) to the wilds of Africa in the nineteenth century. Supported and funded by the Royal Geographic Society, their success greatly encouraged further publications promoting overseas expansion. Things and times have changed and today travel writing too has changed significantly. The collapse of empires, rise of mass tourism, television travel documentaries and 'globalisation' have all contributed towards a reshaping of the writing concerns. There is today for example a more subjective theme, a greater self-awareness and a greater emphasis on subject matter rather than outlines of unknown territories. Issues of 'identity' and 'belonging' can be identified in much of the new writing. Revisiting well-known places is not uncommon. Instead of a focus on the 'exotic', the emphasis now is on examining our widely-shared assumptions and perspectives of these well-known venues to critically discuss any of a number of themes, such as power, sexuality or colour. These are the new 'counter-travellers' as someone put it. They might not be as popular as David Livingstone or Marco Polo but they are certainly more interesting. Our very understanding of 'travel' is under attack, they suggest.

All writers or tourists visiting another country are constrained and inhibited by their cultural and economic circumstances. They cannot simply drop or ignore who they are, their assumptions and beliefs. And these distorted, contradictory and partial subjectivities are what we use to enjoy ourselves and attempt to make sense of our surroundings. Not very encouraging I know but it's the best we can do. There is of course always a sense of learning, of discovery, sometimes of awe and, usually, of pleasure. We experience these reflexively – in a kind of circular process whereby the 'new' or different changes or, if not changes, at least challenges our assumptions and perspectives. Such a view entails introspection and, especially in a country like India, an awareness that one's presence affects the situations and relationships encountered. Again, this is a not too optimistic or easy view of how things work in the social world but it is at least a recognition that 'being a tourist' or 'travel writer' is problematic and needs thinking about.

How well I manage these constraints and problems in the subsequent chapters will have to be judged by the readers. This book though is about travelling around India by myself, ourselves and by those I interviewed. It's a big country and, even with help, there are areas which haven't been visited by any of us (yet). It is also a book about aspects of India itself. Against a backdrop of travel, a number of issues and concerns are examined, however briefly, which to me anyway seemed important and distinctively 'Indian'. Cricket and Bollywood are looked at together with the horrors of Partition, the claims of secularism and the nature and extent of poverty. In the main, the topics examined are oversimplified but they do seem to me to be part of the understandings of modern India. I use the plural of 'understanding' deliberatively as there are many different understandings of this vast, complex country. This will always be the case I would argue, irrespective of which country visited. However, as I discuss in Chapter 3, there is in India today an edge, viciousness and even violence to these 'understandings'. The rise of a muscular, narrowly doctrinaire form of Hinduism – Hindutva – encouraged by the present government of Prime Minister Narendra Modi, is raising concerns in India and elsewhere. In these instances, 'understandings' don't come cheap. But then again, tourism or travelling should not be easy despite the best efforts of the industry's marketing campaigns.

Powering ahead?

Today is a good time to be interested in India. As most of the world realises, India has emerged as a major global player over the last two or three decades. Its most well-known claim to fame at the moment is as the world's fastest growing economy. Even in 2017–18 with major economic wobbles apparent in the global economy, India is steaming ahead. Media headlines abound speculating on when India will overtake China in the growth tables. Engineering technology is seen as a major component of the 'Indian phenomenon'. The software and information technology expertise is well known, millions of top class engineers and scientists are turned out on a regular basis, annual investment is OK and there is an abundance of cheap labour – the so-called 'demographic dividend'. With a mind-boggling 1.3 billion people including a very large number of young people, India has this huge domestic market. Prized above all is the rapid growth of 'the middle class' which has quadrupled over the last decade or so to a total of around 260 million. As the

International Monetary Fund said recently, India's economy is "a bright spot in a cloudy global horizon." The future it seems belongs to India. Or does it?

The economic success story of India is well known. So too is the poverty story. Perhaps even more powerful than images of success are the images of the country's grinding poor. The booming economy of course has substantially reduced the number of poor (some 200 million is a common total) but estimates suggest that 12 million new jobs a year are needed; that's 100 million jobs over the next decade to accommodate the poor and growing population. The scale of challenges facing the country are immense and difficult to comprehend.

Also well known is India's democratic record, the largest democratic country in the world. Reaching decisions in a country with its 29 disparate states reduces the possibility of fast change and reform. Almost alone from Britain's empire, India emerged with liberal and democratic institutions, and almost alone in the world, it is a country where the poorest of the electorate are the most enthusiastic voters. India's success was immediate and came at astonishing speed. Overnight the country became the first poor country in the world to become a full-scale democracy – "the tryst with destiny" as Nehru put it. There is a problem, however, for those outside the country, those visiting the country as well as some of the residents. How does the economic success of the country together with the achievements of its democratic system equate or square with notions of social justice – of its fair or unfair reputation of widespread poverty? It is not an issue particular to India, of course. The recent Brexit and Trump votes in the West in 2016 demonstrate a large angry electorate that has missed out on the supposed 'good times' and that has lost faith in the increasing oligarchic political class. It is India, however, that images of deprivation are commonly associated with, rightly or wrongly. It is a huge, complicated and contested issue, but one that is explored in various chapters.

Other things sometimes figure on the international agenda when the country of India is mentioned. Sometimes we glimpse the popularity and size of 'Bollywood', the Indian film industry or the fanatical love for cricket throughout the country – Sachin Tendulkar is a name many people from outside the country will recognise. As will be Ravi Shankar, the Indian musician known for popularising the sitar and Indian classical music. There will also be other things that we might tend to forget. India is a nuclear power and came close to once using these weapons since Independence. The country has also been involved with – perhaps initiated – five nasty wars and today the military remains very active in different parts of the country. While we might not be too familiar with these events, we would all be likely to recognise and name the Taj Mahal. In fact most of us have 'bumped into' aspects of India at least sometime in the recent past. This awareness and knowledge is likely to increase in the years ahead as India assumes a greater role on the world stage, perhaps as the next 'superpower'. Prime Minister Modi's visit to Britain and to the 60,000 packed Wembley Stadium in 2015 was an example of this growing recognition and presence. As Britain's Prime Minister proclaimed, "Team India, team UK – together we are a winning combination." No irony, no apologies, no history – how times have changed.

There is then much that is happening today that reflects the growing importance and presence of India. It is all happening very quickly. This acceleration, however, contrasts with the rhythms and pace that seem to characterise much of rural life. Scenes of bullocks pulling wooden ploughs through the fields must have been similar hundreds of years ago, maybe longer. Few countries embody this blending of tradition and the ancient with the new and the modern. So yes, it is a good time to be interested in and thinking about India. It's an even better time to be travelling around the country as the discussions in the subsequent chapters suggest.

A vignette: a Colaba walk

In March 2016, I was back in Bombay. My earlier February hotel in the Fort area near to the CST station had been crap. From that experience I learnt that, "The Internet is very slow. You have to wait," really means, "We have no Internet but we don't want to tell you." I decided this time to find a hotel in the Colaba area, further south in the city. I hadn't stayed there since we arrived in India with the children for the first time back in 2003. What a great decision. I had forgotten about the delights, histories and urban adventures that make up this southern finger of the city. I had a working familiarity with the areas south of the CST station from the banking area around Horniman Circle, the Asiatic Society and St Thomas Cathedral across to Churchgate and the greenish cricketing fields of the Oval Maidan. I knew also the roads and alleys down towards the Gateway of India area, passing the museums, university, art galleries and Regal Cinema. South of this along the Colaba Causeway I only vaguely remembered. Back in 2003, we were all in a bit of a daze having arrived from Europe the previous day on our first visit to India. Clutching tightly the hands of the children we did manage a little exploration but overall we were still somewhat shell-shocked.

A number of visits later and many years on, it was different. This time it was like greeting an old friend. What had changed, what was the same, where had this gone, why wasn't this here anymore and those surely weren't the same cows tied to the post at that busy junction? Overall, it was reassuringly similar and I was glad to be back. More confident and relaxed this time, I had found a good hotel with WIFI that worked. The first thing that struck me was the greenery of the area. Lovely giant trees lined the small roads off the Colaba Causeway (or Shahid Bhagat Singh Marg, as it is now called) providing shade throughout the day. Dappled sunshine on most of the quiet side streets provided a lovely contrast to the heat and bustle of the Causeway. There is even a road called Garden Road off the Marg. Go down this short road and there's this lovely little park. It must be around one hundred by thirty metres in size, has no name or opening details and is surrounded by a tall wire fence and sturdy gates secured by a padlock. I found eventually that it opened from around 4.30 in the afternoon until about 7–8 in the evening – I'm not sure about the weekends though. It's a lovely little bit of paradise. Great soaring mature trees dominate the formal pathways that meander around the park, wooden comfortable benches are plentiful, small bushy verges surround the well-watered patches of grass (almost 'lawn') and in the evenings, around a dozen local (I assume) women jog around the pathways all clutching their water bottles. I have no idea who pays for the upkeep of the park or the wages of the 3–4 workers who at this time of the year seem to spend most of their time sweeping up the leaves from the pathways.

The clues to the origins and nature of this little green gem as well as the surrounding streets I guess lie in the extraordinary history of this city. Bombay today is roughly one-third the size of Greater London but has, with a population of around 13 million, nearly twice as many residents as Britain's capital. The metropolitan area of Bombay has around 22 million residents – one of the world's 'megacities'. Its origins over the last five centuries has seen a cluster of seven islands slowly being incorporated into a solid land mass – mainly by the British in the nineteenth century – which is today modern Bombay and more particularly south-western Bombay. Joined by 'causeways' at first and then landfilling between the causeways eventually saw the emergence of modern Bombay from this archipelago. Known by the visiting Greeks as Heptanesia ('Seven Islands'), the city today can trace the influences of Ashoka, the ruler of the Mauryan Empire in the third century, the Chalukya Dynasty of the seventh century (see Elephanta Island) and subsequent political dynasties. Due to its importance as a trading and then military centre, it was the Portuguese for a period of around a hundred years in the 17th and 18th centuries that held sway. It was the British East India Company though that recognised the strategic importance of the city. As the saying goes, 'the rest was history'. In 1661 the islands were given to King Charles II as part of his dowry for his marriage to the Portuguese princess Catherine of Braganza and sold to the British East India Company which made Bombay its headquarters in 1671. By the mid-nineteenth century the British Government had managed to join the city islands into a single landmass and ushered in a period of frenetic urban expansion. As the useful short history of the city in the *Time Out Mumbai* guide remarks, "In the 1860s the British began a construction programme, erecting architecture that was designed to signal to the natives that they were here to stay – a direct response to the Indian uprising of 1857."

And it's in this imperial, historically arrogant expansion of the city over the next decades by the British colonisers that the origins of my little park off Garden Road, the massive trees lining the small roads and the neighbourhoods around the Colaba Causeway have their beginnings. It's not only their beginnings though. A wander around South Mumbai today continues to reveal their stories and experiences of this expansion 150 years ago. Many of the great Indian cities even today have areas that encapsulate the British presence with perhaps Lutyens' Delhi being the outstanding example. South Bombay is another of those areas.

My walk around Colaba and along its Causeway in mid-March 2016 confirmed this but also much more. Down from that most iconic of tourist sights, the Gateway of India – is this India's Eiffel Tower? – is the PJ Ramchandani Marg, or as it seems more commonly called, Strand Road. Overlooking the Gateway of India and its square on the other side of the road is the infamous Taj Mahal Palace Hotel. Opened in 1903 due to the racist policy of the British 'whites only' policy, this beautiful building has since those days welcomed the political and entertainment elite from across the world. It was also one of the targets in the 2008 terrorist attacks which occurred at various locations in Bombay. At least 31 people were killed at the Taj.

Further down from the Taj Hotel along the palm-lined Strand Road is the harbour which forms a boundary to one side of the road. It looked quite busy when I was there with plenty of small leisure boats moored to their buoys. I have my doubts though that sailing is big in Mumbai or even India. The serious-sounding Royal Bombay Yacht Club and the Mumbai Sailing Club have their premises around the Gateway of India area. On the other side of Strand Road and in the streets leading up to Colaba Causeway are grand houses that look like early twentieth century in design and construction. Four-story dwellings decorated with wooden balconies, neat driveways, plenty of columns and ornate towers provide an architectural coherence and historical timeframe for these neighbourhoods. Now and then, there is a modern Soviet-style concrete, quick build apartment block that has replaced one of the original houses. One or two places on Strand Road looked like they were about to physically collapse – empty and derelict. They might not be maintained but they won't be forgotten. As the taxi driver that I was talking to on Strand Road informed me, this was some of the most expensive real estate in the city. Apparently, southern Mumbai is said to be the wealthiest area in all India. Some very rich people owned these houses overlooking the harbour.

I guess that this whole area can trace its origins and character to the booming economic times of the late 19th, early 20th century. These neighbourhoods do have an early 1920–30s look to them, although the foundations of modern Mumbai were clearly detectable a hundred years earlier. The abundance of mature trees and shade in these areas together with an occasional little park reinforce this timeframe. Next time I need to find a local guide who during our walk can reveal all the details and gossip behind the restrained elegance of the area.

Heading up the 300–400 yards from Strand Road to Colaba Causeway is a bit of a shock. The Causeway, perhaps one of the most famous streets in Bombay, stretches south from the super busy roundabout SP Mukherjee Chowk, through to the southernmost point of the peninsula (although it merges into Nanabhai Moos Marg). Walking along it, I guess it might be around 3–4 miles long and is the main eastern route down this reclaimed, landfilled finger of the city. It seems to have been built as a dual carriageway, but today with all the double parking and spread of impromptu market stalls, it is another busy noisy inner-city street. The traffic does get quieter, the shops less numerous and the pavement less crowded the further south you walk as the southern tip of the peninsula is a military or defence base and a dead end, for the public anyway.

The street and area are one of the main shopping centres in the city. There is a scattering of the global brand outlets that can be found elsewhere in the world but also a huge variety of little shops that feature Indian textiles, jewellery and fashion, home furnishings, handicrafts and accessories. I like the lack of a posh feel to the shopping; it has all the shops and all the items you might want but in that characteristic chaotic manner that so defines the urban centres. Exclusive and very expensive outlets lie squeezed between some pretty shabby, rundown premises. Plenty of eateries too can be found along the road ranging from a McDonald's hamburger place, fresh brewed coffee bars through to local Parsi restaurants. Leopold Cafe, a favourite haunt for Western tourists and another one of the sites of the terrorist attacks on the 26th November 2008, is located on the Causeway. So too is another popular eatery, the Delhi Durbar, together with Paradise, a small Parsi outlet.

Walking south along the Causeway can't be rushed. There are too many occasions when you have to move off the pavement on to the road to keep moving. Even if it was physically possible to quicken things up, you shouldn't – too much is missed or glossed over or is unappreciated. My 4–5 hour walk only covered a few miles, and even then, was curtailed because of the midday heat. Most of the locals and traders are only too happy to chat, point out things and suggest new avenues to explore. They appear proud and happy to share their knowledge and history of the area; after all, I might visit their shop and buy some perfume or bangles or carpets when we have finished our discussion.

So I picked my way down the Causeway. It wasn't a stroll or a meander as that suggests a more leisurely and uninterrupted walking experience, and walking anywhere in urban India is far from leisurely. I popped into the Colaba Market which stretched down to the waterside. As might be expected, it was chaotically busy but had everything from fresh vegetables through to antiques, clothing, and of course, street foods. Between the Market and Sassoon Dock – my next stop – were large old buildings, half hidden behind the extensive tree foliage, most of which seem to be undergoing some renovations or maintenance work. Military offices of one sort or another became more common the further south you went. There was a big oldish-looking building for example known as the 'Sassoon Complex. Naval Officers Flats'. At the entrance to the Docks themselves is a new-looking monument by the Mumbai Port Trust at the base of the historic clock tower. The docks today house one of the largest fish markets in the city but visitors have to be there at around 5.30 in the morning to catch all the action – far too early for me.

A little further south down the Causeway was the beginning of the military defence area so I decided to return. Crossing the road, I chose to travel via Wodehouse Road (or as it is now called, Nathalal Parikh Road) which almost runs parallel to Colaba Causeway. It was a good choice. If anything this road was bordered by grander buildings than on the Causeway, many of them rundown, but which I'm sure is still a good address. The pavements were in good repair and the bustle and traffic less noticeable than the Causeway. It had less retail outlets but still had the big trees lining the street and there was an elegant look to the whole area. Again it was just possible to detect this pattern of similar sized and designed residential houses, with long balconies protected by ornate wooden fencing and wooden framed windows thrown open to the weather. They must have been very grand in their heyday. Occasionally there was what looked like Portuguese inspired large buildings of one level, with green corrugated iron roofing stretching low down to the surrounding veranda. A large wooden sign stood at the entrance to one of these buildings – I could only make out the word 'sanatorium'. Sometimes a high concrete wall had been built to hide the houses from the pavement traffic. I continued along Wodehouse Road, nipping into the Church of St John the Evangelist which is better known everywhere as the Afghan Church. Built by the British to commemorate the dead from the First Afghan War and disastrous 1842 retreat from Kabul this is a splendid building with stunning stained-glass panels and surrounded by extensive shady gardens. I was slowing up with the midday sun so pressed on. I had to stop, however, a little further along the road when I came across the big sign announcing the 'Colaba Land Co-operative Housing Society Ltd. (Brady's Flats)'. Here off a side street was a collection of uniform well-maintained flats that presumably were cooperatively owned and perhaps maintained (but maybe not now?). Calm, very green and elegant, there are, from what I could see, ten identical, three-storey flats. They would not have looked out of place in any capital city from around the world.

Things were getting desperate now – the heat and humidity were getting to me, the noise and the traffic had returned and the pavements were busy. I persevered only to stop a little further on at the massive arched entrance to Cusrow Baug ('Baug' means gardens), a housing colony built in 1934 and reserved for members of the city's dwindling Parsi community. I had passed this entrance in previous years, stopped to peer in but never had the courage to confront the watchman guarding the gate. This time, I wandered into the entrance to look at the noticeboard and the watchman was straight across. He gestured for me to approach half a dozen men sitting in the shade. They pulled up a chair and in very good English proceeded to give me a potted history of the emigre community of Iranian Zoroastrians in Bombay known as Parsi.

Bombay has had a reputation as a tolerant, secular city encompassing many varied communities. Few match the influence of the Parsis. Many of the iconic buildings in the historic heart of Bombay were funded or designed by members of this community. Although small in number today – around 50,000 – their presence can still be felt and tasted through the cake shops and restaurants.

I eventually managed to extricate myself from the history lesson and, as suggested by the wise old men, wandered around the sheltered housing complex, as we would probably describe Cusrow Baug today. In contrast to the streets and noise outside, it was all very orderly, controlled and calm. Around five hundred families reside here today. A large rectangular lawn bordered by trees and bougainvillea bushes was surrounded by four-storey blocks of communal apartments. At the far end was the most important and imposing building, the fire temple or *agiary* as it's called. Built in 1836 when Colaba was still an island, the agiary is home to 'sky burials' – on which corpses are placed on open-air towers to be consumed by the city's famous black vultures and other birds of prey. Inside the temple is the inner sanctum with its sacred fire which has burned continuously for 180-plus years. Huge bronze doors at the entrance to the temple are guarded by giant winged sculptures with human faces – all very impressive.

Unfortunately the heat did for me. Tired and wet from the perspiration of the midday sun, I left Cusrow Baug after another short chat with the seated men at the entrance. I made my way across the Colaba Causeway, down Garden Road and back to my hotel. It had been a lovely morning with the delights and intricacies of the city slowly unveiling themselves. I was glad that I had decided to return to Colaba – a little more familiar but with much more to explore next time.

Chapter 2

India for the first time

A working knowledge

My geographical knowledge of India is what I would describe as 'tourist geography'. In other words it has been driven by where we have been or plan to go on our next visit. And it is very basic with bits and bobs added in a piecemeal fashion over the years. It is getting better but is still very patchy and rudimentary. On the other hand the simplicity of this 'working knowledge' gives me some sense of an overview which allows me, to a limited extent at least, to contextualise events such as particular historical episodes, cultural patterns, tourist sites, voting results and transport routes.

After all, India is a huge country or subcontinent with an enormous amount of physical variation. I like to think of it, however, as comprising a number of simple characteristics. Up north you have the wonderful Himalayan range of mountains which extend east to west and form a barrier or deterrent to other 'interested parties' from the rest of Asia that historically have shown some interest in India, came in and stayed for a few centuries. Given the number of television documentaries, books and films that focus on the Himalayas, many people must be as fascinated by these mountains as I am. I would love to spend more time exploring these most iconic of mountain ranges as we have only touched on their majesty in our visits to Shimla in the west, Nepal in the middle and the eastern ranges from Darjeeling. The cold and dampness in the early months of the year have deterred longer stays.

Just below the Himalayas in the north-east, there is the Arakan range of mountains with its great Irrawaddy River, which are mostly in Burma but also encompass parts of India such as Assam, Nagaland and Manipur. These are steep, densely forested areas which again have provided cover for India from those in eastern Asia. At the other side of the country in the north-west there are the infamous Hindu Kush mountains. There are several passes through the Hindu Kush. They have provided the main routes historically and today from the rest of Asia into the plains of India just below the Himalayas. These routes have been the principal gateways into the country which over time have politically and culturally shaped modern India. Nestled into these mountains lies the beautiful but contested Kashmir Valley at just under 2,000 metres high with its tourist 'honeypots' of Leh, Alchi and the stunning Leh to Manali road. "India's earthly paradise," as Jawaharlal Nehru passionately and stubbornly put it.

Immediately below these northern mountainous barriers to the country lies the vast fertile plains of the Ganges River. The Indo-Gangetic Plains as they are known run east to west from the Arabian Sea in the west to the Bay of Bengal in the east, some 3,200 kilometres long and 320 kilometres wide. Extreme temperatures characterise the Plains, very cold in winter and burning hot in summer. We are not as familiar with these great Plains as we would like to be having spent most of our visits and time in the warmer southern half of the country. We have though viewed the rolling, agriculturally rich plains with their abundant rivers from train windows. Three of India's greatest rivers arise in the Himalayas and dominate northern India – the Indus, the Brahmaputra, and of course the Ganges, arguably the most famous river in the world and certainly the most sacred in India. Varanasi (traditionally known as Benares), one of the oldest inhabited cities in the world and a magnet for all tourists, is situated on the banks of the Ganges roughly halfway across the Plains. The mouth of the Ganges or Ganga as it is known in India is the largest delta – the Sundarban Delta – in the world. Famous cities periodically break up the Plains – Delhi in the north-west,

Lucknow further east, and then, Varanasi and Allahabad.

So that's the north of India in my working knowledge of the country. South of the great plains is the triangle-shaped rest of the country – although I have seen it described as diamond shaped. The Vindhya Range of mountains although not technically a single mountain range is generally seen as separating north from south India. Stretching across the country two-thirds of the way up the country the Vindhya and also the parallel Satpura Range of mountains form a collection of disconnected hills, highlands and escarpments and rise to an elevation of around 300 metres. Below these mountainous ranges is the great plateau – the Deccan – which stretches for almost the complete length of 'the triangle', or peninsula, and averages 600 metres in height. A thin green coastal area surrounds the triangle before the sometimes steep rise, on to the Deccan Plateau. Bounding the Deccan Plateau from north to south are the mountainous Eastern and Western Ghats – well known to tourists in their train journeys up and down the coastal routes and almost meeting at the southern tip of India. This is the south of India, culturally, historically and politically distinct from the rest of India. The invaders of India – usually from the north – generally didn't make it past the Satpura and Vindhya Ranges resulting in a small number of India's greatest long-lasting dynasties being located in the south. The Western Ghats protecting the Deccan Plateau block the rain and moisture from the south-west monsoon from reaching the Plateau. Consequently central and southern India is semi-arid with distinct wet and dry seasons.

The east coast of India is washed by the waters from the Bay of Bengal while the Arabian Sea hugs the country's western coast. Huge great mountain ranges, extensive forested areas, five thousand miles of coast and a great plateau – the geography of India in a sentence. I haven't mentioned the deserts – such as the Thar Desert in western North India – primarily because we have not been there but yes, deserts are a part of India.

One or two other geographical characteristics remain part of my 'knowledge', largely because they were part of our travels. I remember for example the Coromandel Coast from my visit to Tamil Nadu. The Coromandel Coast which forms part of the Eastern Coastal Plain stretches down from Andhra Pradesh through to Tamil Nadu – the bottom half of the eastern seaboard, in other words. I have swum in its choppy waters many times. The locals warned me of strong dangerous currents but I was lucky. On the other side of the country is the Western Coastal Plain, that strip of land between the Western Ghats and the Arabian Sea. Very narrow – its widest point is only around 100km wide – the Western Coastal Plain is split into the Konkan Coast in the north and the Malabar Coast running down the bottom half of the western coastal area. Again I have swum at many points along this western coast and travelled up and down much of the coast on various trains and buses at different times. The most memorable journeys were always those that left the humid coast and headed up to the cooler Western Ghats – very scary journeys.

If we move from geographical considerations to cultural matters on this 'working knowledge', a couple of other issues need mentioning. First, India today has 22 official languages. Officially Hindi is the national language of India but its use is mainly confined to the north of the country. A Hindi speaker visiting the south of the country will probably only be able to communicate in English. In the south it is the Dravidian languages – Tamil, Telugu, Kannada and Malayalam – that are common and which are distinct to Hindi which traces its origins to the ancient script of Sanskrit. The arrival in India of the Muslims in the 12th century resulted in Persian-influenced Urdu joining the list of modern Indian languages. The multiplicity of languages reflects strongly of course the diversity of cultures in the subcontinent. Apart from sharing the same geographical space, people from the north of the country had historically and culturally little in common with those from the south – language, diet, clothing, religion, customs and histories were all different. Far from an unchanging Indian culture and tradition as usually portrayed in histories or tales of the British Raj, the opposite was true – imperial 'modernity' did not save an 'unchanging' people and their continent.

The other issue worth mentioning at this stage is a remarkable one that many people know and which has greatly shaped the development of the country, namely religion. As is widely known, India is the home of at least seven of the world's great religions – Hinduism, Buddhism, Islam, Jainism, Sikhism, Zoroastrianism and Christianity. Some 80% of Indians see themselves as Hindus, followed by Islam who total 92 million believers (or 11% of the population). Jainism, Buddhism and Sikhism are all offshoots of Hinduism.

That about concludes my working but hopefully expanding 'tourist knowledge' of India. It allows me to get around the country, make some sense of the Indian newspapers and appreciate some of the current tensions and developments in the country. As mentioned in the previous chapter, this will always be very partial. But however the partiality, this is no barrier to exploring and enjoying the incredible beauty, richness and complexity of the country.

India for the first time

As pointed out in the first chapter, one of things that amazed me on that first trip to the country in 2003 was meeting tourists that had visited India many times. I knew why we had come to India but I was interested in knowing why they had first chosen to visit the country and what it was that kept them returning. So I asked them.

"On our earlier visits to India, we use to zoom about a lot more. If you haven't been shocked and bewildered and delighted and puzzled and intrigued half a dozen times at least before lunchtime, it's a most unusual day. One of my favourite things though is just to watch, step off the main street where for a change you're not being observed and you can just watch others – beautiful. India is charming and friendly but by jove, you won't be alone for long. There are so many people who just enjoy a conversation with you, the companionship… 'Where are you from? How many children do you have? How much do you earn?' They then share their knowledge with you – of where they have visited and, sometimes, a speech from Shakespeare. I'm blowed if I know where it's from but they are immensely proud of their learning," says Tony when I asked him what he enjoyed about his visits to India. Perhaps aware that he might be generalising too much, he continued his response but more cautiously. "After all these visits [20–30 times with his partner, Sheila] I wouldn't say I could understand India or its people very well at all. It's a vast country, the languages and cultures are different in different parts of India. And sometimes when you talk to people, it is difficult to get the truth. I always feel there are a few different versions of the truth. 'Yes, there is a train every day,' says the man at the ticket office. Good, I say. I'll have a ticket for Thursday. 'There is no train on Thursdays,' he replies. But you have just told me that there are trains every day. 'Yes,' he replies, 'there are trains every day except Thursday.' Oh, I see what you mean, I reply. It's a new way of understanding," continues Tony. "And yet India works, somehow it functions. In the West, we believe that our approach to problems is the only way – it's the right way, the only way. I like India because it questions all the things we take for granted in our country."

But why India, I had asked Tony. Why did you come here in the first place? What is it about this country that keeps you coming back? Maybe there are similar groups in different countries who are similar long-stay returners – maybe in south-eastern Asian countries, maybe in Mexico or Peru or parts of Africa. There will be another overlapping group from the West who are long-stay returners I guess who have a second 'holiday home' in another country but they are somewhat different from Tony's group. They are not 'travellers', more semi-permanent residents of another country. But the boundaries of these and similar other groups will be a little blurred – any further examination risks a more sober discussion of 'what is a tourist' and the nature of tourism.

So why did this group of travellers that I talked to happen upon India as opposed to somewhere else all those long years ago? In short and in the main, the answer is by serendipity. 'Serendipity India' has a catchier ring about it than other corporate-inspired slogans such as 'Beautiful India' or 'Shining India'. Anyway, destination India seemed to be a happy discovery arrived at by accident. Gina and Mick, for example, in 1991 wanted to go somewhere warm. "It was a toss-up between Africa and India. As the Gulf War had started, we decided to go to India as there were international flight problems elsewhere. We went on a nineteen-day package tour and loved it." Apart from one year, Gina and Mick have been back every year arranging their own flights, accommodation and sightseeing.

Steven's first visit to India was a similar 'accidental' affair. "In 1992 I returned from Morocco to find a voicemail from my friend Linda who was off to India." Linda's friend had to drop out at the last minute due to medical reasons. "As Linda had no travel insurance she decided to carry on with the trip and asked me if I wanted to come out to India with her. I got the voicemail at the weekend – we were to leave on Wednesday. I had no vaccinations but said yes – I was in between jobs at that time. I had to buy scheduled flight tickets as Linda's friend's tickets were non-transferable. I stayed in India for five weeks, didn't come back but have returned every year since 1996."

Irrespective of the 'whys' and 'hows' of arriving in India, anyone from the West arriving in India for the first time will never forget those first few days. Even our three children, young at the time and nearly a decade ago, today start gushing as the memories flood back. I have travelled to different parts of Africa, bussed through South America and been to countries in Southeast Asia but nowhere compares to the shock of India on that first visit in 2003–4. The introductory sections of the numerous guidebooks have got it right: "a sensory assault", an "unmatched vibrancy", "jarring juxtapositions", "intractable paradoxes", "utterly compelling". Nothing that has been done by way of preparation beforehand – reading the brochures and guides, watching the Indian documentaries on television, talking to Indian friends back home – prepares the international tourist for those few days. For most of these visitors, their first impressions are likely to be of the 'megacities', usually Delhi due to its proximity to the 'Golden Triangle' of Agra with the Taj Mahal, the 'pink city' of Jaipur and Delhi itself. Whether it is Delhi, Calcutta in West Bengal, Mumbai on the west coast or Thiruvananthapuram in the southern western state of Kerala, it is the unrelenting intensity of these Indian cities that usually shapes these first memories that will remain forever. Unlike many tourists, I love cities and especially Indian cities despite the pollution, hassle, noise and hygiene problems. I have never been in a rush to leave as soon as possible. When I do eventually move on, I always have a list of visits, information to seek out and walks that I plan to do on my next visit – always unfinished business. And whatever city it is that you are leaving, within a day's train ride you are in a completely different setting, be it a quiet rural village, the coast or the mountainous regions that stretch across northern India. Surely, no other country in the world can boast of the geographical and climatic diversity of this huge country – maybe the three million square kilometres is really a continent rather than a simple country. Whatever the time of year or landscape preferred, India welcomes you. Except that sometimes, you are not sure that you are in India. The peoples and cultures along the borders, especially in the north and particularly the north-east, seem more 'other' than Indian. Never mind; just more of the jigsaw to puzzle out.

Ultimately, those peoples and cultures of India are for most international visitors the highlights of their experiences of India. The sheer numbers, both in total (1.3 billion) and practically 'on the ground', are difficult to integrate into our circumscribed experience. Likewise, the numbers and vastness are difficult to comprehend. Delhi for example has 15–16 million inhabitants spread throughout 500 square miles. Coming into Mumbai on the train seems to take a couple of hours or so once the outskirts have been reached. So vast are the big Indian conurbations that the term 'city' seems inadequate; it's as though they have burst through and beyond common understandings of the term. And any percentage however small of 1.3 billion when discussing for example voting patterns, the middle class, health visits, education participation rates or housing issues still results in mega totals that are difficult to imagine, never mind grasp. Sometimes it is best not to try; just immerse yourself in this 'massification' at the market, on the local city bus or simply taking a front row seat at one of the great railway stations and watch.

Then there are the different Indians that are met while travelling – educated or illiterate, from this or that caste, from one of the great religions of the world or from one of the 23 official languages in the country that exist alongside the thousands of minor languages and dialects. And they are busy working you out – where are you from, are you married, how many children, how much do you earn – while you are trying to work them out – where is your home village, how long have you been in this city, is the Indian cricket team any good, how do you earn a living. Once these obligatory introductions are over, conversations become more relaxed and discursive; a friendship has been established.

So where do tourists go?

I'm not sure where the eight million (today's figures) foreign tourists visit once they have arrived in India. I suspect that the majority of these visitors are on short-stay visits of around two weeks, are part of a group travel arrangement and focus on a particular geographical area and objective. This might include, for example, a 'beach vacation' (in Goa or southern Kerala), the 'golden triangle' of Delhi, Agra and Jaipur or a tour to the numerous and extravagant architectural monuments of Rajasthan. As was seen from the earlier discussions with the frequent travellers, many of this group first visited India as part of a short organised arrangement before deciding to return as 'independent travellers'. On subsequent visits and with more time on their hands, their itineraries were more ambitious and seemed to cover most parts of the country. Andy for example recounts cheerfully, "From Delhi I got the bus to Dharamsala" in the state of Himachal Pradesh (often abbreviated to HP) – a journey of just under 500 kilometres. Bounded by Punjab on the west, Jammu and Kashmir in the north and Tibet on the east, my image of HP is of mighty mountains and abundant apple orchards in the valleys; such are the simple images of the Western tourist! The hill station of Dharamsala, established by the British between 1815 and 1847, struggles today to cope with the volume of visitors. These visitors in the main are interested in Buddhism, meditation or are sympathetic to the cause of Tibet. And of course the town is the base of the Dalai Lama. For those from the West in particular, the Dalai Lama is a popular figure and draws huge crowds to his visits out of south-east Asia, especially North America. In Dharamsala itself, thousands of Tibetans flock to the town together with nuns and monks from all over India and Nepal to seek his guidance and spiritual blessings. "I had an interest in the Buddhist faith, really," said Andy when asked why he had travelled to north-west India. "It had an element of a pilgrimage. I had seen the Dalai Lama in

South Africa. I then went from Dharamsala to Ladakh. This was in 2002. Ladakh was different to the rest of India. There was more of a Buddhist culture there." Ladakh in fact is often described as 'Little Tibet' (or the last Shangri-La) and has all the Buddhist cultural trappings – the strings of multicoloured prayer flags fluttering everywhere, the white prayer wheels and the white coloured *chortens* at the entrance of villages and monasteries. Ladakh is a region in the neighbouring state of Jammu and Kashmir with the largest town being Leh. Bounded by Pakistan on the west and China and Tibet on the east, the state stretches spectacularly into the Himalayas.

I have never been to India's northernmost and sixth largest state, Jammu and Kashmir, although I have checked the weather and security situation many times. Escaping the British winter weather is not a good time to visit this part of India: most of the roads and passes are only open between late June and October. The temperature drops dramatically after October, apparently often to minus 30 or 40 degrees. The attractions of the state, however, are well known. Indeed by the early 1980s, tourism had overtaken agriculture as the main source of income. The subsequent political disputes since then have, until recently, closed down tourism to the state.

Apart from the geography of this north-west part of the country, another well-known feature of this part of India is the intense religiosity of the region underpinned by simmering ethnic-cultural tensions. Around Jammu in the south-west of the state, for example, it is predominantly a Hindu area while Kashmir is almost exclusively Muslim. In the north-east and occupying some 70% of the state are the followers of Tibetan Buddhism. This combustible mixture resulted from the panicky cynicism and political machinations of the British at the time of Independence in 1947, as will be explored in a later chapter. Ladakh became part of Jammu and Kashmir in independent India 1948 following the first of the three Indian-Pakistani wars fought in the region. Ladakhis today continue to push for separation from Jammu and Kashmir.

Steven too had been to Ladakh as part of a package tour on his first visit to India in 1992, and later in 1999 on a tour with his sister. "It was almost pre-Internet days and I remember it being difficult to arrange coaches, flights and things like that. We got a small plane that had to fly half-empty as the high altitude and air density wouldn't allow a full load of passengers." Throughout the 1990s there had been a simmering insurgency in Kashmir with atrocities committed by both sides. In 1995, five tourists trekking near Pahalgam were kidnapped: one was beheaded and the remaining four tourists were never found. "It was in the middle of the 1999 war," continued Steven. "We kept seeing private coffins coming down the valley – poor dead Indian soldiers. At the airport which was not much more than a Nissen hut, they screened all luggage and coffins. So some poor worker who was busy screening rucksacks then saw skeletons go by presumably with a lump of lead in it somewhere. I really liked Ladakh though. We didn't do any trekking as we had problems of acclimatisation. We hired a 4x4 vehicle." As would be expected in this mountainous terrain, there are some spectacular roads and passes in the Ladakh region. The famous 485-kilometre route for example, from Leh (the capital of Ladakh) south through to Manali (in HP), reaches an altitude of 5,300 metres. Cycling this highway is popular with up to 300 cyclists each year attempting the route before mid-September when the highway officially closes. Steven, however, took the road north out of Leh to the breathtaking Nubra Valley which is apparently the world's highest stretch of driveable road. "We had tea at the top – at Khardung Pass (5,578 metres) – and then down the other side into the Nubra Valley. The geology was awesome," continued Steven. "It was absolutely fantastic – snow, desert, camels, glaciers, everything. On the way back we got to the top and found a British tourist, a hard-arsed cyclist who had actually cycled up there. He had collapsed at the top and was in big danger. He was semi-conscious and we were able to throw his bike on top, lash it down and put him in the back of the 4x4. He would have probably died. No one was particularly bothered. So we took him down the mountain and at various spots he made us stop because on the way up he had been shedding bits of his gear. So he had shed his Primus stove, and left this and left that so that by the time he got to the top he was virtually carrying himself and the bike. An absolutely crazy climb. We had met him in a cafe at Leh earlier in the trip and he had been telling us about his plans so we actually knew him. When we spotted him we recognised him immediately."

Leh, some 3,500 metres above sea level, continues to attract numerous tourists today primarily as a busy base for arriving in the region as well as a base for exploring further parts of the region. It is helped as a tourist centre through its airport links to Delhi, Jammu and Srinagar. Sheila and Tony had also visited Leh, "some twenty years ago. It will be so different now – full of video shops and that."

More recently, Janet and Mike were in Kashmir. "It was quite modern," they recalled. "We were there in 2005 when the earthquake hit." This was October 2005. A 7.6 magnitude earthquake struck Kashmir killing some 73,000 people and injuring hundreds of thousands more in the India-Pakistan region. Srinagar 'the beautiful city' is the summer capital of the Jammu and Kashmir state. Situated in the fabled Kashmir Valley and with huge snow-capped mountains pressing down on three sides of the city, this predominantly Muslim city is home to the famous houseboats and floating gardens on the city's two lakes, Dal Lake and Nageen Lake. Together with the intricate ornamental gardens, water fountains and terraced lawns from the seventeenth-century Mughal period, Srinagar remains a magnet for intrepid travellers. "We were up there (Kashmir) for about ten days," continued Mike. "I had this uneasy feeling in Srinagar so we left. There were no trains. We left at six in the morning and three hours later the earthquake hit. We got the news that Srinagar had shut down – no water, no hospital, nothing." It wasn't the threat of the earthquake that persuaded Mike and Janet to leave Srinagar. Instead, "We were uneasy in Kashmir and in Srinagar. You wouldn't want to be out in the countryside overnight; basically, you get back to Srinagar. Srinagar itself wasn't that welcoming, perhaps because they hadn't seen tourists for some thirty years. We had a look at some of the houseboats on Dal Lake but they were not in a good state of repair. We saw lots of Indian army and police walking around with Second World War rifles. We're Americans and sometimes we get paranoid. Where are you from, we're asked, and we say America. USA is not on very good terms with these folks. In most parts of India we feel very welcomed but in some parts, we feel we're not too welcome due to the way our government operates but as individuals the locals want to welcome you, talk with you and be friendly with you. Part of the problem is that basically everyone you are dealing with is a young male – not with people our age or with women. The countryside though was beautiful. It was autumn and we drove up the road to Jammu. They were harvesting the apples and all the trucks were full of these apples – it was very beautiful."

Maybe one year Susan and I will get to Jammu and Kashmir. We like the mountains and all the written and filmed accounts of the region suggest that this is a very special place. Above all, I think we would enjoy most the cultural and religious diversity that historically characterises the villages and peoples of this most north-western part of the country. We have, however, visited briefly the neighbouring state of Himachal Pradesh. We travelled from Delhi on the train to India's most famous hill station, Shimla, a few years ago. The summer capital of the British at an altitude of just over 2,000 metres is an attractive if sprawling town popular with local tourists coming up from

Delhi. A significant part of the attraction for us was the Shimla 'toy train'. Before ever riding or seeing this 96-kilometre narrow-gauge rail, I felt a 'television' intimacy with its tunnels, bridges, stations and employees. The BBC seems to show its four television episodes of the Indian toy-trains every couple of years – I must have watched them about three times. Eventually, when we did manage to board the train at Kalka I was always on the lookout for some of the employees who starred in the Shimla episode. We visited in February with the weather politely put chilly. We had come up from humidity-drenched Kerala in southern India but in Shimla it was a case of buying jumpers in the market and not moving out of them for the duration of our stay. The 'freshness' of the weather, however, didn't distract from the pleasantness of wandering along the Mall to the main square and savouring the historical distinctiveness of the town. The Ridge was where everyone congregated, and we too sat and watched the strolling tourists, horse riders and children playing, all against the backdrop of huge white-capped Himalayas. While the British architectural presence was still clearly visible in the town, the once-tiny village is now a major holiday resort for domestic tourists. Like the British in the old days, many of the visitors were up from Delhi to escape the sweltering heat and dust. The bazaar was as busy as ever and the Mall (main street) retained enough of its Raj features to provide a glimpse of the past. We were eventually off to Nepal for a trekking adventure; the locals were aghast that we were not pushing further north in HP to trek around the popular Lahaul area (at around 5,000 metres). Next time, we promised them.

The other Indian hill station that we visited a few years later was Darjeeling, this time in the opposite side of the country, in the far north-east state of West Bengal. Catching the train from Calcutta to Siliguri and then via a combination of Jeep, bus and 'toy train' we finally arrived at Darjeeling, 2,200 metres up in the Himalayas and some 600 miles north of Calcutta. The narrow

0.6-gauge rail arguably was even more dramatic than the Shimla journey. It covers 82 kilometres with gradients up to 1 in 19. Its highest point is at Ghoom where it reaches a height of 2,438 metres. We didn't manage the entire journey on the 'toy train' as a small section had been washed away – we had to transfer to a bus. We did, however, pass beside the damaged section and saw for ourselves the engineering skills still required to maintain the line. Similar to Shimla, Darjeeling straddles hillsides and ridges, has its Mall and is thronged with holiday visitors. Even more dramatic than Shimla, Darjeeling has its mountains – great whopping snow-covered peaks that seem to rise a hundred yards from where you're sitting. The Gymkhana Club, the Planters' Club, the New Elgin Hotel and St Joseph's College with of course the numerous tea offices and stores testified to the Raj link. We were in the town for around a week and planned a short trekking tour. Unfortunately the weather was poor. Opening the curtains of the hotel every morning hoping that the hanging damp mist had disappeared tested both our nerves and patience. Visibility for most of the week in the middle of February was never much better than a couple of hundred metres. An unexpected highlight of the visit was waiting anxiously each evening for the complimentary hot water bottles that were delivered to the bedrooms at about seven o'clock each evening. Only after we were sure that the beds were warming up could we relax and venture out for the evening. And then one day, the clouds and mist lifted and there in front of us although not quite in touching distance were some of the highest peaks in the Himalayas set against a clear blue sky and wispy clouds swirling around the summits. Pride amongst the peaks was Kanchenjunga, the third highest mountain in the world. At six in the morning the next day we were off (with half of India, it seemed) to Tiger Hill twelve miles from Darjeeling, to witness the sun rising up over the snow-capped peaks and to ogle at the 360-degree Himalayan panorama, including Everest. As the sun comes up, each range lights up, one at a time – magical.

The shops and stalls along the Mall and the Chowrasta are always busy. Traders seemed to reflect the turbulent political past of the town and region – Nepalese, Tibetans and Gorkha peoples from further east and north in India. The need for warm clothing and lots of it by everyone provided a continuous fashion show for the relatively few Western tourists.

East India and in particular the far north-eastern India is the least visited region in the country. This seems strange. West Bengal for example has so much going for it and is famous throughout the world for its cultural and literary history, its turbulent political past (and present) and the wonderful city of Calcutta. And then there is the Sunderbans Tiger Reserve, another World Heritage Site, in the south of the state with the largest mangrove swamps in the world, supposedly 300 Bengal tigers and the wonderful Ganges River and its tributary, the Hugli entering the Bay of Bengal.

Sheila and Tony, however, had visited the Sunderbans. It was during the Gulf War and in their twenty-plus visits to India, this was the only occasion that they had been part of an unhappy experience. "It was a bit strange," began Sheila. "People with placards and posters were supporting Saddam Hussein. And then the police accused us of being spies and stupid stuff like that. It felt dangerous. We should have taken an organised tour (through the Sundarbans). We did it ourselves – booked the boat and train and everything. And the language was a bit of a problem."

Mike and Janet similarly had been to West Bengal and many times to Calcutta. However, in their case, their stays in West Bengal largely were a transit experience on their way to the far reaches of north-east India – namely, Sikkim, Assam and Nagaland. Why these north-eastern states receive so few tourists is again a little puzzling. Perhaps it has something to do with the military sensitivities of the region. There are disputed borders with mighty China. It might be the bureaucracy and complexities of getting permits and visas, the complex and volatile political atmosphere resulting from secessionist groups or simply the lack of a tourist infrastructure that makes travel more difficult than elsewhere in India. The north-east does suffer from being off the main tourist routes of Delhi, the west coast and southern India, and after all, India is a big place. Perhaps the differences – culturally, historically, politically – of the north-east to the rest of India deters travellers. Which is a shame as arguably this region is seen by many as the most beautiful area in the country. Surrounded by Nepal, Bhutan, Tibet, Burma and Bangladesh there are landscapes ranging from the high Himalayas, deep forests through to flat low-lying agricultural valleys – rich with rice, apple and orange groves. It is a real frontier region with its ethnically and linguistically diversity resulting in one of the most culturally differentiated areas in the world. Nagaland for example is almost entirely made up of people from fifteen distinct Tibet-Burma groups but are collectively known as the Nagas. Recognised as respected warriors, the Nagas are skilled farmers growing twenty different species of rice. Although each of the fifteen 'tribal' groupings has its own distinct dialect, a hybrid language drawing on the various local languages has developed into a common Naga tongue. In Arunachal Pradesh, perhaps India's most remote state lying north even of Assam and Nagaland, there are 26 tribal groupings each with its own culture, dialect, dress, social structure and traditions. One of the state's claims to fame includes the 500 species of orchid. Another less auspicious claim is the Indian military humiliation in 1962 when the Chinese invaded Arunachal Pradesh and pushed 300 kilometres into Assam, a painful blow to Indian nationalism and military bravado. And in Assam, the ethnic origins of the people range from Mongoloid groups through to Indians found elsewhere in the country. People movements continue as ever – Muslims settlers from Bengal moving into Assam over the last hundred years, Nepalese into Sikkim and Bangladeshis into a number of the smaller north-east states. Apart from the beauty and spectacular landscapes of the region together with the cultural diversity of its people, there is as might be expected a strong spiritual history and architectural dimension to the area. Sikkim for example was an isolated independent Buddhist kingdom until hostilities between India and China in the early 1960s resulted in its annexation by India in 1975. Today Sikkim is predominantly Hindu but the state remains an important source of Buddhism and is home to a multitude of historic monasteries (over two hundred). Generally, though, there is this blend of Hindu and Buddhism in the region, as is apparent in wandering around Guwahati, the capital of Assam on the banks of the Brahmaputra River.

It was in 2012 that Janet and Mike spent about a month in the north-eastern states. Previously, they had visited Sikkim and Assam but this year "decided to go further east. So we went to Calcutta and got the train to Guwahati, capital of Assam and went out from there," blithely said Mike. According to maps that I have looked at, the train journey is just over 1,000 kilometres and must have involved numerous changes of train. Anyway, "we were prepared to get special visas but as it turned out, we didn't need them. We had to get one for Itanagar (capital of Arunachal Pradesh) but not for Nagaland. The north-east is a different part of India. We found it much more Asian, oriental than Indian. It was the same as you got up into Sikkim. The women wear saris but they are different, more oriental. It's the same in Tawang (Arunachal Pradesh) and in northern Nagaland."

"We like the countryside," continued Janet. "We live in the countryside in Colorado, and we like the countryside in India. Our favourite towns here are probably those places with a population of 40,000 people or less. We don't like to be in big cities although we've been in Calcutta several times to get to the north-east. And we tend to enjoy the tribal areas. We've been back three times to south-western Orissa."

Orissa is the large state south of West Bengal, along the eastern coast. A quarter of this economically poor state's population are *adivasi* (meaning 'first people') or 'tribal people'. In general, *adivasi* is a term for a heterogeneous set of ethnic groups claiming to be the original population of India. The term *adivasi* has gained popularity over the last couple of decades and has sometimes been used by ethnic groupings themselves such as in Kerala, although not by other ethnic groupings. However, *adivasi* is not equivalent to tribe. Recognised within the Indian Constitution as 'Scheduled Tribes' (together with 'Scheduled Castes' and 'Other Backward Classes'), *adivasi* constitute just under 9% of India's population. Legislatively, there are 744 tribes across 22 states. According to the 2011 Indian Census, Scheduled Tribes number some 104 million people. Central India (including, for example, the states of Chhattisgarh, Madhya Pradesh, Orissa and, to a lesser extent, Andhra Pradesh on the eastern coast) has the largest concentration of tribal people – some 75% of the total tribal population. There is also a spread of tribal groupings in other parts of northern India and in particular areas in the foothills of the Himalayas such as Jammu and Kashmir and in Uttarakhand in the west.

'Tribal' groupings and 'scheduled castes' appear frequently in the media reports and in the tourist literature. However, substantial controversies surround definitions and use of 'tribe' and associated terms such as 'Scheduled Castes'. Firstly, these are to some extent due to the discriminatory behaviour and attitudes towards these peoples by the majority, and secondly, because of the positive electoral arrangements provided for recognised ethnic groupings. Groups labelled 'Scheduled Tribes' are those formerly called 'tribes' by the British, points out Peggy Froerer, an anthropologist working in Chhattisgarh. As she notes, "The identification of 'tribes' thus involved a relationship between the British concept of a more 'civilised' Hindu society, defined by their understanding of the caste system, and the 'primitive', wild periphery which dotted the edges of its social and geographical domain. Groups that could not be classified into major caste or religious categories were labelled instead on the basis of the general impression about their physical and socio-cultural isolation from mainstream, caste-bound Indian society."

However, there is a broader social and political agenda that involves tribal peoples. Whether it is maternal or child mortality, access to drinking water, income, size of agricultural holdings or educational status, tribal communities lag far behind the general population. A flavour of this larger agenda was the report in the international press in August 2013 of the Dongria Kondh tribe rejecting overwhelmingly the plans by the British multinational mining company Vedanta Resources for an open-pit bauxite mine on their sacred lands. The struggle, supported by a number of British celebrities such as Michael Palin and Joanna Lumley, was seen as an unprecedented triumph for indigenous rights in India. During consultations ordered by the Indian Supreme Court, the Dongria Kondh people argued that the mine would destroy the forests and disrupt the rivers in the Niyamgiri Hills in the state of Orissa. Both the forests and rivers are central to the livelihood and identity of the 8,000-strong tribe. This good news, however, was preceded by the bad news in March of the same year that the central government was removing substantially the need to obtain consent from indigenous people and forest dwellers before losing their lands and forests to industry. On 15th February, the government stated that major 'linear projects' such as roads, railways, electricity lines, canal systems and pipelines do not need to obtain consent from affected forest populations before clearing their lands.

India of course is not alone when reviewing indigenous people's struggles, especially against mineral multinational companies. A quick review of the media reveals similar struggles in the Chiapas region of Mexico, the Klamath people over water rights in Oregon, USA, illegal logging companies threatening the cave dwellers and their 20,000-year-old ancient cave art in Papua New Guinea, the Maya's struggle to maintain rights to their rainforest against oil companies, including US Capital Energy and finally, the Musqueam people's recent victory against the British Columbia Government in Canada over the construction of apartments at a historic village and burial site in the heart of Musqueam traditional, unceded territory. The situation in India, however, seems to attract a disproportionate amount of international media attention. This attention is to be welcomed but little mention is made of the other struggles outside of India. Perhaps one of the reasons is, as a recent report from Human Rights Watch notes, that "the scale of lawlessness that prevails in India's mining sector is hard to overstate." Official figures apparently indicate that there were more than 82,000 instances of illegal mining in 2010 alone. The report argues that an even bigger problem than this is "the failure of key regulatory mechanisms that even legal mine operators comply with the law and respect human rights." Mining and ancestral lands don't mix easily as the aggressive activities of mining companies such as Vedanta and Posco indicate, and the huge dams of the Narmada and Damodar Valley projects which submerged thousands of Adivasi villages illustrate. The "Proud not Primitive" campaign established recently by Survival International is an attempt to engage with the reality of the situation confronting Adivasi people.

Most of the tourists I talked to in India were aware to some extent of the Adivasi struggles. Occasionally, particular episodes are reported in the world's press and contribute to maintaining the long continuing but low profile of these struggles.

Anyway, largely missing from my discussions with the 'regular returners' on where they had been in India was the east coast. The three big Indian states along the eastern coast

54

– Orissa, Andhra Pradesh and to a lesser extent Tamil Nadu – were rarely mentioned. This is reflected to some degree in the guidebooks – less attention is given to these areas, especially the north-eastern coast. In Orissa, one of India's poorest states, there is another 'golden triangle' of Puri, Konark and Bhubaneswar boasting the highest concentration of historical and religious monuments in the country. A few Westerners are visible here but rarely elsewhere. Perhaps the beaches don't compare with the west coast although Puri's beaches pull in the crowds from Calcutta. Perhaps the remote, sparsely populated interior or densely forested hills or heat throughout the year put people off. Incidentally in June 2014, the 29th state in India was formed – Telangana. Following many decades of agitation the new state was formed from north-western Andhra Pradesh. Hyderabad is to remain as the capital for both states "for a period of ten years".

Further down the south-eastern coast, however, Tamil Nadu is a different proposition. Flat coastal plains give rise to the Eastern Ghats with the 'blue mountains' of the Nilgiris providing relief from the heat and hot, dry dusty plains. Famous tea hill stations at 'snooty' Ooty and Kodai high up the mountains provide a cool contrast to the coastal heat of southern east and western India. As the country's second most industrial state – mainly textiles but increasingly mineral ores – the Tamil-speaking population (India's oldest living language) in Tamil Nadu is the country's Dravidian Hindu heartland. The great Tamil temples form part of a large network of sacred sites connected by ancient pilgrim routes. A strong nationalist political current is fuelled through the cities of Chennai (or Madras, as it is still commonly called), Madurai and Pondicherry. This is a state with a lot happening. Not surprisingly, it figures regularly in newspaper and media reports – too big, contrary and important to be kept quiet for long although not a major focus for Western tourists.

Its neighbour on the west coast – Kerala – has by contrast proved a magnet for visitors over many centuries and today is experiencing somewhat of a boom for package visits from the West. All my 'regular returners' had been to Kerala, often a few times. It's not difficult to see why. Stretching 550 kilometres along the coast, the state is divided between the dense forested mountains of the Western Ghats in the east through to humid, lush but narrow coastal plains. Paddy fields and coconut palms seem to cover any spare opening down on the plains while the same is true with coffee, tea and rubber plantations up on the highlands. Scoring high on most welfare indicators and boasting an enviable literacy rate, the residents of Kerala seem at ease with its influx of foreign tourists. Known for its laid-back pace of life, its cities are smaller than elsewhere in India, and in the main, provide the amenities required by outside tourists in a relaxed and friendly manner. The famed 'backwaters' of Kerala, however, are what bring in the visitors from around the world. Stretching 75 kilometres north of Kollam to Cochin up the coast, the perplexing labyrinth of waterways, lakes, canals and rivers, lined thick with tropical greenery, provide the perfect 'getaway', as the brochures put it, aboard a houseboat or wooden barge. Local ferries or canoes provide a sample of backwater pleasures without committing to longer periods of stay. Today the 'houseboat' industry is a very serious business and, as such, has initiated equally serious ecological problems.

Compared to Tamil Nadu, Kerala is the poor neighbour when focussing on religious or historical monuments. Its festivals, dance and theatre activities, however, are renowned throughout India while some of its beaches – such as Kovalam and Varkala – match those of Goa, further north. The heavy marketing campaign by the state throughout the West is likely to increase foreign tourist visitors in the future.

It's interesting – I've noticed that most of what I have written above is about those areas of the country that we *haven't* visited. It's mainly about the north and we have spent most of our time down south. Maybe this reflects an unconscious agenda of where

I would like to go or where I wished we had already visited. As it turns out, this doesn't really matter as I discuss our travels and experiences down south in subsequent chapters. The other thing that occurred to me was the value of the discussions with my little group of frequent travellers. Informal and unscientific as they might be, these discussions opened up to me parts of India that were both delightful and insightful. After listening and reading them again, I wanted to be off to the places they mentioned in the forlorn hope of experiencing some of the adventures and encounters they discovered. I guess that's part of the 'tourist experience' – the excitement, anticipation and sheer foolhardiness of some journeys. As they say in the million-selling self-help manuals, 'nothing ventured nothing gained'.

The Tourist business in India

Finding out where my little group of 'India returners' had visited in the country was illuminating. It alerted me to places that I hadn't thought of and might never visit. They also illustrated what it was and is that they find so absorbing about India. Their responses will continue to inform later chapters. I remember being struck, however, in those discussions about the reasons they gave for choosing India in the first place – that is, often accidentally or by chance. As mentioned earlier, for the 'India returners' it wasn't initially a calculated priority destination. Rather it was accompanying a friend at short notice, a stopover on a longer journey or one destination from a list of other possible countries. Today, however, things have changed from those times in the 1980s or 1990s. Increasingly, global tourism is a competitive business. Numbers of foreign tourists to India continue to edge up. In September 2015 for example, some 6.8 million visitors arrived in India, down a little from the previous year. Two years later, the number of foreign arrivals had crept up to around 8 million. Overseas visitors from 2000–2015 averaged some 4 million tourists per year. 2014 was a bumper year.

As would be expected tourist numbers reflect wider global concerns about a particular country as is currently the case, for example, in Egypt, Pakistan or Zimbabwe. In the first three months of 2013 foreign tourists arriving in India dropped by 25% largely because of the fears about the risk of sexual assault. The number of female foreign tourists fell by 35%. This fear probably was the result of the widespread global publicity of the fatal gang-rape of the physiotherapy student on a Delhi bus in December 2012 despite a senior government tourist officer stating that it was "still unclear" why there was this dramatic fall in the foreign tourist numbers in early 2013. In 2014 the falling number of women tourists continued. India wasn't 'incredible' anymore. In fact, over the last few years it has attracted global attention as a country unsafe for women. As the *Indiatimes* put it in 2015, "Given India's rape epidemic (there's honestly no other way to term it), countries and travel organizations around the world are increasingly wary about women visiting India." Gender issues remain a major concern socially and domestically in India, and will also play an important part in influencing choices made of destinations by outside tourists. It contributes towards contextualising foreign tourist numbers but is not likely to be the major factor in explaining overall numbers.

It is unlikely that any statistical tool can capture or trace the value of tourism to any country although numbers of visitors remain the most commonly used indicator. Tourism is a complex industry to manage and understand within a broader industrial policy. Unlike the automotive, shipbuilding or leather industries for example, tourism is a complicated value chain that incorporates and cuts across a number of disparate policy areas such as regulatory provision, labour markets, tourist infrastructures and hospitality. Coordinating and developing a coherent strategic direction for the tourist industry in any country is fraught with difficulties. Despite these complications, most countries recognise the importance of this sector as an important financial contribution to the economy and as a generator of jobs. The aggressively marketed "Incredible India" campaign by the Indian government in the early years of this century together with more recent marketing efforts has resulted in just under 8 million foreign tourists arriving in the country in 2016–17. Overall, there has been a steady increase in foreign tourist arrivals. In 1997 for example, there were 2.4 million arrivals. Despite the increasing numbers, the last few years have seen a smaller than anticipated increase – a plateau of sorts is appearing.

The two 'biggies' when looking at where the majority of these foreign tourists came from are the United States – about a million (16%) – followed by Britain (12.6%). A number of other countries follow but with much smaller numbers: Bangladesh, Sri Lanka (0.29%), Canada (0.25%), Germany (0.25%), France (0.24%), Japan (0.22%) and Australia. Surprisingly and not mentioned yet are Russian, Ukrainian and Eastern European visitors. The explosion of Russian-speaking tourists anywhere hot during their own winter in places such as Egypt and West Africa saw this group dramatically entering the 'top ten' a few years ago before falling away recently due to the economic circumstances back home. The later chapter on Goa confirms this pattern.

India's share of the international tourist market continues to average around 0.64%. The smaller countries of Southeast Asia attract far more visitors. When using the fashionable management speak of 'benchmarks', India is an underperforming country. The recent decline in tourist inflow is a worry for India. Ranked 38th among the top global destinations for international travel, since 2002 the tourist sector has not expanded to the extent expected. Around seven million out of a total of around 983 million tourists globally can be seen as leaving plenty of room for improvement. Despite these trends, the industry remains a vital part of the Indian economy contributing around 6.5% to the country's total wealth and responsible for about 40 million jobs.

Given the growing numbers and economic importance of

tourism globally, India's total can be seen as a worry. While there are obviously many different ways of calculating 'foreign visitors', the overall trends are clear-ish. The latest figures confirm the incremental increases.

There are many reasons which have been listed as contributing to these small numbers. European Union residents for example are in general reluctant to travel too far from home, with between 50–60% preferring to enjoy their holidays in their own country. Given the popularity of sea and beach vacations, Spain, France and Italy are Europe's favourite destinations. Despite such reasons, the foreign tourist numbers for India are low. Thailand for example attracts some 25 million foreign tourists a year. The dramatic increase in Chinese tourists in the last couple of years (although down recently) is likely to increase the importance of tourism in Southeast Asia but not India.

Leaving these tourist numbers aside for the moment, it's quite interesting to map out officially where these tourists chose to go when in India. The state of Maharashtra on the west coast with Bombay as its capital is the most popular destination (around 25% of total foreign visitors). This huge wealthy state with a population of 112 million is home to a number of big cities, obviously Mumbai but also Nagpur, Pune and Nashik. There are a number of major tourist attractions in the state such as the UNESCO World Heritage sites of Ajanta Caves and Ellora Caves, the National Parks and the various delights of Mumbai, but I suspect that its popularity may also be due to its country entry/exit importance through its international airport. The state of Tamil Nadu down in the south-east of the country is next in popularity attracting 17% of foreign visitors. With more than 34,000 temples, an extensive network of sacred sites and with five UNESCO World Heritage sites, it is easy to see why this is a popular part of the country. The stunning temples of Mamallapuram together with the Meenakshi Amman Temple in the 2,500-year-old city of Madurai continue to be important tourist venues. Then there are the big coastal cities of Chennai and old French capital of Pondicherry and, inland, the majestic Eastern Ghats mountain range which runs up the eastern coast of India almost reaching West Bengal. Up here in the mountains is the Nilgiri Mountain Railway, the only narrow-gauge line in India built by the British that we have not enjoyed. The acclaimed cinema, food and cultural activities (especially dance) make Tamil Nadu a difficult state to leave. Unsurprisingly, Delhi is the third most visited area in India with 11% of total foreign visits. One of the great cities of the world, Delhi's attractions are well known. The British imprint on the city with the India Gate, the Parliamentary buildings, Connaught Place and Lodhi Gardens are only the most recent added layers to this most historic of cities. Surely, not many people who have read William Dalrymple's *City of Djinns: A Year in Delhi* will fail to place the city near the top of their must-visit 'wish list'. The city of Agra with the Taj Mahal and that most holiest of Hindu cities Varanasi probably contribute significantly to the state of Uttar Pradesh being next in the list of foreign tourist destinations. Rajasthan with its royal palaces of the maharajas is the next most visited state (7% of the total) followed by West Bengal, Bihar and Kerala in popularity rankings. In each case, there are obvious touristic reasons for their inclusion on such a list. The problem for any visitor from outside India is that wherever you go it is difficult to get away once you begin immersing yourself in the local sites, cultures and histories of a particular area of India. It is such a huge country with so rich a varied and complex tradition. Asking others who have visited the country many times is one way of short-cutting this dilemma.

As already mentioned, using statistics and lists to try and capture aspects of foreign tourist experiences and preferences in India is a crude and blunt methodology. However, it does have the merit of situating and contextualising, from a bird's eye view, what is going on. But perhaps the most important aspect of these touristic happenings in India hasn't yet been mentioned. To put it bluntly, the number of foreign 'Western' tourists to India are hardly worth getting out of bed for, especially when compared to the rising figures of places such as Vietnam, Burma (Myanmar), the ever-popular Thailand and even Cambodia. The country might have the fastest growing economy in the world but it lags far behind in attracting foreign tourists. But help is on the horizon.

If Western foreign visitor numbers have been a little iffy in recent years, the spectacular rise of the domestic traveller has not only arrived to cheer the industry at a time of Western austerity but also to pose fundamental questions over the nature and direction of the sector as a whole. Statistical reports suggest around 18 million foreign visits (a different calculation to foreign Western visitors) in 2010 while the number of domestic tourist visits was around a mind-blowing 740 million, an increase of around 19% on the previous year. However, this domestic tourism pivots around 'temple tourism', as they call it in the business; that is, pilgrims or visitors interested in religious or spiritual issues. So the state of Andhra Pradesh north of Tamil Nadu on the east coast, which doesn't even feature on the 'top ten' for Western foreign tourists, attracted 155 million visits in 2010 and was top in India for total tourist visits. Even when compared to Tamil Nadu, Andhra Pradesh boasts a greater number of pilgrimage destinations.

2002 was the year that was seen as heralding the policy turn towards domestic tourism. But as recent studies have begun to realise, 'foreign' and 'domestic' tourism cannot simply be equated with each other. The Taj Mahal for example is not a priority for domestic visitors, unlike foreign visitors. More generally the two groups have different tastes with regards to tourist sites and experiences. The most popular sites for the domestics are around Delhi and North India while for foreign visitors it is in the south. They are interested in two different types of India. It was only in recent years that the national tourist agencies recognised the overwhelming policy emphasis given to Western foreign tourism at the expense of the domestic market and began to encourage advertising and promotion at the local state level. A greater ownership and responsibility at local level on tourism resulted in new funding and budgets, a different focus and attention to transport infrastructure as well as associated issues such as accommodation facilities. The recent arrival of India's 'middle class', 'mass tourism' and 'weekend breaks' raises a completely different set of choices and priorities than those associated with the traditional Western tourist 'high-end' market. Given the generally low income of pilgrims when compared to Westerners, how many beds can be built and by whom at the expense of a five-star, air-conditioned hotel that will be only reached through some international airport? Apparently, a number of mid-scale hotel chains are beginning to emerge that fills some elements of the gap in the market. And temples too that are rarely poor due to the offerings made by the pilgrims are beginning to provide cheap dormitory arrangements on a large scale. Instead of islands of luxury catering only to a small segment of the market, there has been a turn towards accommodating and encouraging the internal mass market. Spin-offs in this new focus include non-religious destinations such as Goa with its emphasis on all-year attractions aimed at domestic visitors ("Goa in the Rains") and Kerala ("Dream Season").

Travel and tourism remains as the largest service industry in India. As the government's tourist site puts it, "It provides heritage, cultural, medical, business and sports tourism." It contributes over $100 billion to the nation's GDP each year, around 7% of the total GDP. It is expected, the government promises, to grow substantially in the years ahead, with new investment projects and the promotion of 'niche' areas such as medical tourism.

Being a tourist

There is another issue, however, that underpins this discussion of tourism in India. Who exactly are 'tourists'? Are all 'tourists' the same or are there different types of tourists? What is the essence or nature of 'tourism', and how is it different from other closely related experiences? What exactly are we talking about?

As might be expected, tourism is big business. In fact, it is the world's largest single industry and growing fast. According to a 2016 report from the United Nations World Tourism Organisation (UNWTO), international tourist arrivals were up 5% in 2015 to a record 1.2 billion. A quick glance at some of the literature and reports surrounding either national or global tourism risks being drowned in a sea of statistics. The contribution to the Gross Domestic Product (GDP), the number of people employed in the industry, destinations for 'outbound' and 'inbound' tourists, the percentage contribution to exports and the amount of money domestically generated by the industry are all outlined in loving detail.

For the UNWTO as might be expected, the dominant focus is on tourism and poverty alleviation. Tourism is seen as the proverbial 'magical bullet'. As it mentions in one of its recent reports, "In many countries, tourism acts as an engine for development through foreign exchange earnings and the creation of direct and indirect employment... it is the most viable and sustainable economic development option."

This is I'm sure all true, especially when it lists the positive as well as the negative consequences of the industry. However, they take us only along a little of the route that deserves consideration when discussing 'being a tourist'. As mentioned in the opening chapter, the big growth of tourism studies or hospitality studies within higher education tends to share in, uncritically, this 'development led' approach to the subject area. There is a wealth of empirical studies and reports on how to achieve a 'competitive advantage', designing ways of 'maximising revenues' or on various marketing or brand strategies.

Understanding or defining what or who is a 'tourist', though, is not a straightforward issue. Many commentators simply accept the widely accepted UNWTO definition – that is, as "temporary visitors staying in a place outside their usual place of residence for a continuous period of at least 24 hours but less than one year, for leisure, business or other purposes". There are many problems associated with this or similar technical definitions. It's very wide-ranging and seems to encompass almost everyone; it reduces tourism to an economic activity and minimises or ignores the cultural and social aspects of the activity. What if any are the differences for example between 'tourists' and other categories of similar activity such as 'travellers', 'explorers', 'backpackers', 'pilgrims', 'outsiders' or 'hippies'? What these and other labels suggest is that understandings of 'being a tourist' are socially constructed and multidimensional rather than being a technical or practical matter. 'Tourism' encompasses different groups of people (according to gender, social class, colour, age, nationality for example) with different agendas and seeking different experiences. Acknowledging the complicated nature of 'being a tourist', a number of scholars have attempted to outline various categories that differentiate between touristic experiences. An early example is Cohen's 1979 distinction between recreational, diversionary, experiential, experimental and existential tourists. Others such as Plog distinguish between allocentric travellers (those seeking exotic or untouched destinations) and psychocentric tourists (non-risk taking and going to established destinations). There are many other illustrations over the last few decades of conceptual efforts to nail down the nature of 'being a tourist' or of 'the tourist experience'. McCabe (2005) for example provides a summary of some of these approaches. As a frequent tourist myself, they make for an interesting read. I and possibly the other 'returners' that I interviewed can recognise many of the behaviours, intercultural exchanges and contacts and experiences discussed in the studies. I am less keen, however, on the linking of 'tourism' to 'identity formation' that seems popular in recent years. I acknowledge that it is very difficult to pin down the nature and experiences of 'being a tourist' although I will inevitably in this text employ certain assumptions and perspectives on this issue. The questions I chose to ask and the discussions reported here necessarily imply a particular view of 'tourism', "a particular view" that I am not going to explore further beyond a recognition of its problematic nature. My overall focus is on visiting India rather than the nature of tourism. And an important aspect of this focus is on the historical dimensions – the subject of the next chapter – that inevitably, especially for the British, shape these visits.

Chapter 3

Fighting over the past

Navigating history; Akbar and the Mughals

"Why did you first come to India? Where did you go? How many times have you returned to India?" were some of the questions I asked the 'regular returners'. Other people who I haven't talked to or even know have some answers. "It seems to me that nowhere on Earth can you find all human histories, from the Stone Age to the global village, still thriving, as you can in India," as Michael Wood puts it in his wonderful television series *The Story of India*. Most visitors both foreign and domestic would probably agree with Wood. It is one of the great attractions about the country. On the other hand, getting a feel for 'all these human histories' is no easy task. So dramatic and dominant are the stories of India in the twentieth century – famine, Independence, Partition, assassinations – that they risk overwhelming all other understandings and dramas. Comfortable definitions and narratives seem impossible to grasp – re-evaluating and reconsidering are par for the course. In the main, however, our ignorance as foreign tourists is always evident and often a great source of frustration. It's rare for example to visit say the ruined city of Vijayanagara (commonly known as Hampi, in the southern state of Karnataka) and not leave a day or two later exhilarated and exhausted but also painfully aware of a lack of any historical narrative that allows you to situate the rise and fall of the Vijayanagar Empire. The almost surreal, boulder-strewn, once-dazzling Hindu capital of the Vijayanagar Empire spread over 26 kilometres reached its peak of power in the 15th century with a population of over 1.5 million people. What happened to the Empire? What are the archaeologists working on the site today looking for and expecting to find? Where does Hampi fit in with other earlier and later Empires? I keep buying these guidebooks at the sites but rarely finish them as I'm soon off on the train somewhere else. I do have, however, a wonderful collection of these guides on the bookshelves at home.

Unlike Britain with its more 'theme park' conception and practice towards its 'heritage industry', India's civilisation, or its particular historical forms of social development, appears real and continuing – an everyday experience that links the past with the present. Few countries manage to infuse these meanings and rituals of the past in pointing to acceptable boundaries and behaviours of the present. While the unlocking of British culture and history is largely a detailed exercise in class analysis, the situation is altogether more complex and mysterious in India, to the outsider anyway. At times, this everyday weight of the often-distant past can seem a little overwhelming. The seemingly simple task 'of being a tourist' risks mental exhaustion and often frustrations in that more questions and puzzles are raised than answered. Take for example the Taj Mahal, arguably the most iconic tourist site in the world, although only ranked Number 10 in the world's top ten tourist sites with 2.5 million visitors a year. Few overseas visitors leave India without a visit to "the teardrop on the face of humanity". Irrespective of the hassles on arrival by train at Agra with the 'guides', the crowds, the queues, the heat... it is all soon forgotten. Everything about a visit to the Tomb is cliché-ridden and yet these clichés seem to capture many of the experiences and sensations of the visitors, including ourselves. Just watching the expressions on the faces of the steady stream of tourists (mainly, Indian) as they come round the corner of the massive red sandstone gateway and see for the first time the luminescent white marble of the Taj laid out before them rekindles faith in the discoveries and joys of old-fashioned tourism. Most of these visitors will have a general understanding of the Taj Mahal story – the grief-stricken Mughal emperor's memorial to his recently departed wife Mumtaz Mahal who died at the age of 39 in 1631 while giving birth to their 14th child. This story will be examined in more detail once inside the tomb. Here at the viewpoint at the gateway though, the 64 raised gardens are not visible, the cypress and fruit trees hidden – only visible is the raised pool and the tomb itself. Nothing is allowed to intrude, complicate or detract from this first sight. Inevitably and seemingly uncontrollably, people stop to gawp in an attempt to 'capture' this special moment. Like us, they will have worked out the best time to visit so as to maximise the constantly changing hue of the white marble against the changing light. And like us, they will be aware that the Taj is seen as the jewel of Muslim art in India.

It is only later, while reflecting on the time in front of that bulbous dome protected by its four minarets, that other issues begin to emerge such as questions between the 'then' of 1631 and the 'now'. Who were the Mughals and where do they fit within the wider historical development of India? What contribution did Islamic influences – architecturally, spiritually or culturally – make to modern Hindu India? What sort of 'India' made possible the Taj Mahal and associated artistic endeavours, and how are they understood today? How did the British react to this and other monuments and behaviours that confronted and challenged their 'civilised' mercantilist rationales? Who were the Muslims of then and where do they fit in within the rising Hindu nationalism in today's India? It's always safer to de-contextualise tourist sites through an exclusive focus on the 'then' divorced from the 'now', and yet in today's India there have been some violent confrontations over this legacy. Perhaps at the end of the day, it's best not to move from the particular to the general; just enjoy another bottle of Cobra or Kingfisher. After all we are tourists, visitors, or perhaps travellers. But it is difficult, especially in India where ancient but continuing cultural configurations appear as essential aspects of the Indian pathway to modernity, and eventually perhaps, a world economic power. Could any other country, for example, have as one of its recent towering historical figures Mahatma Gandhi? What is there about this country that raises Gandhi to a semi-god status while most countries would have locked him away as a dangerous loose cannon? For the outsider, Gandhi seemed to embody this ancient with the modern, albeit in a highly original and particular manner much to the bewilderment and frustrations of the imperial British political class and their aristocratic outriders.

It was in fact our Taj Mahal visit that led to my continuing but intermittent interest in the Mughal Empire. When back in England for example, I'll spend a relaxing hour or so on YouTube flicking through some of the numerous videos that focus on the Mughals. Or I'll seek out the appropriate rooms in the British Museum while I am down in London. It was on one of these visits that I learnt about the museum's interactive, 3D videos on aspects of Mughal history such as the Taj Mahal. Moreover, Michael Wood's enthusiasm and wanderings around relevant spots and sites in modern India in his search for a dynasty whose rulers were, as he puts it, "among the greatest and most glamorous rulers in the world," can't but enthuse visitors or those interested in the history of the country. For any tourist and especially foreign tourists to India today, it is impossible not to see a landscape that is dominated by the beauty and grandeur of this Mughal legacy. Most of the memorable snapshots of India retained in the years after a visit or even the images used in the country's marketing publicity stem from the nearly two centuries rule by the Mughals – Taj Mahal, the Red Fort or the ghostly splendour of the old Mughal capital Fatehpur-Sikri. It is this city of Agra that perhaps best represents the pinnacle of Mughal architectural masterpieces and continues today to pull in the tourists. But it is not only some foosty old history that leads to the Mughals; the language, customs, dress and food of today's India incorporate the Mughal influence. And unlike most of the earlier episodes in the country's history, the rule and achievements of the Mughals can be deciphered from a wealth of diverse sources including written documents (biographies, poetry) and paintings from many of the leading lights of the period through to visiting Europeans.

There is one name from this period that I kept coming across – namely, Akbar (1542–1605). The achievements of the founder of the Mughal Empire, Babur (1483–1530), are recognised widely in the historical accounts of "one of the most glorious and fascinating episodes in Indian history". But it was Akbar that kept reappearing and who dominates the histories. The accolades for Akbar from then to now could fill another book. "The reign of Akbar is one of the most significant and decisive epochs in the history of India" (Sinharaja Tammita-Delgoda) or "one of the most extraordinary figures in Indian and world history" (Michael Wood) or "Akbar bestrides all accounts of the Great Mughals... because without him there might not have been a Mughal empire" (John Keay). What then in a nutshell characterised this major figure of "world history"?

Decisively in his forty-year reign, Akbar was a soldier and warrior. Although only 13 years of age when coming to the throne, his conquests led to the consolidation of Mughal power that eventually incorporated most of India. Similar to most conquering armies in India, the Mughals arrived from central Asia. Babur managed to subdue the north of today's India and established an empire stretching from Afghanistan through to Bengal. Akbar militarily extended this empire (brutally in a number of instances) south into the Deccan plateau. It wasn't only military conquest, however, that was important – perhaps of greater significance was what followed in the aftermath of conquest. As Akbar's biographer of the time noted, "The emperor was aware of the fanatical hatred between Hindus and Muslims." Through a number of imaginative initiatives over subsequent decades, these divisions were confronted and minimised. "Ignorance above all was the cause of this 'fanatical hatred'," Akbar reasoned. No religion be it Hindu or Muslim could claim absolute truth. Violence in the name of religion, forced conversions or intolerance of other faiths had no place in a civilised society. Moreover, religious divisions threatened the stability and functioning of a stable society. "Justice and reason should be our guide," argued Akbar. Discussions were held with all the major religious faiths be they Hindus, Muslims, Christians, Buddhists, Parsis or Jains. In contrast to previous Muslim conquerors in India, Hindu temples were safeguarded from destruction and the building of new temples encouraged. Two particular taxes – a pilgrimage tax and the hated jizya tax – seen as oppressive by most Hindus were abolished.

Being seen as 'the protector of the people and guardian of all', however, required Akbar moving beyond the religious realm. Marriage alliances and personal privileges were used to incorporate the old enemy – the Rajputs who assumed governing and military roles in the new empire.

And in his spare time Akbar turned to the issue of statecraft. Underpinning these initiatives dealing with religion was above all his 'political nous', as we might put it today. His empire which by now covered most of today's India (apart from the far south) and included parts of Pakistan and Afghanistan was given a firm basis with a clearly developed, organised system of government. Characterised by an extensive centralised bureaucracy with the king as the unquestioned authoritative centre, the empire was divided into eighteen provinces each with its own governor. A new civil service was created and arranged into 33 grades with fixed salaries. A new tax system based on land revenue was introduced. Recording all cultivated land, their use and potential was seen as providing a fairer, more efficient and more effective means of delivering the revenue needed to fund the state apparatus.

As Michael Wood writes, "No Renaissance ruler in Europe,

not even the brilliant Elizabeth I, tried so consistently as Akbar to bring in the rule of reason... it is an idea whose time has yet to come."

And all from an innocent touristic visit to the Taj Mahal. Things might have been a bit more relaxed if we missed Agra on our travels.

The 'Indic civilisation'

Whether it is the Taj Mahal and the Mughals, Mahatma Gandhi, Hinduism, the hymns and chants of the Vedas or even of Bollywood movies, there is this encouragement to the outsider to examine the new and recent through the prism of the past. Why we are who we are continues to inform and drive most people's curiosity, arguments and inquiries; in the case of India, the effort promises rich dividends in any analysis of the tourist experience.

In between our visits to India, I have found numerous texts and videos that have gradually, and without needing any specialised knowledge, introduced me to some of the intricacies of this complex and earliest of civilisations. Goran Therborn's recent book *The World: A Beginner's Guide* for example situates this history through using the wider notion of 'civilisations'. It's the big comparative picture that he is after and, like my 'working geographical knowledge' of India, provided me with a basis of 'working historical knowledge' of the country's civilisation. He understands civilisations as those "large, enduring cultural configurations, pertinent to our contemporary world". Five ancient major civilisations of enduring importance are identified. These are first, the Sinic civilisation (centred in China and encompassing Korea, Japan and Vietnam). There is then the Western Asian civilisation (origins in the Arab peninsula but incorporating Istanbul and Western cultural centres in Cordoba, Spain, Fez in Morocco, Tunis and Cairo through to Persia and Uzbekistan in the east). Thirdly is the European civilisation followed fourthly, by the sub-Saharan civilisations, and finally, the Indic civilisation. Centred in India, the Indic civilisation incorporated Sri Lanka, moved eastwards through to Bali and Java, Burma, Thailand, Laos, Cambodia and southern Vietnam and northwards across the Himalayas into Nepal and Tibet. Indic civilisation, suggests Therborn, emerged around 3,500 years ago but had no known direct connection with the earlier Indus valley civilisation despite both originating around the River Indus, in today's Pakistan. From these origins in the north-west, the Indic civilisation spread eastwards along the Ganges river plain, reaching southern India much later.

Although knowing nothing about these very early civilisations, I found Therborn's periodisation interesting – not only because of historical inadequacies on my part but, more importantly, because of raging arguments and controversies happening today in India over the early origins and nature of modern India. Associated recently with the rise to government of the Bharatiya Janata Party (BJP) with Narendra Modi as Prime Minister, this is a hot, hot topic. Bitter disputes between intellectuals, passionate newspaper editorials, controversial political appointments and vindictive articles today characterise this seemingly arcane issue on the origins and nature of the country.

In terms of making sense of Indian culture today, Therborn identifies a number of distinctive features that characterises the Indic civilisation. First, it "is soaked in religion". It permeated everyday life and was remarked upon by early visitors such as the Greeks. So nothing new, then. It was importantly a religiosity that was pluralistic; a variety of religions were managed and tolerated. Given that Hinduism is a polytheistic religion – a belief or worship of more than one god – it coexisted with the gods and beliefs of other great religions such as Buddhism, Christianity, Judaism or Islam. Secondly and perhaps most distinctively, the Indic civilisation has this central notion of transmigration or the rebirth of souls. Common to both Hinduism and Buddhism, there is this idea that lives today are determined by incarnations of things done in a previous life. It is this view of transmigration that morally and religiously underpins the hierarchical social division or caste system that even today baffles visitors to India. This *varna* or caste system will be explored in a later chapter when discussing everyday life in modern India. It is not, however, the only or the most visible feature of this religious character to the Indic civilisation; pride of place for outside tourists probably are the extraordinary religious rituals and performances that pepper travels around the country. These range, for example, from the pilgrims visiting some of the great devotional temples or sacred rivers through to the various 'holy men' or wandering *sadhus*. Thinking of these *sadhus* reminds me of the time in 2013 when I was poring over the daily newspapers on another great religious theatrical spectacular – the Maha Kumbh Mela in Allahabad, North India. Lasting 55 days and held every 12 years at the confluence of the holy rivers of the Ganges, Yamuna and Saraswati, the 2013 Mela attracted some 100 million pilgrims. How many Londons, New Yorks or Tokyos is that? Watching the ritual bathing and the mass feeding of the holy men and women on Indian television was mesmerising – only in India, I kept thinking.

However, it was not only religion that characterised the Indic civilisation, continued Therborn. As distinctive as its religious features was its political character – namely, the absence of an established imperial head or centre. Astonishingly, until 1947 what is now the Indian Union had never been politically united. Historically as Michael Wood points out in his *Story of India* television documentary, the major rulers and leaders were the Buddhist Asoka in the third century, the great Muslim Mughals of the seventeenth century and then eventually, from the nineteenth century until 1947, the British who were Christian. It wasn't political empires or a historical awareness arrived at through historical texts that provided a unified Indic civilisation, argues Therborn. It was uniquely this set of religious conceptions and practices – rebirth, the ten obligations of *dharma*, the rituals associated with *karma*, the Brahmin 'gatekeepers' with their inherited knowledge of sacred rites and rituals conveyed in the elite language of Sanskrit – that defined and provided the continuity of the Indic civilisation. As Wood puts it, it was "the ten thousand year epic" of the "world's oldest and most influential civilisation."

Wandering around Varanasi – or Benares as it is still traditionally known, perhaps the holiest city in India for Hindus – in 2011 seems to confirm this legacy but also its relevance today. Mark Twain in 1896 described beautifully the city as "older than history, older than tradition, older even than legend, and looks twice as old than all of them put together." This great northern city in Uttar Pradesh on the banks of the Ganges is a magnet for travellers. As one of the oldest living cities in the world and one of the holiest places for Hindus, it manages to encompass most aspects of this religiosity – an hour or two at night-time on the ghats on the side of the Ganges will never be forgotten as the lights come on and the pilgrims just keep on coming to immerse themselves in the waters of the river. Washing in the (heavily polluted) Mother Ganges is said to wash away all sin. To die next to the river or to have one's ashes scattered into the waters and so guaranteeing release from the eternal cycle of birth and rebirth is the goal of every devout Hindu. Seen as the home to the god of creation and destruction Lord Shiva, the city's life revolves around the seven kilometres of ghats that line the west bank of the Ganges. Around one hundred of these ghats provide the focus for one of the most devotional sites in the world. Sitting on the rooftop of our lodgings amongst the ghats on the side of the river provided us with a continuing spectacle of bathers covered in soap suds immersing themselves in the river, Brahmin priests holding forth under palm umbrellas, pavement barbers shaving the heads of their customers and *sadhus* in their minimal orange loincloths passing on their wisdom and gratefully receiving gifts of food. We were close enough to one of the 'burning ghats' – Manikarnika Ghat – on the edge of the Ganges to see the great pyres of wood burning away releasing yet another soul to the gods. Daybreak or evening time in Varanasi must be one of the most dramatic and lingering memories of any visit to India.

The attention to rituals and practices of birth, death and purification that are so 'in your face' evident in Varanasi have a lineage that Therborn would happily find room for in his outline of the five great civilisations of long ago.

The Indus Valley civilisation

The Indic civilisation of 3,500 years ago that Therborn refers to has been in the news more recently, in fact a couple of decades ago, and Varanasi hasn't anything to do with this breaking news. To a large extent, modern India can trace its archaeological origins to the cities of Harappa and Mohenjo-Daro. Commonly referred to as the Indus Valley civilisation (named after the great River Indus which gave India its name) this civilisation lasted about 1,000 years evolving from around 5,000 years ago and reaching its peak around 3500 BCE (Before Common Era/AD) although its origins remain a little vague and was based, as mentioned above, around the great cities of Harappa and Mohenjo-Daro. Tracing its origin from the earliest known civilisations of Egypt and Mesopotamia, the Indus Valley civilisation (sometimes referred to as the Harappan civilisation) covered a huge area stretching across what is today Pakistan, north-west India and eastern Afghanistan. Today there are some 70 excavated sites with more currently being explored by Indian and Pakistani archaeologists. Discovered accidentally by two British engineers only in 1856, it was in 1921 that the first excavation took place. Overnight almost, the birth of India was lengthened another 1,000 years. Almost overnight, world history had to be rewritten – staggering. The last 90-odd years have continued to provide a steady stream of discoveries, excitement and discussion about the sophisticated, carefully planned and well-ordered world of the Indus people. Why did it disappear, what led to its collapse, and where did everyone go were some of the tantalising questions raised and discussed around the world in subsequent years. The *Los Angeles Times* for example in 2012 had an article on this mysterious decline and disappearance of the Harappans, using the latest satellite technology. They reached two conclusions; first, that the eastward drift of the monsoons which provided the water for the extensive agriculture projects left a dependency on local rains which were insufficient to sustain a large agricultural surplus which was needed for food and trade. As the article puts it, "The cities dried out, the writing was lost, trade halted and the Harappan civilisation was no more." Secondly, the team believed that they have solved the mystery surrounding the mythical river, the Sarasvati. The ancient Indian scriptures – the Vedas – described the Sarasvati as "surpassing in might and majesty all other waters" and "pure in her course from the mountains to the ocean". The new data from the recent study, however, suggests that there was no such great river fed by the Himalayan glaciers. If there was such a river, it was a river like others of that time fed by monsoon waters. A quick search around, however, suggests that controversies and debates about the mysterious Sarasvati River continue today unabated.

I am no archaeologist but I remember my amazement and excitement when watching Michael Wood wandering around Harappa and Mohenjo-Daro in his television series on India. Michael Wood is an enthusiastic and knowledgeable commentator on India (among many other subject matters) and I remember being riveted while he wandered around what remains today of the "sensational finds" as he put it, accompanied by various Indian experts. As is his manner, we get a lot of information but also a lot of questions and links to everyday life today in the Indus regions. Despite the recent accidental stumbling upon one of the earliest great ancient civilisations, a lot seems to be already known. The well-planned, uniform, almost regimented cities, the gridiron street plan with streets divided into blocks of roughly equal size, the hierarchical arrangement of the burnt brick (no stone) two-roomed tenements through to the palatial mansions all with their careful planned bathrooms and elaborate drainage systems all contribute towards suggesting a system of local government and town planning, unknown before and perhaps unmatched until the Romans many years into the future. The pottery remains together with the size and number of vast granaries suggest a thriving agricultural economy, huge surpluses, a high standard of living and a well-developed system of trade and commerce, suggests Sinharaja Tammita-Delgoda in his very readable *A Traveller's History of India*. As he points out, the process of spinning cotton into yarn and weaving it into cloth was first developed by the Indus people at around the 2500 BCE period. "This discovery ranks amongst India's greatest gifts to the world." Since these first awakenings for me of the Indus Valley civilisation from the televised series, I have always kept an eye on the media reports of excavations and discoveries. What a continuing detective story.

But here is something. Even today apparently, the written script of the Indus civilisation remains a complete mystery. Comprising a total of 400 characters which remained almost unchanged throughout its history of about 1,000 years, all efforts to decipher the language have failed. As a result, little is known about the Indus people themselves. Until further efforts at unlocking the language are successful, tantalising suggestions of this non-violent, conflict-resolving society which honoured women will remain unresolved. Mother Goddess for example was the most important of the many gods, and women were seen as the origin of life, the font of fertility from which everything – man, animals, trees and plants – sprang. The seemingly enhanced role of women in Indus society is particularly striking.

The Ashoka discoveries

During our visit to Calcutta in 2012, I stumbled upon (not literally unfortunately) another early towering figure in India's history – Ashoka or Ashoka the Great who ruled most of the Indian subcontinent from around 260–232 BCE. The walk from our hotel in Calcutta passed the Asiatic Society just off Park Street. The name rang a bell. Moreover while wandering around the wonderful, shady South Park Cemetery I noticed that recent renovations had been funded by this Asiatic Society. Founded in 1784 by Sir William Jones, the Asiatic Society of Bengal was once a world centre of archaeologists, geologists, linguists and historians with the aim of "inquiring into the history, civil and natural, the antiquities, arts, sciences and literature of Asia." It seemed that it was members of the Society together with people from the Archaeological Survey of India that unearthed (literally) the forgotten Ashoka; and all very recently in the eighteenth and nineteenth centuries. I did go into the Society's building, up the dark stairs and into the entrance foyer. There was no one there apart from the security guard and it looked a little rundown and foreboding so I didn't go further. I remember, however, the excitement of reading Charles Allen's *Ashoka: The Search for India's Lost Emperor* (2012) around that time. It was like a popular detective novel as layer upon layer of evidence was uncovered by these British orientalists. We now know that Ashoka was the Indian Emperor of the Maurya Dynasty who ruled most of the Indian subcontinent from around 269–232 BCE. For over a hundred years in the nineteenth century, a series of scholars unearthed the missing history of Ashoka, and what a history it was. After conquests and complete domination over the whole of the subcontinent from eastern Afghanistan, Ashoka seemed overcome with remorse at the violence and savagery required in the consolidation of the Mauryan Empire. He embraced the new emerging religion of Buddhism with its emphasis on compassion and non-violence. A *Dharma* or universal law based on Buddha's teachings was proclaimed throughout the Empire. Non-violence, tolerance, helping one another together with animals, hospitality to others and respect for the environment were some of the espoused sentiments. The means of propagating these new, strange views were through inscribing edicts on the face of cliffs, huge rocks or giant pillars and all written in Prakrit, a non-standard vernacular language of North India popular at that time. Bizarrely though, despite the far-reaching consequences of Ashoka's rule and enlightened practices (for most of the time anyway), Ashoka disappeared from the history books. Far from being a celebrated figure, he was ignored and invisible for the next two thousand years or so. It wasn't really until the twentieth century that his achievements and distinctiveness were recognised worldwide. Arguments and debates continue today in attempting to explain this invisibility. One argument for example has it that while Buddha was incorporated into Hinduism, there was less tolerance of Buddhism as a religious faith by an assertive Hinduism. Furthermore, Buddhism always had a greater reach and audience outside of India, and in this Buddhist literature, there is a recognition of Ashoka's importance. Apart from the stone and rock edifices displaying Ashoka's edicts in India, much other evidence has disappeared over time. Again similar to the Harappan civilisation, no one could understand or decipher the language inscribed on the pillars or rock faces. Despite their undoubted imperial motives, it was the formidable skills and passion of orientalists working through the Asiatic Society of Bengal and Indian Archaeological agencies that in 1837 unlocked the language on the edifices, mapped out the history, dates and achievements of the Mauryan Empire and identified and preserved a number of stupas and rock edicts. Today as Burjor Avari points out there are, in all, 14 major rock edicts, three minor rock edicts and seven pillar edicts spread across 30 sites throughout the subcontinent – national treasures supported by government funding. Given that the uncovering of

Ashoka and the Mayans was at the same time, an uncovering of the historical Buddha himself added to the global significance of these breakthroughs. An amazing story that comes alive when for example gazing upon an Ashoka column in Delhi.

Ajanta and Ellora Caves

I was reminded of these Ashoka discoveries and stories as I sat on the train leaving Bombay and heading towards Aurangabad, some 350 kilometres east of the city. It was early 2016 and I was off to see the fabled painted caves of Ajanta, another of India's UNESCO World Heritage Sites. My guidebook had whetted my anticipation but it was William Dalrymple's article in a 2014 edition of the *New York Review of Books* that really set me going. Here was another of those wonderful India stories of archaeological discovery, serendipity, global significance, mystery and splendour. The Ajanta Caves comprise 31 caves dug into an amphitheatre of solid rock. Excavated between 90–70 BCE (it is believed today) shortly after the collapse of Ashoka's great empire, the Caves, as Dalrymple puts it, "contained probably the greatest picture gallery to survive from the ancient world, and along with the frescos of Pompeii, the fabulous murals of Livia's Garden House outside Rome, and the encaustic wax portraits of the Egyptian Fayum, (the) walls represented perhaps the most comprehensive depiction of civilised life to survive from antiquity."

Phew – who wouldn't want to make a visit – and I wasn't disappointed. Although it was very hot with very few visitors about, I managed to view "the most beautiful and ancient paintings in Buddhist art" in around half the caves – art that as Dalrymple put it, "rank as some of the greatest masterpieces of art produced by mankind in any century." Engulfed in darkness, the caves are filled with wall murals, sculptures, carved pillars and ceiling paintings showing tales from the life of Buddha. Representing lifelike, detailed aspects of everyday life – military battles, Buddhist themes, dancing women, animist gods, hunting parties – the Caves unveiled understandings of an earlier Buddhism, devoid of texts that are seen as essential today in practising Buddhism. Each of the caves has their own physical characteristics and layout although all suggest a monastery with residential facilities. Cave One, for example, has what appears to be a square congregational area with an adjacent aisle leading to fourteen chambers, has 20 carved and painted pillars, ceiling paintings and the large shrine of the Buddha at the rear of the cave.

Twenty-six of the thirty-one caves – all the most elaborate ones – were developed in the fifth century, some six hundred years after the first ones were excavated. By now under a wider Hindu influence, these later cave developments were, it is argued, constructed at high speed in a mere sixteen years – amazing if true. By this time, Buddhism was in decline and the 'new caves' were built to commemorate wealthy individuals and patrons although still clearly of a Buddhist nature.

As in all good India stories, mysteries remain. Why were some of the later cave paintings unfinished, what purpose did the caves serve, was it possible to build so many caves so quickly in the fifth century, who were the foreigners depicted in some of the paintings – of different skin colour, in strange clothes, hairdos – and what was their role and why were the caves abandoned are some of the questions left hanging in the air.

And again as in many good Indian archaeological stories, there is a touch of bewilderment about its discovery, just as in Ashoka's or Harappa's case. It was in 1819 that a British hunting party following a tiger bumbled into the rock-cut temples known today as the Ajanta Caves. Cut into the face of a mountain high above the Wangorah River, the caves formed a horseshoe shape that even today remain pretty well camouflaged. Although local people used the caves for prayer and shelter, in the main, the caves were overrun with tangled undergrowth, piles of collapsed rubble and home to bats, birds and larger animals. News of the caves was announced to the wider world through publications from the Royal Asiatic Society in 1829. Subsequently a number of dedicated archaeologists such as Dr James Burgess, James Fergusson in the early days and more recently, and above all, Walter Spink have worked with Indian specialists in preserving and documenting the unique collection from the caves.

Two or three hours' drive from the Ajanta caves are the Ellora caves which the Archaeological Survey of India says are one "of the largest rock hewn monastic-temple complexes in the entire world". The most famous of these caves – Cave 16, known as Kailasa – is the world's largest single piece of rock cutting and all with primitive tools that date back thousands of years. 200,000 tonnes of rock were removed and it took some hundred years to complete. Comprising 34 caves and constructed between the fifth and tenth centuries, the 'caves' are structures chipped out of the vertical face of the Charanandri Hills up in the Western Ghats. Many other caves are evident apparently but not open to tourists. The historical and cultural significance of the Ellora complex, however, is the religious harmony suggested by the caves; 12 Buddhist caves are followed by 17 Hindu caves with the remaining 5 caves being of Jain influence. In one visit and along a two-kilometre stretch, visitors can study and compare the differing architectural splendours and artistic expressions and representations from the three great religions. Unlike the Ajanta caves, those at Ellora have been in continual use over the centuries with written texts recording numerous visits by royal visitors as well as traders. Instead of destroying the religious buildings of other beliefs, the Ellora caves suggest an earlier period of tolerance, coexistence and acceptance of other religions.

Down south – the temple trail and their dynasties

Chennai, or Madras as it is still popularly known, is India's fourth largest city and proud capital of Tamil Nadu. I was there in 2014 arriving by train from Bangalore. I didn't stay too long – I had only arrived in the country a couple of weeks ago and was still a little overwhelmed by the heat and crowds. As mentioned in the previous chapter, I probably didn't give myself enough time to explore the city's histories and delights. I needed instead some time to 'adjust' and, anyway, I had the whole of Tamil Nadu's famed 'temple trail' ahead of me. A week later as I wandered around the Shore Temple at the coastal town of Mahabalipuram (now officially renamed to Mamallapuram) south of Chennai and located on white sands of the Coromandel Coast, I felt that I had made the right decision. As an introduction to this Tamil-speaking (India's oldest living language), cinema mad, creamy rice pudding eating land, and of course, to the temple towns of Kanchipuram and Madurai, Mahabalipuram was an ideal spot to rest and plan the next steps. However, the sheer spectacle, extent and excellence of the astonishing legacy of the monolithic rock-cut temples, caves and reliefs in this one town alone resulted in another experience of 'picking up history on the hoof'. It's not possible to visit, for example, Kanchipuram with its thousand-odd temples or the fortress-like towering Meenakshi Temple in Madurai without coming across references to the ancient dynasties of the Cholas, the Pandyas and the Cheras. More great dynasties and empires from the past – I was flagging on my history stuff. Distinct from the great northern kingdoms, the southern dynasties provided and continues to provide the distinctive culture, language, cuisine, dance, literature of India's south-east.

As mentioned, Mamallapuram was a good place to rest up a bit. It is today an important fishing village with a natural unspoilt beach. Its claim to fame throughout the world, however, is as a centre of stone carving and craftsmanship. Wandering around the town demonstrates the numerous stone carving activities still continued today. About 200 metres from my room on the second floor of this little, local homestay was the Shore Temple perched beside the sea. Built in the eighth century, the Temple is considered to be the earliest stone temple in southern India and the greatest construction of the Pallava Dynasty. The maritime activities of the Pallava rulers ensured that their influence spread throughout India and to neighbouring countries. Although not fully developed as recognisable Hindu temples, the stone-built sculptures around Mamallapuram constitute a kind of experimental laboratory centred on stone as a devotional art. The Hindu gods of Shiva and Vishnu are everywhere evident but the varied collection of boulder sculptures, temples, man-made caves and chariots (*rathas*) used in temple processions (and carved from single pieces of rock) suggest a spiritual rather than a strict religious focus. Rather than religious practices, the Pallava constructions suggested the centrality of religion in everyday life and observance. Massive rock bas-reliefs carved in enormous detail on the side of gigantic slabs of rock continue to provide debate and controversy over their significance. Irrespective of the debates about this storytelling, the influence of the Mamallapuram structures influenced subsequent devotional architecture throughout the south and eventually throughout India. Design and sculptures not only shaped subsequent Hindu temple developments but also temples culturally as places of feasts, festivals, dancing and devotion. Songs sung then are still recited and sung today, some thousand years later. Similarly, the inner sanctum of the temple – the sanctuary – was developed by later dynasties and came to be regarded as a sacred space. The Chola empire for example carried out the next architectural temple development at their capital Thanjavur, from the ninth century onwards. The Brihadishwara Temple for example is arguably the most breathtaking treasure of the Cholas and moved temple developments significantly along. Less grandiose than later temples, those at Thanjavur continued the architectural innovations with courtyards, extensive inscriptions on the temple walls, gopura (monumental towers at the entrance to the temple) tapering in a pyramid shape and carved figures. The carvings were bronze castings, with the figure of the dancing Shiva standing on one leg encircled by flames on a circular frame an image found around the world. These bronze castings were but one of the lasting artistic legacies from the Chola Empire and continue today in Thanjavur in a process almost unchanged from those times. Built 300 years after the Shore Temple and monumental in size, the Brihadishwara Temple through the inscriptions outlined for the first time detailed rules, finances, administrative arrangements and ritual activity. Shiva, Vishnu and their cohorts still dominated the iconograph but religion or more particularly Hinduism was becoming more structured and codified.

In terms of fame and photography, though, it is the Meenakshi Temple in the ancient city of Madurai that grabs all the attention. Mentioned by visiting Greeks and Romans some thousands of years ago, Madurai has long been a city of commercial importance, trade, Tamil culture and worship. Today it is the state's second city after Chennai and has a population of about a million people. It was the capital of the Pandyan Empire for over a thousand years. The Pandyans were the most southern of the three great historical cultures of Tamil Nadu. It was the wealth from this trade that provided the means for the Pandyan Empire's greatest creation – the Meenakshi Temple. Here we have maybe the most outstanding example of Tamil architecture, as distinctive in the Tamil south as the Gothic cathedral is in Europe. My hotel was down by the market area in the city, quite close to the Temple. It was incidentally my first experience of 'a business hotel' – you book in at any time of day or night and have a period of 24 hours before leaving or extending your stay. It was all a little confusing at first. In this downtown area, everything is dominated by the Temple. It is huge. Covering an area equivalent to 25 football pitches and with some 14 towers, the Temple is a maze of courtyards, halls, and shrines. It is a city within a city. It is a Shiva temple but is dedicated to Shiva's wife, Meenakshi, or Minakshi as she is sometimes called. It is she who is the patron deity of Madurai. Michael Wood in *The Story of India* states that the goddess of Madurai is mentioned in Tamil poetry dating back to Roman times but that her name and attributes may point to a more distant connection with the culture of the Bronze Age and earlier. Dominating the Temple profile – and much India tourist brochures and literature – are the magnificent gate towers, some 250 feet high and ornately decorated in garish and lurid coloured plaster characters and scenes from the *Mahabharata,* the national epic. It is a staggering building and from all the photographs I had seen had always been one of my 'must visit' sites in India. And here I was. I spent a day wandering around inside the Temple. It was both exhausting and wonderful. I was unable to do justice to the symbolism, sculptures and ritual activity surrounding me due to my own inadequacies. More importantly though I was able to witness how these most ancient of features still remain vital to people, worshipped as living deities and still a part of everyday life.

After returning home from Tamil Nadu I watched a three-part television series on the BBC entitled *Treasures of the Indus* presented by Sona Datta, a curator from the British Museum. They were wonderful programmes on first the Harappa discoveries, then the Mughals and, finally, the temple cultures of Tamil Nadu. I wished I had seen the series before my visit to Tamil Nadu. One of the dominant themes linking across the programmes was the complexity of spirituality and the evolving religiosity in Southeast Asia as exemplified in these three instances at three different times. What emerges is the evolution of Hinduism from a cultural experience to a more organised, ritualised and codified religion. Always complicated with the multitude of deities and narratives – often competing and contradictory – Hinduism emerged as one of the world's great religions replacing Buddhism in the process. Adaptive to changed circumstances, absorbing influences and different beliefs and interrelating the profane with the divine, emerging Hinduism not only was defined by its tolerance and respect for others but also by its peaceful progression over the millennium. Above all it is a story of the blurring of the illusionary with reality in everyday life and observance. And at the centre of these devotional practices was the temple that has provided a focus for over thousands of years. It's not surprising that this flowering of temple building and architecture ushered in an explosion of artistic expression, and best seen in the Tamil Nadu temple trail.

In trying to fathom the complexities and intricacies of southern India, I got talking while in Madurai to this Indian young woman from Chennai. She was a student and was down in Madurai on a sightseeing visit. She knew her Indian history. For most of its history, India was a weak state, she pointed out. The numerous empires and dynasties that were swirling around my head and that provided some rough timeline and storyline for me were, she continued, symptomatic of its weaknesses. I felt a little deflated after all my efforts to make sense of my visits to this or that part of India. Yes, she argued, there were glorious periods, 'golden ages', enlightened rulers and dynasties, stunning cultural endeavours and achievements, substantial economic successes and global respect from other trading powers at different times in the country's history. She was really in her stride by now. But the fundamental weakness that bedevilled historic India then and today, she argued, was the absence of any empire or ruler capable of unifying all its peoples and territories. There was as a consequence an absence of institutions, political legitimacy and bureaucracy necessary to establish a viable functioning state. The very diversity that we foreign tourists find remarkable and welcoming has been India's Achilles heel. When compared to say China or European countries, India failed historically to create the political infrastructure that managed to incorporate this huge diversity – linguistically and religiously. This fragmentation was exacerbated by the proliferation of local rulers who were happy to go about their business provided there was no interference.

Phew, I thought and ordered another beer – my reflex action when I need time to think. However, and notwithstanding these insightful comments by my student friend from Chennai, for most overseas visitors to India, the country's history and culture is grasped imperfectly through a number of dates and episodes that shaped world history not in the third or eleventh century but in the twentieth century. This more recent history of India – dramatic, brutal and momentous – will be discussed in more detail in later chapters. Most obviously for example is the Independence of India itself in August 1947, the withdrawal of the British and the terrible human costs of the Partition in the creation of Pakistan. The one to two million deaths and eleven million people leaving their ancestral homes to flee to safer venues in the ensuing Hindu-Muslim bloodbath constitute one of the defining global historical episodes of the last hundred years.

History in the crossfire

As mentioned earlier, the notion of 'civilisation' is a difficult one to grasp or understand even though it is used extensively when discussing India. It seems to be one of those elastic terms which means whatever the authors want it to mean. You have for example 'Indu civilisation', 'Indian civilisation', 'Western civilisation' or 'Eastern civilisation', all suggesting many different understandings. Most people probably will associate 'civilisation' as something to do with history, language, culture and institutions. Our tourist books confidently talk about the Mughal or Chola civilisations. 'Civilisations', or 'dynasties' or 'empires' seem to be a convenient shorthand for separating great clumps of history into manageable chunks. For serious historians, however, such crude periodisation must be infuriating (but, whisper it, very useful for us tourists). The nature of history, 'what it is' and its methodologies have always been subject to lively discussions and debates in India and elsewhere. In recent years, however, and as hinted above, being clearer on what is meant by 'civilisation' has moved out of narrow academic concerns into more mainstream media agendas. The heated and occasionally violent discussions around aspects of Indian history have been fuelled by a wider global debate. For example, Samuel P. Huntington, an influential American academic, published in 1993 his seminal article entitled "The Clash of Civilizations?" which he later followed with his book, *The Clash of Civilizations: And the Remaking of World Order*. Focussing on an understanding of the post-Cold War period, Huntington argued that attention to 'civilisations' was a better way of understanding the world rather the previous attention given to 'ideologies'. Given the 'end of history' as an American colleague of Huntington described the fall of the Soviet Union, Huntington outlined his argument precisely and clearly. "The twentieth-century conflicts between liberal democracy and Marxist-Leninism," he wrote, "is only a fleeting and superficial historical phenomena compared to the continuing and deeply conflictual relation between Islam and Christianity." Religion he argues is the key primary element in "civilizational identity". Given the "War on Terror" from the world's superpowers and the subsequent invasions of Iraq and Afghanistan, the mess that is Libya today, anti-Islamic sentiment, and brutal dictatorship in Egypt and the tragedy that characterises contemporary Syria, Huntington's arguments provided ready and easy answers that appeared to legitimate the dangerous world turmoil and the actions of the West. 'Islamophobia' was a new term that entered the media's lexicon.

Adding fuel to this fire was the British historian Niall Ferguson. Describing himself as a "fully paid-up member of the neo-imperialist gang", his book *Empire: How Britain Made the Modern World* (2003) and later in 2013, *Civilisation: The West and the Rest*, made the British Empire respectable once again. As a flattering review in the British *Daily Mail* newspaper put it, Britain's Empire stood out "as a beacon of tolerance, decency and the rule of law." Colonised people such as those in India, Ferguson argued in his later text, would not have had their most valuable ideas and institutions – parliamentary democracy, individual freedom and the English language – without the 'humanitarian' rule of the British. As might be expected the arguments of 'how Britain made the world great' provoked heated and extensive debate not only in the West but in India too. Some of the best of these debates are between Ferguson and Pankaj Mishra that run across many years and are to be found in a number of journals.

However, it wasn't the writings of Ferguson and many other Western defenders of Britain's military and ideological adventures in various parts of the world that were the main stimuli behind the re-emergence of 'civilisation' as a focus of interest in the popular press, and especially in India. Instead it was the election of the Hindu nationalist party, the Bharatiya Janata Party (BJP) under Prime Minister Narendra Modi in 2014, that has generated excitement and, also, a deep foreboding within the country. The BJP's sweeping victory was not totally unexpected given the torpor, stagnation and inactivity of the last years of the Congress government under Manmohan Singh, but the complete collapse of the Congress Party was nevertheless dramatic. Bereft of any significant grassroot organisation unlike the BJP, the Congress party was already faced with formidable obstacles in the overwhelming corporate and small business support for Modi, the sycophantic media support for Modi and a grumbling middle class who felt that Congress had concentrated far too much on the country's poor. It appeared that most of the country yearned for a new champion in the march towards neoliberal solutions in the country's stalled economic progress and they seem to have found it in the BJP.

Later chapters look more closely at the rise of the BJP. Here, the focus is more directed to the purposeful, hateful and divisive atmosphere that has enveloped 'history' as its focus. Worries had been expressed by an increasing number of Indian intellectuals of the religious and ideological baggage that is, and has been, associated with the BJP and its more hidden allies. In an article in the *Times of India* entitled "Journey towards soft fascism", and written a week before the 2014 election for example, Kanti Bajpai warns of the dangers of a majority-led government under Modi. He describes this as "soft fascism", which is, he argues, "simply a society marked by less authoritarianism, intimidation, chauvinism, submission and social Darwinism" than "hard fascism". More ominously, he suggests that soft fascism: "rises, establishes itself and consolidates its hold through the structures and systems of democracy." 'Soft fascism' maybe a little over the top to put it mildly but it illustrates some of the fears that have been aroused by the rise of the BJP.

Established just over thirty years ago, the BJP is generally seen as reactionary party (rather than a progressive right-wing Party), chauvinist and with an ugly communal outlook (i.e. anti-Muslim). If BJP's nationalist 'masculine' Hindu outlook was not enough of a worry, there is the larger issue of the influence within the BJP of the Rashtriya Swayamsevak Sangh (RSS), founded as a direct imitation of European fascist organisations. The RSS is, argues Amit Chaudhuri, a "disciplinarian, quasi-militant, extreme right wing outfit." The promotion of a fundamentalist, literal brand of Hinduism is resulting, he suggests, in leading to "the political, instrumental use of Hinduism to defend and assert identity while assailing other identities." Given that India at the time of Independence opted for 'secularism' to prevent religious strife, the implications of a move towards Hinduism rather than secularism as the dominant paradigm in the near future has grave and dangerous implications. Hinduism with its incredibly rich, creative and fluid legacy as a non-organised religion is to be replaced as a narrow, literal, dogmatic, monitored and puritanical collection of 'truths'. For most scholars and believers, Hinduism is far from being a monolithic belief system. It has no founder, no single canonical text and no ecclesiastical structure. Based on archaeological and linguistic evidence, the evolution of Hinduism traditionally has been seen as a complex pattern of groups, cults, ideas and sects interacting with other religions such as Muslims at different times, in different contexts and in different ways. Instead we have today an attempt to replace this complex, rich myriad history with a simple historical narrative of India defined by two antagonistic religious communities with a glorious Hindu 'golden age' followed by the 'dark ages' with the arrival of the brutal Mughals. Today it is the focus on a single god – the warrior god Ram – that is promoted and used as the mobiliser of true Hindus against the outsiders and invaders, the Muslims. India has become the land of Ram. Myth and fiction is asserted as historical fact – a 'post-truth' in today's political lexicon.

And today, one of the centres of these battles is the ancient Harappan civilisation. For today's Hindutva warriors, the people of the Harappan civilisation was home not to migrants or invaders but to indigenous people who participated in the great Vedic Age. Propaganda and assertion replace study and painstaking discovery and discussion. And unfortunately, it is also by intimidation, physical destruction (of museums, artefacts) and mass mobilisations that increasingly characterise the march of this militant Hinduism.

It's not surprising then that the celebrated Indian artist MF Husain (the 'Picasso of India') was chased out of India in 2006 because of his nude depictions of Hindu goddesses or Penguin Books' decision to pulp the international scholar Wendy Doniger's book *The Hindus: An Alternative History* in 2014 because of the campaign by militant 'Hindus', the third book to be withdrawn over a number of weeks. The message seems to be not to fall out with these militant Hindu groups, these "fanatics" as Pankaj Mishra describes them who see "traditional Indian religions as a threat to their project of a culturally homogenous and militant nation-state."

Given the linguistic, religious, cultural and historical diversity of the peoples who reside in India, an accepted version of 'Indian civilisation' is difficult. On a variety of different measures for example North India is very different from the south. These difficulties as mentioned above have not prevented the BJP and its associated organisations from aggressively promoting a version of 'Hindu civilisation' based on Hindutva throughout the whole of the country. Communalism is a widely used term in South Asia and highlights differences (usually religious) between people. Followers of a particular religion or 'community' are seen increasingly as incompatible, antagonistic and hostile. Hindutva is an Islamophobic, religious-communal, intolerant prejudice. The successful campaign by the BJP in the 2014 national elections was India's most communal campaign ever. Not surprisingly, India's Parliament (Lok Sabha) today has its lowest ever Muslim representation and without a single Muslim member from the state of Uttar Pradesh, which has around 40 million Muslims. 'What it is to be an Indian today' is not some academic conference title or philosophical tract; instead, it is the subject of political demonstrations, riots in the street, ransacking and destroying libraries and mass rallies. As William Dalrymple put it in an excellent summary and review of various Indian books in the *New York Review of Books* (in 2005 before the 2014 election of the BJP), the "roots of the current conflict can be traced back to two rival conceptions of history which began to diverge in the 1930s, in the struggle for freedom from the British Raj." On the one hand there was the push for national unity between Hindus and Muslims under Mahatma Gandhi and Jawaharlal Nehru. In contrast there were the extreme

Hindu nationalists some of whom established the paramilitary RSS, who campaigned for the return of what they saw as the lost Hindu golden age of national strength and purity. The BJP was created as the political wing of the RSS. The problem for Hindutva promoters and historians though was India's Muslims and the spread of Islam and, secondly, the religious tolerance of many of the Muslim Mughal rulers, especially Akbar (1542–1605). There was another small historical problem. The early Harappan settlers in India the evidence suggested, and as most people agree, were Aryan who arrived in India from Iran. Wrong, argued the guru of Hindutva, Madhav Golwalkar (an admirer of fascism and Nazism). "The Hindus came into this land from nowhere, but are indigenous children of the soil always, from times immemorial," he wrote.

The solution from the mid-1980s onwards was simply to rewrite history demonising Islam and the Muslims and asserting Hindu glory and, more recently, rewrite school history books peppered with ahistorical myths, intimidate and threaten those who disagree, take over the regulating scholarly bodies and research institutes, challenge physically and through the courts scholarly texts which are anti-Hindutva, subvert the judiciary and broadcasting institutions, destroying religious buildings and so on. It's called the 'saffronisation' of society. Legitimating the Hindutva past provides the basis for political tasks today, to manipulate identities with the object of the 'Hinduisation of everything'.

In contrast to these Hindutva warriors, the dominant and perhaps most memorable view on Indian history and 'civilisation' was from that of those heroes of independent India, Jawaharlal Nehru and Mahatma Gandhi. Yet there is that famous but ambiguous quote from Nehru's book published on the eve of Independence in 1947 *The Discovery of India*, where he writes of "the continuity of a cultural tradition through five thousand years of history." British rule he continued was a mere blip in the long continuous history of the country. The key to modern India, he argued perhaps confusingly, was "ancient India." The key to understanding Indian civilisation was its past. Despite communal differences between Muslims and Hindus (especially around the time of Independence) Nehru argued that: "Indian civilisation... was essentially based on stability and security and from this point of view it was far more successful than any that arose in the West." What united the different elements of this civilisation was the "same national heritage and the same set of moral and mental qualities." As with Nehru, Gandhi dismissed Western civilisation – "a civilisation only in name." Indian civilisation by contrast was characterised by its "traditional" qualities. Its strengths were its continuity and unchangeability based on its village communities within the framework of beneficial caste divisions. Later chapters will look more closely at both Nehru and Gandhi.

Until recently, states in India did not have fixed or clearly demarcated boundaries. Instead, areas under the control of particular dynasties or empires flowed and ebbed over time, growing and contracting according to internal developments and external influences. Adding to these complexities is the natural understandable continuing process of rewriting history in the light of new evidence, discoveries and perspectives. The situation today though is of a different order to those traditionally characterising the historian's craft, and a lot more worrying. The communal interpretation of history into Hindu and Muslim periods might have been seen as sufficient for the occupying British colonial administration but surely is unacceptable in the twenty-first century. Interpreting the history of India through the use of crude religious stereotypes risks damaging a rich heritage defined by its very opposite – its rich cultural, religious, linguistic and ethnic diversity.

For the overseas tourist as well as those from within the country, the history of India is as Michael Wood puts it, "a tale of incredible drama, of great inventions and phenomenal creativity, and of the biggest ideas." It is a country of big history. For the regular returners to the country, maybe this is part of the reason – and one of their secrets – on why they keep coming back. Recent political developments, however, seem threatened by this notion of 'big history'.

Chapter 4

Konkani blues

Magical Goa

For nearly everyone, Goa punches above its weight. For many overseas tourists, Goa is India. For Indians themselves it is more complicated – proud that a part of their country attracts so many overseas tourists yet bewildered, bemused and ultimately baffled at the sometimes hedonistic behaviour and narrow interests of these visitors. The marketing brochures and daily stories appearing in the media do little to disturb the caricatures of widespread extremes in the single-minded pursuit of 'pleasure'. Certainly, there are activities and issues that not only warrant anger and protest by locals and visitors alike in Goa, but civilised behaviour as we know it is not ending (yet). For young people from abroad, it is not difficult to see the allure of Goa. Wonderful beaches, many of them unspoilt, cheap accommodation, alcohol and good food together with unchanging blue skies and dependable sunshine all contribute towards 'partying' in the middle of Western winters. For the older visitors, the attractions are similar but with less of the partying, I assume. There are few places in the world that provide this mixture of beach, climate, affordability and relaxation although Southeast Asia is fast coming up behind Goa. Anyone visiting other coastlines in India, especially the Bay of Bengal eastern coast, immediately notices the differences. In the main, Indians don't do beaches but they do in Goa, big time.

In Goa, even those travelling as part of a package tour are unlikely to remain within their hotel complex. Instead they will be out and about, savouring and exploring experiences unplanned a few weeks ago. For most people, and especially tourists, Goa is its beaches. The coastal area probably accounts for 90 plus per cent of all tourists with its extensive tourist infrastructure that caters to its customers' wants, whether this be drink, travel, food or 'experiences'. It might be a little ramshackled, unorganised and sometimes unreliable but it all seems to work. No one anyway is in a hurry. And in general, it is a safe place although there are periodic incidents that shatter any complacency and that go 'viral'.

At the centre of this infrastructure are the local inhabitants, often non-Goans. Noticeable is an easy-going confidence and friendliness that characterises relationships and conversations between locals and their visitors, again unlike the rest of India where there is less confidence and a greater reticence. Familiarity and experience provide the bedrock of this friendliness. In Goa as in most of the rest of the developing world, participation in the tourist industry in any way possible is not only better than options back 'home' but also can be very financially rewarding. Families or at least women and their children from Kashmir are common sellers of tourist clothing on roadside stalls, extended families from Nepal run a number of restaurants in particular locations and women from particular villages in the neighbouring state of Karnataka seem to dominate beach sales. Most of the visiting workers return 'home' around April, once the main tourist season has finished and come back in September or October. This regular routine is a way of life and seems to result in this working knowledge of tourist culture, language and behaviour. The number of non-Goans working in Goa are a persistent grumble in the newspapers. Some estimates put the number of non-Goans living in Goa at around 40% and fuel a continuing debate and controversy about 'who is a Goan' and 'where is Goa heading'.

In many ways, Goa is a tourist bubble, distinct from the rest of the country and yet part of that country. Ironically it is this contradictory character of the state that provides much of the interest for me at least. Everything in Goa seems part of, yet different from, India – the culture, its history, the food, the alcohol laws, its religion as well as its aspirations and grumbles.

I never wanted to visit Goa. The reputation and hype surrounding the state in the 1970s onwards put me off not only Goa but India in general. Forty years on and I've changed my mind. Maybe a little late but eventually I got there. I enjoy visiting India and Goa. Much of the hype surrounding Goa is still there but it is less intense than in the early days. Perhaps this is due today to different categories of tourists visiting the state – people on short package tours and, above all, Indian tourists from the nearby large metropolitan centres such as Mumbai or Bangalore. The cliché that is often repeated about 'Goa not being India' contains much that is true; but then again, there are different Goas. For such a small state, Goa offers a wide diversity of experiences and its many tourists must find in general what they are looking for – be that the nightlife, the sunshine, birdwatching, noisy parties or the warm sea waters on unspoilt beaches of the Arabian Sea. India's smallest state (with a population of only around a million and half people) faces the warm Arabian Sea and is bounded by Maharashtra in the north and Karnataka to the east and south. Most of Goa is part of a rugged coastline escarpment known as the Konkan, that part of India that separates the western coastline from the mountainous Western Ghats which run up India's western coastline. Since obtaining state status within India in 1987, Konkani has been recognised as the sole official language of Goa. It is spoken by around 70% of the population and is understood by most Goans.

Goa of course is very closely associated with tourism, and for very good reasons. The palm-fringed beaches pictured in all the holiday brochures actually do exist. Prices over the years have remained low and the climate is dependably hot. In the south of the state – the area that I am most familiar with – there remains a relaxed, informal and unhurried pace to life for visitors. Major outside capital projects such as luxurious hotels or 'resorts' have not greatly impacted (yet) on the numerous, family-run 'homestays' or rented room accommodation. 'Time share' developments are increasingly attracting domestic tourists (from Bombay and Bangalore especially) as well as those from overseas. Most of the tourists, however, tend to visit and appreciate the local, make-do facilities rather than the all-encompassing services of the hotel or timeshare. The famed 'shacks' alongside parts of the beaches continue to provide a major focus for the tourists. Because of the numerous regulations centred on what can and cannot be done near to the sea, the beachfronts themselves remain remarkably underdeveloped, sometimes scruffy but in the main beautiful. Away from the beaches, tourist stalls and shops are proliferating, all selling a similar narrow range of goods. Most of the stalls are managed, but perhaps not owned, by non-Goans who work long hours seven days a week throughout the tourist season before returning 'home' to other parts of India between April and September. Christmas is the peak period with thousands of foreigners and domestic tourists arriving for a short stay of 1–2 weeks. Festival decorations largely Christian go up a day or two before Christmas, tourist stalls are open as usual throughout the vacation – including Christmas day – and some of the restaurants would advertise a 'special' Christmas lunch – all very relaxed. New Year is a bigger celebration with varied firework displays starting in the early hours of the new year.

Celebrations and life in general are likely to be more hectic and intense in some of the bigger tourist spots, perhaps confirming the 'hedonistic traveller' image in places such as Anjuna, Calangute and Baga in north Goa, and in Palolem and Colva in the south. Almost inevitably, tourist developments over the last decade or so are benefiting the new Indian middle class, big hotel owners and shady characters looking to exploit corrupt state mechanisms as well as capturing some of the 'tourist dollar' (or 'rouble'). Village economies, the environment and small vendors are usually the losers in the development of tourism in the state. The absence of Goans benefiting significantly from the economic gains in the state over the last couple of decades remains a continuing and festering issue in the media and amongst Goans.

When entering Goa for the first time by train or at the airport there is an immediate and noticeable difference to other parts of India. Panjim, the capital of the state, is a pleasant, old-fashioned and unhurried place that is of an ideal size to walk around. The splendid Mandovi River provides a handy northern boundary to the city. Originating in the Western Ghat mountains some 77 kilometres upstream, the river is at its widest and most majestic at Panjim. The river waterfront has a walkway covered in shade from the trees and with plenty of seating to take in the views of the river. On the other side of the road alongside the river is the Hotel Mandovi, a favourite of ours. Although the hotel has seen better times, the second-floor balcony or veranda overlooks the river, serves pots of tea or coffee and is rarely busy. The bookshop on the ground floor provides a good choice of local Goan literature and naturalist guides. As might be expected the huge whitewashed Church of Our Lady of the Immaculate Conception near the Municipal Gardens dominates views of Panjim but provides a useful landmark when ambling around. It was closed for repairs when we were last there but the nearby Hindu Mahalaxmi Temple provided an alternative venue to rest and watch. The cake and coffee houses, bookshops and numerous restaurants give central Panjim a slow and relaxed feel different to other cities in the country. I hate to admit it, but there is a more European feel to the town.

Along the road thirty minutes from Panjim is Old Goa, the former capital of the state. Still attracting busloads of local tourists and schoolchildren, it is today a rather dusty and faded centre of a once fabled glory. Historically spice and slaves provided the great wealth that characterised this capital city. Today all that remains are a collection of significant Portuguese colonial and religious buildings. Its most famous building is the Basilica of Bom Jesus, a UNESCO World Heritage site. The absence of shops, accommodation and anything to do with everyday life gives Old Goa a rather eerie feel but the splendour of its religious architecture helps overcome these peculiarities. Wide avenues and parched gardens connect the churches, chapels and monasteries. The mixture of Portuguese colonial power and a once-dominant Catholicism pervades the old city, even today.

While we were visiting Goa at the beginning of January 2015, it was surprising to see that the most important event according to the newspapers seemed to be the public veneration of the Sacred Relics of Saint Francis Xavier as part of the 17th decennial Exposition. The 44-day mega event at the Se Cathedral in Old Goa was the context for numerous articles about St Francis Xavier, his arrival in India in 1683, and also, the implied influence today of the Catholic Church. Some 200,000 visitors a day, it was reported, were visiting the silver casket containing the saint's relics.

Portugal, Goa and India

The defining feature of Goa, old and new, is of course Portugal. After all, it was only on the 19th December 1961 that Portugal then under the rule of the fascist dictator Salazar was thrown out of Goa. It became part of the Indian nation, first as a Union Territory. On the 30th May 1987, Goa finally became a state of India with Konkani as its official language. Prior to the arrival of Portugal, waves of conquerors from overseas empires as well as neighbouring kingdoms sought control of the territory as both a prized port and as an entry to the rich hinterlands. In 1497, Vasco da Gama landed south of Goa, at Calicut. In 1510, Alfonso de Albuquerque seized what is now Old Goa. By the end of the sixteenth century, Goa (or Estado da India as it was known by the Portuguese) had developed into one of the world's most important trading centres, and also a site of missionary activity by the Catholic Church. Corn, potatoes, chillies, cashews, papayas and other fruit were introduced, believe it or not, into India for the first time. By the mid-nineteenth century, the city on the banks of the Mandovi River was one of the richest places in the world and was bigger than London or Paris – quite incredible.

Today, most people associate Portugal's adventures in India only with Goa. Given the spectacular 'success' of the Raj, Portugal's role and history in India has tended to be both diminished and overlooked. Within fifty years of Vasco da Gama's arrival, however, Portuguese conquests were far more extensive than Goa. They controlled 60 miles of the coast around Goa and up to 30 miles inland. Northwards from Bombay through to Damao and Diu and to parts of Gujarat was Portuguese. Southwards from Goa, they held a long loosely-linked chain of seaport fortresses and trading posts such as Oner, Barcelor, Mangalore, Cochin and Quilon. Pepper, ginger and cinnamon were their prizes. On the eastern coast, military posts were established at San Thome for example, and Portuguese control even extended to Hooghly in West Bengal. Envoys and resident ambassadors were exchanged with other major states on the continent and peace treaties agreed with other powers in the region, such as the Mughal and Vijayanagar kingdoms. The Portuguese in India were more than just the Portuguese in Goa, as it is not generally recognised, and were the last foreign power to leave in the 1960s.

In the fifteenth century Portugal was one of two invading forces in India, both of which had far-reaching consequences for the continent. The other conquerors were the Mughals who, as pointed out earlier, had a recognised lasting influence on subsequent political, administrative and cultural developments in the continent. The Portuguese essentially were a sea power and used this military and commercial advantage to open new trade routes. It was the Portuguese that effectively created the beginnings of the global system of trade and, often, exploitation. By way of Lisbon, India was linked to the Portuguese colony of Brazil and with their settlements in West Africa. The Portuguese not only linked India with Europe, Africa and the Americas, they also tied India more closely to other Asian markets.

Significant as these historical economic developments were, it was in the cultural sphere that Portugal's influence is clearest today. Like the British later, there was never that large a number of Portuguese settlers, but unlike the British, Portugal encouraged marriage with the local inhabitants and saw the areas where they lived as 'home' – they were not a transient, temporary presence distancing themselves socially and culturally from the locals. It was a presence nevertheless backed by the use of military violence where required. Underpinning this domination was of course the Catholic Church with its narrow, oppressive strictures and practices, especially after the arrival of the Inquisition in Goa. The subsequent atrocities on the local population in the name of the Inquisition and the destruction in 1540, for example, of all Hindu temples significantly increased indigenous resentment towards the Portuguese. The growth of the Mughals especially under Akbar further pressured Portuguese influence on the continent. Low wages and rampant corruption characterised the search for fortunes. Later, Brazil rather than India became the choice of plunder for the Portuguese. The rise and competition from other European imperial powers finally sealed the Portuguese decline on the continent.

In Portuguese Goa, however, an affluent middle class had emerged long before elsewhere in India. Rural villages often with generous courtyards were created and large villas with extensive verandas, tiled roofs held up by wooden rafters and large windows were built. Many of them remain today, a little rundown and dwarfed by trees that have grown wild and huge. The distinctive Goan-Portuguese style of architecture as it is known is celebrated at the Museum of Houses of Goa, close to

Panjim. The best remaining example of this architecture is said to be the Menezes Braganza House, a private home with the family tracing its roots back to the sixteenth century. In 2014 we finally managed to find the house and had a guided tour around it. Located in the Chandor village just south of Margao in southern Goa, this 350-year-old house is a magnificent collection of chandeliers, porcelain, paintings, crystal, period furniture and other varied antiques. We walked through the ballroom, gazed at the baroque chapel, admired the Italian marble floors and browsed the leather-bound volumes arranged in the rosewood bookcases in the library. Three hundred and fifty-year-old Ming vases stand quietly in the corner of one room, unguarded and without alarms. The land upon which the house was built was apparently given to the family by the then king of Portugal in the 17th century. A family member from the same time represented Goa in the Portuguese government and was a vice-consul general in Spain. Today the house which has been split into two halves is still inhabited by descendants of the families. After the Portuguese left India in the 1960s, some of the 'grand' families were allowed to keep their houses although most had their extensive lands confiscated. The Braganza family had made their wealth from farming the coconut and rice on their large estates. In 1962 when the family surrendered these lands, they lost the primary source of income. One particular family member Luis de Menezes Braganza was a campaigner for Goa freedom and was one of the few settlers to oppose Portuguese rule. With the escalating political violence around anti-Portuguese issues, he was forced to flee the house and Chandor in the 1950s.

And then there is the Catholic Church – another reminder when in Goa that this is a different place with a distinctive culture from the rest of India. Along the coastal region these vast and whitewashed church landmarks appear at regular intervals. On most days and not only on Sundays, they are busy with people. And yet, despite the Portuguese Inquisition lasting some

250 years through to 1812, Hindus have always constituted the majority population of Goa and today account for about 65% of Goans. In contrast Muslims have always been a small minority. The Catholicism of Goa, however, seems to have always been a hybrid religion – recognising caste differences and incorporating a mystical, goddess-centred Christianity with traces reaching back to pre-colonial times.

For Goans today, the 'Portugal' link remains an important but largely unspoken issue. In December 2010 for example, there began a year-long celebration in Goa to mark the fifty years since the end of Portuguese rule. Reading reports from local and national Indian newspapers, it was clear that some of the events "brought to the surface an ever present, palpable and deep Goan divide" as one of the papers put it. "There are those here who see the Portuguese as benevolent fairy god-uncles who infinitely enriched and transformed Goa, who will always be joined with them in the deep longing for a shared, poignant past," reported one commentator. On the other hand, "There are as many, perhaps more, who see the Portuguese simply and starkly as imperial conquerors – divisive, coercive, plundering and cruel," he continued.

Those beaches

For the majority of visitors to Goa, however, it is not the tranquillity and order of the rural villages or the extensive, well-maintained evidence of a previously fierce Catholicism or the fading charms of once powerful Luso-Indian families and their mansions that is the attraction of the state. Instead it is the beaches. For most people and especially tourists, Goa is its beaches. Goa throughout the world is synonymous with palm tree lined beaches of soft white sand, the warm waters of the Arabian Sea and, for some, hedonistic extravaganzas. The weather is almost a given – an unremitting average of around 30 degrees and undisturbed blue skies. A gentle breeze is often available on the beaches but not elsewhere. The best weather is said to be in the last months of the year; March and April getting hotter with the approaching monsoon period raising the humidity levels. Early mornings through to about 10 in the morning together with late afternoons are the activity periods, for walking, visiting, shopping or perhaps birdwatching. Nights are warm with no need for bed covers – a fan in the room on a slow speed is usually sufficient. The 'season' for overseas tourists usually begins in October and closes down in March and April. It is not only the tourists that have their routines and patterns. Many of the workers are from out of state, from neighbouring Karnataka or further afield such as Nepal. Jobs and responsibilities have to be attended to back home either in the fields or with family duties. Kiosks and eating places are dismantled until returned to in September or October.

And those beaches that dominate the marketing literature are there – they are real. They are not some fancy fiction that often characterises our holiday brochures. And you can choose which sort of beach you want – from the hectic, built-up party chaos of a Palolem experience in south Goa, or Calangute and Baga in the north through to the almost lonely beaches of Mandrem, Keri or Utorda. Somewhere in the state's 125 kilometres of coastline you can find what you want.

Beaches, however, are often a proxy for a number of other things – a wider pattern of experiences. There is for example the plentiful accommodation at any desired budget range. Small family-run 'home-stays' are popular amongst long-stayers while five-star corporate hotels are beginning to congregate in particular areas. Then there is the cuisine particular to Goa and, again, shaped by the Portuguese but with distinct Hindu influences. It's a bit like a southern Mediterranean diet with its staple ingredients of chicken, spiced sausages and meats but mixed up with spicy flavours and locally available vegetables. Pork vindaloo, chicken xacuti (roasted grated coconut with chunks of meat in a thick gravy) and cafreal might sound a little familiar to some British tourists but the flavours and spices are not. Beans and cashews are common as of course is the chilli pepper, introduced all those centuries ago by the Portuguese. Fish curries today seem to be less common or popular than in the past, replaced instead by a variety of plainer, less tasty, safer 'seafood dishes', although rice dishes remain popular as do prawn curries. Common to all the eating places today is that hybrid categorisation of dishes and menus into 'Indian', 'Goan', 'Chinese' and 'International'. It's a shame but I assume that it's 'what the market wants'. And then there is the wonderful bebinca, worth a trip to Goa if for nothing else. Served at every restaurant, this sixteen-layer cake of flour, ghee, egg yolk, coconut milk, sugar and almond slivers is usually served warm with ice cream on the side. It is a staple for all ceremonies and celebrations. Each layer can only be added to when the lower layer has cooked and cooled. It's a rich dish as its ingredients suggest, so portions are small, but it provides a wonderful sweet contrast to a spicy main dish. And given that we are now concentrating on Goan particularities, mention should be made of completing the meal with a glug of Feni, a spirit produced only in Goa. Regulated as a 'country liquor', the coconut feni or cashew feni can't be produced outside of Goa and is often still distilled in the traditional earthen pot. Traditional coconut feni is distilled from fermented toddy collected from the coconut palm by a toddy tapper called a 'rendier' and its collection is a craft to be found throughout India and Southeast Asia. A skilled task that has been continued over the centuries, the toddy is collected every alternate day in the early morning and late evenings in late February through to mid-May for the cashew variety and throughout the year for the coconut feni. Given the ubiquitous nature of the coconut palm throughout Goa, the toddy collector is not an uncommon sight. The business seems to remain as a local, unorganised industry characterised by numerous small producers who supply distillers or bars through long-standing relationships.

The allure of the 'beach-life' for most, perhaps all, visitors to Goa is, however, more than the feni – it is almost uniquely, in India, the friendly and widespread alcohol availability. For the Western visitors this largely means cold lager beers, and for many of the Indian tourists means rum and whiskey. As an increasing number of states in India restrict or ban alcohol sales, Goa's attractions increase. Alcohol is available elsewhere in India but at a considerable cost of effort, camouflage (in Kerala, it is served in teapots), travel and finance. In Goa it is plentiful and cheap. And it goes down well with the sun and the beaches.

As mentioned earlier, the Colva beach or the beach running along the Salcete coastal region in south Goa is the beach I know best. This 24-kilometre stretch of white sands is almost completely palm fringed and includes villages such as Cansaulim and Betalbatim in the north through to Colva and Benaulim in the middle, and then down to Varca and Mobor at the mouth of the Sal River, in the south. A favourite walk that I don't like to miss on my visits is from Mobor up to Benaulim – about 8–9 kilometres. As usual the heat can be a bit of a problem. I reckon that I'm quite a good walker, but I've had to give up on previous walks trying to reach Cansaulim on the northern stretch of the beach due to feeling faint with the heat in the midday sun.

I usually manage, however, the Mobor to Benaulim walk provided I make an early morning start. I catch a bus from Benaulim down to Mobor – a lovely ride provided you can get a seat. It gets quieter and less busy on the bus once past Varca and the further south you go. At Mobor you leave the bus, walk alongside the big posh Leela Resort and on to the beach, turn right and keep going for about 3–4 hours.

It's a lovely walk. When I last did it in March 2016, the tide was out but was on its way back. The beach is wide, about 70 metres I would guess with two levels defined by the high tide mark. On the bottom level is the still-damp sand which is ideal for walking. Higher up is the soft, dry, strength-sapping stuff which makes the going hard. At the edge of the beach is the thick greenery – the inevitable palm trees but also rows of trees that reminded me and look like but are not yew trees. Sometime in the past, the edge of the whole beach has been planted with foliage to prevent erosion. Now mature and up an embankment, these trees provide a lovely line and definition to the entire beach. Occasionally through my 'yew' trees you can see small plantations of bananas and wild mango trees. It's all very dense, green and natural. In this stretch of the coast and almost up to Varca, there is little to no sign of human development. There are three or four big, foreign 'corporate' hotels on the walk but they are set away from the beach and are not the usual eyesore. Instead it's very tranquil with, at the beginning anyway, few other swimmers or walkers around. The sea is usually calm and always available when it gets too hot. The incoming tide brings on to the shore a line of debris – driftwood, small dark coconut fruit, some plastic bottles, a flip-flop sandal here and there, and plastic leftovers from people's picnics. Not too bad. At each of the villages along the walk are the beach shacks – maybe a half-dozen temporary structures that each attract their regular customers for their daily fix of drink, board games, food, friendships and sea. In the early morning, the shacks are empty and only begin to show life at around 10–11 in the morning. Apart from the weekends, most of the visitors are Westerners. Even with some of the bigger villages such as Cavelossim there is no sign of permanent buildings from the beach. They are set away from the beach and hidden by the greenery.

Up early though are the municipal (I assume) workers making their way down the beach clearing up the rubbish and plastics. They are decked out smartly in green or orange fluorescent jackets. It's a low-tech operation, involving the pulling of a plastic shallow bowl along on a stretch of rope. Once filled, the bowl is periodically thrown into the bordering beach foliage. Nearer to Varca – the big village along this stretch of the coast – are big, green rubbish bins standing in the middle of the beach at 300 or so metre intervals. Given the furore over rubbish and plastics throughout Goa, this is a very welcome new initiative even though there was little evidence of them being regularly used. 'Privatised' individual collectors with their hessian sacks for the plastic bottles were also busy walking the beach. Together with the green bins more people become visible – groups of young schoolchildren standing around, a game of cricket or football here and there, and the beach loungers under the umbrellas beginning to fill up. Once past these spots, things quieten down again with only occasional walkers greeting each other. A cold drink here and there at a shack provides the opportunity for a restful stop and an opportunity to catch up with the gossip on tourist business with the workers or owners – who's here this year, who's missing, what's business like, what fish is available and so on.

After 3–4 hours you are back on home beach hot and sweaty, at 'your' shack but ready for a light lunch snack. As I said earlier, a lovely walk – nothing too ambitious but something accomplished and enjoyed.

Green Goa

It is the beaches that are synonymous from around the world with Goa. Less appreciated are the forests and trees of the state. A study of the map showing the distribution of forests in the state indicates how widespread and important are the rich flora and fauna. There are six Wildlife Sanctuaries and one National Park. Moist, mixed deciduous forests, subtropical hill forests through to evergreen forests provide the storehouse for the rivers and natural resources within the state. This biodiversity is common to the Western Ghats running through western India and through Goa. As a percentage of total area in Goa, forest and tree cover is some 66% in south Goa, which is significant. Forget the beaches; trees rule OK.

Walking or travelling around the busy coastal villages or largely tourist-deserted hinterland, you come across one of the wonders of India (for me, anyway) – the huge Banyan trees. Next to the Baobab tree of sub-Saharan Africa, the Banyan tree must be one of the world's most iconic trees and, unsurprisingly, is the national tree of India. I have many photographs on my camera of these great monsters often from under their vast canopies, looking upwards. The nearer to settlements the more likely is the damage to the tree. Unfortunately, there are plenty of examples of trees with huge branches which have been lopped off because they block the light or are in the way of electricity lines.

The name 'Banyan' is thought to derive from the word 'banya', which means 'trader'. Maybe in earlier times, Hindu travelling traders would rest and do their business within the shade of these trees. Irrespective of the source of the name, once identified and seen the Banyan trees are never forgotten. They are easily recognised. They are the trees with the numerous vertical hanging vines or roots which spread out from their branches and reach down into the ground below where they take root. On an old tree, and most of the trees we have seen are old, there is this mass and mess of hanging aerial roots which over time become thick and twisted but all remain connected to the main trunk. It is sometimes difficult to identify the original trunk of a particular tree. The leaves are large and leathery and look similar to the fig tree or bush. The younger leaves have this reddish tinge and provide a contrast with the older dark green elliptical-shaped glossy leaves. Apart from the hanging vines or roots, there are two other features of the tree which are remarkable. First, the older trees are usually huge. The jungle of the vertical aerial roots provides a stability for the tree that stretches over a significant territory. The canopy shade provided by the tree consequently is staggering. In the literature, there are stories of 7,000 soldiers sheltering under the tree, and early British colonialists identified and described Banyan trees covering an area of 846 metres. Apparently, one individual specimen in Andhra Pradesh provides cover and shade over some 19,000 square metres. The shade from the canopy cover provides an ideal playground for children, a shady spot to sit for travellers and passers-by and as a natural community centre for the villages in rural areas.

It is not only the size of the tree, however, that is of interest. The Banyan tree is often described as a 'type of strangling fig' and is I think a member of the fig family. Like the common fig, the tree produces little berries in pairs that are attached to the base of leaves from the stem. The berries are bright red when ripe. The seeds are dropped by feeding birds on the ground, on a tree or in a crack in a building. The forest ground is not a hospitable environment, but other trees, garden walls and buildings are more promising. The seeds start germinating, young saplings begin growing, continue to grow around the host trunk, and eventually, strangle the host through the considerable pressure on the host's trunk. It eventually rots away often leaving a hollow central core. With the older trees that we have visited, there is no absent centre; the Banyan tree has expanded to fill the space and provide wonderful pictures of numerous twisted, contorted thick trunks that now form the main support of the tree.

Perhaps the most famous images of this 'strangling' characteristic of the tree is not from India but from Cambodia. Angkor Wat, the Khmer temple and city started in the late twelfth and early thirteenth centuries, was left undisturbed from around the seventeenth century (the fall of the Khmer empire) until very recently. Dramatically visible at various parts of the complex are these gigantic trees rising above the stone walls and temple roofs which have enveloped the structures. The undisturbed periods have allowed the surrounding jungle to enter the temples and the Banyan trees to do their business. Thick roots spread down from great heights and creep out over the stone floors. In some places, the thick stone walls have been pushed aside leaving rubbles of stone. So dramatic are these images of the power and influence of these trees that they are hopefully likely to be left alone in the restoration work recently begun at Angkor.

While Susan and I were in Calcutta in 2012, we took the bus to the Indian Botanic Garden to see its most famous specimen 'The Great Banyan', said to be the largest tree in the world measuring more than 330 metres in circumference. The garden, from 2009 renamed as the Acharya Jagadish Chandra Bose Indian Botanic Garden, is the proud home to this 200–250-year-old tree. The bus journey was, as ever, a bit of an adventure with local people and animals entering and leaving at intervals with their huge loads of produce and wares on their way to market. Crossing the cantilever designed Howrah Bridge over the Hooghly River we goggled at the packed pedestrian lanes crammed with bicycles carrying huge cloth-covered bundles of stuff and things. The Garden itself was a little disappointing. Established in 1787 by an army officer Colonel Robert Kyd of the East India Company the Garden has evolved over the last 250 years and is today a popular public park as well as an important venue for scientific study. The Garden's collections of orchids, bamboos and palms are well-known collections from among its 12,000 specimens.

Today, however, the Garden is a little rundown with, I seem to remember, an absence of useable toilets! The Great Banyan Tree was not as visually dramatic as we had thought due to being struck by lightning in the early 1920s. The tree became diseased and in 1925 the middle of the tree was removed in order to save the remaining tree. There is no clear history of the tree but it is mentioned in early travel books and journals. So today, the world's largest tree is not a single tree but a series of trees or colony, all linked to the original tree. The Great Banyan Tree today looks more like a forest than a single tree. The present crown of the tree has a circumference of about one kilometre

– plenty of shade, then! A 330-metre road was built around the base of the tree as a form of protection but the tree continues to spread beyond the road.

It is not only the Banyan trees, however, that are worth finding and visiting in Goa. Another tree, for example, that fills my camera's memory card is the Peepal Tree. It too appears to be a member of the fig tree family. Not quite so distinctive as the Banyan tree, this is a medium-sized, fast-growing deciduous tree. It has heart-shaped leaves and has a pair of small fig fruits growing just below the leaves. One of its major assets is its large crown with wonderful, wide-spreading branches – shade again.

The importance of both trees extends beyond their shade-providing qualities, important as that is. The Peepal tree for example is very important to all Indians and especially Buddhists who see the tree as the personification of Buddha. The tree is regarded as a sacred tree as Buddha attained enlightenment meditating under a Peepal tree. There is a saying attributed to Buddha which states, "He who worships the Peepal Tree will receive the same reward as if he worshiped me in person." Hindus in India also hold great spiritual reverence for the Peepal tree as they regard it as the tree beneath which Vishnu was born. It is also a 'wish-fulfilling tree', and therefore it is not uncommon to find ribbons and cloth wrapped around the trunk of the tree.

Together with the shade and religious associations, both trees are important sources for many Ayurvedic medicines and also for commercial usage. Papermaking and rope fibres, for example, come from the Banyan tree.

Rapid social and economic change in the recent past is almost a given in Goa. The faster the pace of change the more intractable it seems are the competing claims of what and where Goa needs to go in the years ahead. It is therefore pleasant to be able to report on a small development that focuses on the opposite direction: namely, uncovering and recording Goa's past – not so much its history but more about its past working lives, cultural items and transport forms. This is the Goa Chitra Museum which was opened around 2009 and has over 4,000 items representing traditional farming methods, arts, tools and crafts from 'old' Goa. Situated inland in south Goa and driven by the affectious enthusiasm and expertise of Victor Hugo Gomes, the museum is part of an organic farm and is an amazing collection of ethnographic utensils reflecting everyday life in a Goa largely before the arrival of electricity. All the items are fully described, using information and data obtained often from interviews and photographic evidence. The predominant focus as would be expected is on agricultural, rural trades – especially the coconut industry. Once second in importance after rice production in the state, today believe or not Goa depends on coconut supplies from outside the state. Tools (from farmers, tailors, barbers, masons, carpenters, for example), storage implements, weights and scales, modes of transport and religious items are some of the themes characterising the collections and rooms of the museum. It is a museum that on a local scale matches the quality, detail and breadth of any other from around the world. It doesn't have the 'must have' technological sophistication that seems to characterise other modern museums and is better for this absence. Instead of this omission, it has space (lots of it) and an unhurried atmosphere all driven by a friendly and knowledgeable staff. Here in this one site visitors (with a lot of time on their hands) can get a real feeling and understanding of the old agrarian ways, their craftsmanship and materiality. It's difficult to believe that this wonderful opening to the old ways of Goa has been developed and driven by one man Victor, helped by his wife Aldina. If 'the wisdom of the past' which drives the collection could be matched by 'the wisdom for the future' in regard to Goa's future developments, things would be good. Unfortunately this wisdom is in short supply.

Goa and tourism – dark clouds in the blue sky?

As might be expected, Goa is an important part of the Indian tourist sector. However, it is not as dominant as might be expected given the historical coverage in the Western media. It attracts around 13% of all foreign tourist arrivals to India. When domestic tourists are included, this totals around 2–3 million visitors a year. As a tourist destination for either foreign or domestic travellers in India, Goa does not figure in the 'top ten' destinations. The three most popular states for foreign tourists in 2011 were Maharashtra (25%), Tamil Nadu (17%) and Delhi (11%). For domestic tourists, they were Uttar Pradesh (18%), Andhra Pradesh (18%) and Tamil Nadu (16%). Such bald figures obviously mask a number of different agendas which will be explored later. Nevertheless, it is surprising and encouraging that for foreign travellers India does not simply mean Goa.

The growth of tourism in Goa is fairly recent. When the state first joined the Indian Union in the 1960s, its main industry was rich ores of iron and manganese exports. Further development was limited and tourism was introduced not only to increase incomes and employment but also to create non-manual employment opportunities. It was only in the 1980s that the first charter flight landed in the state. In 1985 there were around 700,000 tourists a year, mainly from other parts of India. In 2000, numbers crept up to around a million and then doubled three years later. The big times had arrived.

So who is going to Goa today? Beyond bald numbers, it's difficult to answer this question with any confidence – different perspectives seem to arise depending on where you are based or visit. One of the major travel guides to India mentions the state being the "preserve of working class Brits and Scandinavians". Perhaps. Certainly I remember discussing long-distance lorry driving in Britain on the beach in Goa with an elderly British tourist. He had been returning to the same coastal village in Goa for decades during the European winter, seemed to know everyone and had his daily routines which rarely changed. My own experiences suggested an elderly tourist, predominantly British and who treats their visits, people and village as their second home. Some of them have been staying with the same families, homestay or hotel for many years. They have seen the local family children grow up and in some cases attended their weddings. When I glance over the daily Goan newspapers, however, I realise how partial and limited is my experience. Reported stories and events mainly in the north of Goa, it must be said, didn't fit with my observations. Maybe I am in bed too early most evenings but the 'raves', 'wild parties' and 'happenings' have not been part of my visits. Instead, talking and arguing late into the night with a steady supply of Cobra beers seems the norm.

I did come across an interesting survey which explored this topic more systematically than my own limited experiences. It was quite revealing. For all tourists to the state, the overwhelming number are males, single or groups of females; they constitute only around 7% of the total visitor numbers. The average length of stay again for all tourists is between one week and a month, although longer stays of 3–6 months are much more popular with foreign tourists. The most popular type of domestic tourism is package tours, followed by 'individual explorer' and 'leisure' visitors. For the overseas tourists, the overwhelming category is the 'individual explorer', followed by package and leisure types. Bottom of the list is sports and health tourism. In terms of the occupations of these visitors, the most common categories for both groups was the service sector, followed by business jobs for domestic visitors and students for the international tourist. The 2010 figures reveal that more than half the tourists are under the age of 30, while a large minority are between 50–60 years of age. Missing are the group between 30–50.

However, all is not well. Goa today is struggling to keep pace with India's growing tourist industry. Over the last five years, the state's growth has been less than 1%. The attraction of sunny beaches has not been sufficient to keep Goa in the top 20 destinations for domestic tourists and is not in the top ten destinations for foreign tourists. While other popular destinations such as Rajasthan and Kerala have forged ahead as attractive destinations for overseas visitors (around 8% growth rates), Goa saw only 1% growth. Talking to any of the Western 'returners' about Goa elicits a very similar response about decline and degradation. As always, things were much better in the past; the beaches were less polluted and less crowded, the coastal villages are now overrun with package tourist hotels and facilities, local people have been squeezed out and replaced by outsiders from other parts of India who are keen on making a quick buck, timeshare developments are everywhere, vendors of tourist goods are overrunning villages – the list could go on. There will be a lot of truth in these observations, but on the other hand, most other tourist hotspots will also be very different today – things change. However, a number of research reports and a regular diet of negative news in the Indian newspapers do contribute towards a growing realisation that things today are not going well. Typical are the following comments from *Outlook* magazine: "The worst affected are the 34 beaches along the 105 kilometre coastal stretch. The coastal areas have changed from virtually wilderness in the 70s to haphazardly developed structures. A stroll down Calangute," the magazine continues, "is enough to bear that out. The shop-lined stretch to the beach feels like a dirty, grimy lane... Just behind the many beach shacks lies a huge ugly dump of plastic and waste. The lack of garbage management continues to be an eternal woe." It's not difficult to find other comments in a similar vein. "It used to be a long, pleasant walk from Sinquerim all the way to Calangute. Now, Candolim and Calangute have become trash bins," said a local resident.

However, the explosion of mass tourism to Goa over the last

couple of decades has been breathtaking. In the case of Russian-speaking and Eastern European tourists for example, the Goa's tourist website reports an increase from 13% in 2010 to 30% in 2011, the highest jump of any nationality. In 2008–9 there were 179 charter flights a year. A year later this figure had risen to 259 charter flights. In 2013, there were 996. The *Times of India* reported that 1,400 charter flights will link Goa to the West in 2013, while an increasing flow from the rest of India will continue. Russian-speaking tourists are making up for the shortfall of visitors from the UK and elsewhere. There are other stories. The *EPW* (*Economic and Political Weekly*) in 2013 for example reported, "tensions simmering for some years now between the local population and the Israeli and Russian speaking tourists accused of setting up 'exclusives' in Goa where Indians are not welcome." "Russian mafia" and "Israeli mafia" are terms used quite frequently in the media. And in some places like Morjim in the north, it is all Russian speakers apparently.

However, things can change quickly. I was in Goa in January 2015 and 2016. Due to the Ukrainian-Russian issues, the collapse of oil prices and the tightening of Western economic sanctions, the Russian rouble was in freefall. The number of visitors from Eastern Europe and Russia had collapsed. Rumours abounded of the number of cancelled flights coming into Goa. It wasn't only from these destinations. Charter flights from Germany via Condor Airlines to Goa were discontinued in 2015 after a period of 30 years. The reasons given by Condor was "all-round disenchantment with the State" and the high costs of using the state airport.

But it isn't only the pesky tourists. Mining companies, most of which are illegal, continued to operate quite openly. The Shah Commission set up in September 2013 to look at this problem suggested that "around 90% of the mining leases in Goa are being operated illegally." The demand for iron ore from China has fuelled an export bonanza with nearly a four-fold increase in little over a decade. A few years ago there were around 22,000 trucks involved in the transportation of ore to the landing jetties. From here the ore is moved in barges to the ports; there are 357 barges operating recently, up from 136 fifteen years ago. This unprecedented boom in mining and disregard for the law and regulations within the state could only have been possible through the involvement of politicians and civil servants as most locals acknowledged. Historically the mining lobby, interests and influence have been a powerful and intimidating force in Goa. A compliant and submissive media helped sustain this power. Resentment against the environmental damage, unaccountability and financial exploitation of the sector had been growing for some time. Hardly a week passed without another anti-mining story. News media outlets, campaigning groups and local activists are challenging these powerful interest groups. Recently for example, villagers in the Quepem area in south Goa halted all mining activities as the company was operating without proper clearance.

However, the power and influence of the mining industry in Goa is significant. The contrast between images of its wonderful beaches with the pock-marked interior is stark. Open mine operations have left and continue to leave an indelible legacy of flattened hills, razed forests and fields and roads marred by silt runoff from waste sites and processing plants. A recent report written by the Centre for Science and Environment (CSE), which looks at the possibility of sustainable mining, indicates the magnitude of the problem – "With less than 0.1% of the geographical area of the country, this state already has 8% of its land area under mine leases, and produces 15% of the country's iron ore." It warns that if all applications for leases in varying stages of processing are cleared, as much as one-quarter of the state will be under mining. And yet in October 2013, a major investigation into illegal mining practices that had already resulted in the arrest of public officials for corruption was wound up without explanation. Vijay Pratap, convenor of the thinktank *South-Asian Dialogue on Ecological Democracy*, is convinced that it was closed due to the extent of corruption uncovered in the country's mining sector. "The commission was exposing too much corruption at government level and risked undermining tightly woven corporate collusion with the political class, which has sadly become endemic in the mining industry. This is why the government aborted the investigation." In September 2012, however, this pressure paid off. Environmental clearance for all mining was suspended "for alleged violation of rules." But surprise, surprise. On April 2014, the Supreme Court of India lifted the ban on mining in Goa, albeit with a temporary cap on the volume of extracted ore. Goa's story of battles over its mineral-rich region is a story repeated from around the world – economic imperatives pushing aside environmental, health and social concerns.

And it is not only the mining of iron ore. In an article in 2013 from the excellent newspaper *The Goan*, there is an account of the illegal sand mining business. A local owner says, "I have the power, I can show my strength. If you are doing legal business you won't even be able to buy a scooter. You think I got all this (points to his house) just like that?" Although banned by the Supreme Court in February 2012, the article details the political patronage that allows a flourishing sand mining industry to grow in "Goa's sand mafia-dom" as the article puts it. Twenty sand miners make up the Goa's sand mining mafiascope – all their names and location details are provided in the article, as well as the fate of those local people who challenged their illegal activities. In a 2012 report by *Human Rights Watch* on the regulatory failure of the mining industry across India (82,000 instances of illegal mining throughout India, according to official figures), evidence is documented in Goa of the destroyed or contaminated water sources, the punctured water table, the illegally heaped waste rock and other mine waste near the banks of streams and rivers, the endless streams of overloaded trucks passing along narrow village roads and the widespread coating of metallic dust on homes and crops. Little if any of the income amounting to "hundreds of millions of dollars" finds it way in to the state coffers.

It was not only illegal mining that prompted negative stories around Goa. On 31st October 2013, a new Goan story hit the world headlines. A Nigerian national was found dead in the village of Parra in north Goa. On the same day, over 200 Nigerians took over the NH-17 Highway near Porvorim, overturning vehicles, damaging the police van carrying the body to the government hospital and refusing to let the police constables take the body for an autopsy. Despite the racist remarks by a Goan minister, the incident has brought to the surface at least two problems that have simmered for some time in the state – the drug wars and the transformation of large swathes of the state into foreign strongholds. The local *Herald* paper in an editorial said, "We have seen Americans, British, Germans, Italians, Israelis and of late, the Russians and Nigerians come and go but the narcotic trade continues unabated. This is primarily because the major drug barons are local Goans and not the foreigners." Drug peddling, gang violence and a number of murders every year provide a glimpse into the seamy side of Goa.

Goa is India's good-time state. But says the general secretary of the Shack Owners Welfare Society (SOWS), "Goa needs a better class of tourists." The recently-elected Chief Minister for Goa agreed that change must come soon. "After drugs and prostitution, garbage is the third biggest hurdle keeping away high spending tourists. Three new rubbish plants will be opened within the year," he promises. "There is a lot of nexus between the politicians and the police and the anti-social activities that are going on. This corruption cannot be weeded out in a short time."

We'll see. Controls on nightclubs and outdoor parties, police remaining on the beaches until midnight and enforcement of alcohol restrictions after ten at night in eateries are some of the new measures recently introduced in 'hotspots'. From a perusal of the local daily and weekly newspapers in Goa, it does appear that there is widespread concern among people in the state that 'something' needs to be done to arrest the unsavoury and sometimes violent activities together with the constant stream of negative stories about the state. 'Tourism' has become an election issue. 'Crisis', 'slippery slope' and 'tipping point' are the new contextual frames for discussion of the issues. Again, we'll see.

For most of the tourists visiting Goa, however, most of these unsavoury features are unseen or unknown. Most of the locals don't like to disparage the state and are reluctant to discuss issues of illegal mining or refuse problems. And there are illustrations of improvements in this or that village together with local campaigns to address grievances. But in Goa, India, Britain or elsewhere there are formidable and powerful forces determined (sometimes violently) to maintain their 'get rich quick' ways at all costs.

And the Goans themselves – being a Goan

As mentioned above, and as any foreign or domestic tourist is aware, Goa was not that long ago a Portuguese colony. This 451-year period of colonialism brought Catholicism, the Portuguese language, culinary and assorted culturally practices as well as centuries of economic stagnation. Although today around one-third of Goans are from other parts of India and Catholics only constitute about a quarter of the population, Catholics have always dominated life in the state. According to the geographer Arun Saldanha, "it is not difficult to find common themes of Goan-Catholic patriotism: nostalgia, sentimentality, faith, community, folklore, kinship and morality."

But it is around the issue of tourism that the cracks and

tensions within Goa today begin to emerge. 'What to do' about the accelerating problems of tourism begin to illustrate these differences. The dominant framework as in the rest of the world is that tourism=development=wealth. And as in the rest of the world and in India at large, the primary beneficiaries of this tourism are domestic and foreign big capital – the big hotel owners and multinational corporations together with those jobs dependent on this investment such as builders, tax collectors and a variety of shady operators. Ranged against this powerful and dominating narrative are a collection of critical actors. There are for example sections of the media which act as persistent watchdogs of developments, such as *The Goan on Saturday*. Then there are various activist, village and citizen groups that campaign around an assorted number of issues such as water, rubbish and corruption issues. There are also Christian-inspired human rights groups which criticise aspects of tourism from a predominantly moral perspective. A number of nongovernment organisations (NGOs), such as the *Goa Foundation* founded in 1986, concentrate on environmental issues and have the resources and credibility to use the High and Supreme Courts of India in their campaigns for conservation of Goa's natural environment. A number of local groups have been campaigning against 'irresponsible tourism' for many years. There are also a number of popular authors, celebrities and academics that regularly comment on the tourist industry. Then there is the considerable Goan diaspora who from afar continue a commentary that harks back to some undiluted, pure-like past.

As would be expected 'the Goas' that these and other groups seek to defend or promote are not identical; there are different understandings of 'what Goa is' and 'who Goans are'. Indeed as Saldanha argues, all these criticisms of tourism "lead to a struggle over the meaning of Goa – Goa's community, Goa's culture, Goa's future." The issue of 'being a Goan' is complicated. After all, historically the State of Goa is the result of the interplay between Portugal, Britain, India and the rest of the world; to put it another way, between colonialism, nationalism and capitalism. More simply, what is the dominant allegiance of 'indigenous' Goans today – to India, Portugal or some hybrid 'identity' (as it seems to be termed today)? The answer to this question begins to unlock some of the ambiguities and differences towards 'tourism' and 'the tourists'. The 'Indianness' of Goa and the inclusion of Goa into the wider India has not been straightforward – indeed, it has been contested. It is noticeable for example that tourist marketing images of Goa appear to ignore the wider India and instead present a very Westernised, gendered and racialised (white women in bikinis etc) series of images, often with reference to its Portuguese past. The contrived 'fun-loving' destination could be anywhere in the world; the uniqueness of Goa and of Goa as part of India is absent. Sociologically, Goa is 'disembedded'. Underpinning such a positioning of the State is the politically dominant Portuguese-Catholic view of the world and of themselves. And the criticism of tourism as centred on sex, parties, drugs and immorality especially by young domestic tourists flows from these perspectives. Foreign tourists are preferred and, especially, rich tourists in search of sanitised, five-star holidays. A strong puritanism permeates the criticisms. The primary focus of this dominant critique is on the hedonism of young Westerners; largely absent is a concern for displaced villagers, scarce water resources and environmental issues resulting from the large luxury hotel complexes with their accompanying golf courses.

For other Goans there is a different perspective on changes. For local villagers for example, the threat of losing a steady income from young tourists staying in their houses or vacant rooms is viewed with alarm. Many of the Western tourists are now family friends returning frequently to the same village accommodation, attending family weddings and catching up on the local news and developments. Familiarity and understandings are constructed which have little to do with the stereotypes of sex, drugs and rock 'n' roll.

In a way, tourism represents a contested issue for Goans that is almost unique in India. It is a proxy issue that masks deeper, more fundamental issues that are wrapped up in the state's (almost unique colonial) history, culture and aspirations. Put bluntly, there is this tension between those who still attach significance to the – or at least a Portuguese – past and a more pragmatic majority whose primary attachment is to India, rather than some Portuguese sentimentality. This tension rivets the state – in its understanding of the past, in the composition and priorities of the political elite, in its religion and strongly in its culture. Many of *The Goan* daily newspaper articles and long-running grumbles have to be read through this prism. The cleavages which continue to characterise Goa lead to a disputed type of patriotism within the state. Understandably this leads to different views on what should be happening in the future. Nowhere is this clearer than in comments on the aims and 'hidden agenda' of the Bharatiya Janata Party (BJP) whose recent rise to political office in Goa from 2012 was not only a surprise but seems to be strengthening since the elections. As argued in the previous chapter, the BJP under Narendra Modi is generally seen as an aggressive, right-wing Hindu party. Its success in the state elections from 2012 has resulted in much soul-searching especially in Luso-Catholic circles, such as daily Goan newspaper the *Herald* ("The Voice of Goa since 1900"). The resentment against the continuing 'Indianisation' of Goa by the influential but small old guard seems to be weakening – individual Catholics although not the Church itself are moving away from the traditional political parties. For the traditionalists, this is simply another example of the takeover of Goa. Because Goan landowning and business families were slow to realise the economic potential inherent within the rise of the tourist industry from the 1980s onwards, big capital from outside the state (Mumbai and Bangalore, for example) moved in. Big hotels, shopping malls, restaurants, holiday apartments and resorts steamed ahead.

Central to this contested, complex mix that is Goa unsurprisingly has been the tourist sector. Are 'hippies' and 'sossegado' – easy-going, fun-loving, laid-back ambience – to be promoted or ignored? Is 'fun' in Goa to be marketed or downplayed? Should there be more emphasis on domestic tourism at the expense of foreigners? If the publicity material for Goa or tourist Internet sites are examined, there seems to be a clear answer. Patriotic pride in the global popularity of the state seems to outweigh any moral misgivings. Maybe another way of formulating this ambiguity is the simple recognition that the 'bottom line' always wins, or at least at the moment.

The sheer scale of tourist numbers domestic or international arriving every year until recently in Goa requires strategic decisions that focus on long-term plans and developments. Private capital initiatives from either a state, national or multinational source will only acerbate the problems without direction and regulation; infrastructural initiatives are not headline news and rubbish collections don't generate the same financial returns as does tourism. Yet it is the construction and delivery of such strategic thinking that is likely to bedevil tourism in the state in the years ahead. The politics are too complicated and too contested. And underlying this contestation are the competing notions of 'being a Goan' – that is, of Goan identity.

A vignette: the Great India Roadtrip

While Braganza House might be the most sumptuous of the Portuguese mansions remaining in Goa (referred to as "The lost Versailles of the jungle" by one British journalist), it is not the only one. Many other examples, more humble and less grandiose, are not difficult to find. Wandering around on the back roads even when lost is never wasted time as smaller and more dilapidated villas keep popping up around most corners.

They contribute towards reminding you of Goa's particular and distinctive history.

Most tourists staying in Goa rent a scooter or motorbike. Some prefer a bicycle but being mobile seems to be part of spending time in Goa. Safety is getting better slowly and insurance cover and helmets are no longer met with vacant stares. While most tourists settle for a scooter there are those that cannot resist riding one of the most iconic and oldest of British motorbikes, the Royal Enfield. Now manufactured in Chennai (on the east coast and formerly known as Madras) these single cylinder bikes are instantly recognisable – very old-fashioned, heavy tank-like design and probably leaking oil – and you can hear them chug chug chugging away long before they are in sight. The Royal Enfield Bullet is probably the most famous model having been produced continuously since 1948. The lack of Japanese competition for most of this period together with the closure of the British company in 1970 ensured that the 'Indian' Royal Enfield maintained its iconic status. It is not unusual to see advertisements for Royal Enfield Tours in India in the British motorcycle press. Lasting a couple of weeks these tours on the bikes cover great distances in some beautiful parts of North India. Mechanics, doctors, guides and accommodation are all provided. Up into the foothills of the Himalayas, across the dusty hot plains of eastern India or meandering through the Ganga valleys must be some trip.

Inspired by these adventures, I decided to do my own 'Great India Roadtrip'. It wasn't quite as ambitious as the Royal Enfield epics – instead of the 2,000-odd kilometres, it was only a 40-kilometre Goan coastal journey on a beat-up scooter but what a lovely route. I have done this journey a few times and always look forward to the next time. It provides a wonderful uncovering of Goa far away from the beaches and crowds, and also, an insight into the complicated historical past and present of Goa. The secret of this particular 'Great India Roadtrip' is taking it slowly, stopping frequently for cold drinks, a chat with locals if possible and sightseeing; instead of completing the journey in an hour, done properly the 40 kilometres should take the day. Anything quicker suggests a rushed trip. Like the best of all tourist experiences, the slower the better.

The route is in south Goa and starts halfway down the magnificent 24-kilometre beach lining the administrative region of Salcette, passes the northern edges of the Quepem region in Goa before finishing at the coastal village of Agonda in the Canacona region. They say that the essence of Goa is in its villages and this is a village route, largely through an unbusy countryside with little traffic, lots of shade from the overhanging trees and a lovely twisty up and down road. This is a glimpse of an older unhurried Goa with few signs of Western tourists outside of one or two coastal resorts such as Cavelossim. Occasional lumbering trucks carrying water, sand or quarried building blocks of laterite were the only nuisances and disturbances I encountered on my 2016 February trip.

The first part of the route is comparatively busy, down towards Varca before leaving the coastal road to cut inland so as to get over the Sal River before rejoining the small coastal road. Just beyond the village of Chinchinim, you leave the road and head down towards the villages of Assona, Ambelim, Betul (on the banks of the Sal River) and south towards Cola and Saleri before reaching Agonda. The further south you go, the quieter it becomes. Around Varca at the start of the journey, there are the schoolkids on their way to or from school, traders getting into the market or buses on their way to Margao, the big city in south Goa. Once you get over the Sal River, you are on your own. Dried paddy fields (at this time of the year) are common as are salt ponds with their brilliant white heaps of drying salt alongside the Sal River. Unused concrete irrigation channels spread out on one side of the road while the Western Ghats are visible on the eastern skyline. Some of the fields have recently been burnt, presumably to encourage new growth with the approaching rains during the monsoon. When entering each of the villages, there is usually a sign from the elected village official (the *sarpanch* who is in charge of the local government of the village – the *panchayat*) welcoming you to the settlement. When arriving at Betul I usually stop at the same general store on the main road for a drink. A large proud notice announces the Rolina General Store. The store is down in a dip and has a seat outside and is in the shade. From here I can watch the comings and goings in the store. Fishing seems to be the main work in the village, and from the bridge spanning the wide, mangrove-lined Sal River when entering the village, there is a lovely view of the boats and houses (some on stilts) on the side of the river. A campaign to clean up the Sal River from pollution has been running now for a few years.

My favourite part of my Great India Roadtrip, however, is the road just south of Betul. Here the road winds around, up and down through thick groves of coconut trees or old wild mango trees with their bright new lime green leaves providing a contrast with the old dull and dusty growth from previous years. Their hard, green mango fruit is visible but small – another four or five months' growth is needed before they are ready. After Malorem up a steep road is the cashew nut plantation. You can smell the approaching trees and fruit as the scooter struggles up the hills. Like the mangoes, it's a little early for cashews but there are early large, reddish-yellowish squashed fruit on the road. Their unripe fruit is largely hidden behind the large leaves of the tree. You have to stop to examine the evidence. They have a most distinctive shaped fruit – a large, fleshy, kidney-shaped fruit with a toxic shell. And that distinctive smell, a little pungent with a touch of sweetness. Some of the trees beside the road are huge and look semi-wild. Their branches with their evergreen leathery leaves, however, bend low to the ground and are not always helpful for shade purposes. The cashew tree plantation finishes once a treeless, parched plateau is reached. Saleri is the next village I look forward to nosing around. Previously, it was possible to stop on the plateau and see the coastline and Agonda stretched down below you. Unfortunately now, the foliage and bushes are too thick and the panorama has gone.

At Saleri in 2016, my nosiness was rewarded. There was a lot of unusual activity around the local health centre. Scooters were parked everywhere and mainly women clutching their babies in one hand and letters and papers in the other queued to enter the centre. It seemed to be a vaccination day and it looked like people had arrived from many neighbouring villages. It was all very exciting and demonstrated the functioning of a rural health facility, in Goa anyway. No one bothered me as I sat on my scooter watching with interest this important day in the lives of the young patients.

Leaving Saleri, you go down the hill and cross almost immediately the River Saleri on the outskirts of the coastal village of Agonda. The river is biggish and sluggish at this point and is an estuary on the Arabian Sea. Fishing huts and well-used wooden fishing boats lie up on the mud flats. Small fish are dried in the sun on plastic sheets. A local told me that after the tourist season finishes in Agonda (in another 4–6 weeks) the workers from the hotels and restaurants take up fishing during the monsoon and summer months. They go out in the family boats mainly up the River rather than out to sea, and help to keep some money coming in during the quiet tourist period.

And then you are in Agonda. This is our favourite beach in Goa and is a beautiful crescent-shaped wide beach about a mile long, with elevated rocks and forested woods at each end of the beach. The trees, mainly coconut trees, come down to the beach edge and all the beach huts and rooms are hidden beneath the trees. Unspoilt, unsophisticated, friendly and above all shady, it is lovely waking every morning overlooking the beach or at least a few metres from the beach. And there are protected turtle spots on the beach. We have never seen them, but apparently, they are the endangered Olive Ridley turtles and are a lot more common on the Indian east coast. There are reports from Agonda of them coming ashore around April, laying their eggs at night and, five days later, 50-odd baby turtles making their way down the sea. How magical must that be?

Fifty yards behind the beachfront is the only road through the village. Tourist shops and kiosks together with restaurants cramp either side of the road – all a bit busy and to be avoided when possible. Apart from the wonderful beachfront, two events, however, characterise Agonda for us. First are the nesting sea eagles high up on the southern rocks. They seem to have been there for a few years. I think we saw them on our 2016 visit but I can't be sure as they are so similar to the more plentiful Brahminy kites that patrol the sea waters just offshore looking for dead fish and other prey. They differ in size and in their tail feather shapes but they both have that lovely reddish brown, chestnutty plumage with a contrasting white head and breast. Beautiful birds, so don't forget the bins!

The most famous site in Agonda, however, are the bat trees. Located along the northern bit of the road through Agonda, many hundred and possibly thousands of giant fruit bats hang upside down from branches on three trees beside a smelly, polluted tributary of the River Saleri. They are sometimes referred to as 'flying foxes', have dark snouts and rusty brown faces. They are silent throughout the day but at around six in the evening they start stirring, begin their screeching calls, stretch out their wings disturbing their neighbours before flying off for a circular test run. I've watched (from a poo-safe spot) their evening stirrings for up to a couple of hours at a time. By the time it is dark and difficult to see what is happening, about half have left the trees for their night feeding. The noise is deafening and they are huge in size. When a crow or raven passes nearby, you get some indication of their massive size. The first time we saw the bats I'm sure they were only in one tree. Now they are crowded in three trees, the largest one being a huge eucalyptus tree. A 'birder' told me that the fruit bat is one of four different bats found in India. We have only seen this species and it is a mesmerising sight. Unforgettable.

However, it is not the villages or the trees or the bats or beautiful Agonda that is the most memorable aspect of this Great India Roadtrip. By contrast it is something completely different that opens up and reveals the most distinctive feature of Goa – namely, its Portuguese and Catholic Church history, as touched on above. In almost each of the villages that line the route is a pristine, whitewashed church, often with an attached school. Given that some of the churches have a date going back to the seventeenth century, my humble little road trip must have been along a route or horse track stretching back four or five hundred years. It was a little spooky thinking that this road I was pootling along on my scooter probably had horse-drawn carriages carrying the local Portuguese dignitaries, colonial officers or Church officials many hundreds of years ago. The Goa Chitra Museum, which I mentioned earlier, has an entire hall devoted to wooden carriages of various designs, intricacies, sophistication and technology that were pulled by oxen or horses. Perhaps one or more of them travelled along my little coastal route down to Agonda to inspect the cashew nut, mango or coconut crop for that year!

The Portuguese hugged the coastline, built their churches along the coast (leaving the interior to the Hindu majority) and built their houses in the coastal villages. It is noticeable, however, that evidence of these houses become rarer the further south one goes in Goa. Around Varca in the Salcette region up to Margao city are numerous examples of these magnificent colonial structures; less evidence is apparent in Canacona. When it comes to the churches, however, there was no holding back. Every little village seemed to have some church edifice still dominating the village. In Varca for example there is the grandiose Cathedral, all white apart from its features picked out in blue. Three levels high with a grand courtyard surrounded by a small wall, the church dominates the village. At Canaguinim, there is St Sebastian Church perched up on the hill with the road below. A large signpost depicting the crucifixion has as its main message, 'Drive with Care. Make Accident Rare' (sic). St Sebastian Church itself overlooking the village and surrounded by coconut trees seems to incorporate living accommodation and again has recently been painted white with dark blue colours around the window and door frames.

Perhaps the most elaborate church buildings are at Assolna village. Built in 1616, Our Lady Queen of Martyrs was built on the ruins of a Portuguese fortress on the banks of the River Sal. The church itself is a substantial building, pristine white and seemed to have anticipated large congregations. In the church courtyard is a huge statue of Christ with two angels blowing their trumpets and surrounded by four apostles – all in marble. Originally, this agricultural village depended on rice and coconut crops with harvests of mangoes and jackfruit in the summer months. Today agriculture has largely disappeared and the money sustaining the village is from exiled workers in the Gulf States or on the tourist boats – a very Goan experience today. Attached to the church is the school – the Regina Martyrum High School – with a banner over the entrance proclaiming "400 Years of Faith". Across the road from the church is an elaborate covered cemetery surrounded by a six-foot wall. The memorial comments on the burial grounds are in Portuguese and, more recently, English. All in all, the Catholic Church has had and continues to play an influential role in the village and possibly region.

And then there is St Anne's Church in Agonda itself or Holy Trinity Church or the Church of St John the Baptist in Benaulim, Salcete.

The interest I have, however, is not in the documentation of the extent and nature of the Catholic Church in southern Goa, but rather in understanding a little more clearly the currents and issues underpinning Goan 'identity' today and its place within wider India. The continuing historical weight of the Portuguese in Goa seems clear-ish. What is less clear is the current situation. Interestingly, this particular road trip to Agonda seemed to confirm for me the continuing authority and influence of Catholicism in Goa today. It did more than this though. It illustrated (in a very pleasant manner, I must admit) how distinctive and different – culturally, religiously, historically, materially – this part of India is from the rest of the country.

Chapter 5

That Empire – then and now

Calcutta delights

Calcutta, one of the great cities of the world, is always hot, always dusty and always busy. It doesn't seem to figure strongly in most Western travellers' itineraries to India but for me this city with its 15 million inhabitants provided some of the most lasting memories of all the great Indian urban centres. The response of others who have visited Calcutta seems similar – they liked it. We stayed in a small hotel round the corner from Park Street, just south of the city centre. We familiarised ourselves quite quickly with the local Bengal eating places around the maze of stalls that made up the New Market, the legendary cake and tea shop at Flurys on Park Street, the wonderful Oxford Bookstore and the local rickshaw pullers who never gave up trying to get us on onboard. Most mornings we were up early and off to sit for an hour or so in the local small enclosed park and gardens on Park Street. The local residents from the overlooking apartments were out enjoying the early morning sunshine, like us. Children before off to school were playing, stacked plastic chairs were unstacked and pulled into a circle for chat and gossip, joggers hurried around the small perimeter track and breakfast sandwiches eaten. We too were soon included in the sandwich rituals as they welcomed us to 'their' gardens. After the park, most days involved a tram ride to some different part of the city. Sometimes it was to nowhere in particular – the purpose and joy simply was sitting in the tram and enjoying the inside and outside goings-on.

I'm not sure why Calcutta 'out-memorises' Delhi, Chennai, Bangalore or some other cities – perhaps expectations were not that great or the compact nature of the city centre encouraged a greater pedestrian feel to everything when contrasted with other cities. It might also result from the accessible nature of narratives for Western tourists. While Calcutta is clearly a very Indian city it was also quite visibly the old capital of the Raj. More than any other city apart from New Delhi we were reminded, it seemed, of this British presence. Calcutta was after all the second city in the British Empire after London. There are obviously other claims to fame for Calcutta – its contemporary cultural activities, its pride as 'the intellectual capital of India', the cinema of Satyajit Ray or, until 2011, the rule of the Communist Party. However, the British had left an indelible footprint that is not only difficult to ignore but which raises numerous questions which this chapter explores.

A couple of kilometres down Park Street is the celebrated South Park Street Cemetery. We visited the cemetery a few times in 2012 to escape the heat but also to examine more closely the stories and implications of this historical venue. The cemetery covers some eight acres, is enclosed by a high brick wall, has some 1,600 tombs, and has been substantially restored and renovated in recent years. Ancient rambling trees and flower beds and pots provide a shady canopy for the extravagant array of monuments, urns, pyramids, carvings, obelisks, raised plinths and fluted columns. Opened in 1767 and closed around 1831 for the employees of the East India Company, the cemetery can boast links one way or another to the likes of Rudyard Kipling, William Thackeray and Charles Dickens. Each of the tombstones seemed to tell its own story of disease, battles, shipwrecks and politics. One of my photographs is a tombstone of a "Collector of Revenues" who died aged 29. There is this interesting inscription on the tomb headed "In His Public Capacity". "He accomplished by a system of Conciliation what never be affected by Military Coercion. He civilized a Savage Race of Mountaineers who for Ages had existed in a state of Barbarism And eluded every Exertion that had been practised against them." Insights into the work and beliefs of these early colonisers are evident throughout the graveyard.

Incidentally, it was the South Park Street Cemetery that introduced me to the *Asiatic Society*. A plaque by the entrance gate announced that recent clear-up schemes and cemetery alterations had been funded by the Society. Delving into the history of the Society, I came across a number of names that I would meet in subsequent readings especially over the archaeological discoveries relating to Ashoka the Great who ruled around 230 BCE. Most prominent of these names was of course Sir William Jones. Founded in 1784 the Society's extensive and valuable library together with its museum both in Calcutta remain on my list of visits to do when next in the city. I think it remains today as a viable organisation although its website is a little dated.

Most of Calcutta's landmarks drip with variations of the sentiments carved into the stones of the South Park Cemetery. The white marbled Victoria Memorial for example (or the VM as it is commonly known) with its mixtures of Italianate and Mughal architecture was completed in 1921 and in 25 galleries houses the glories and triumphs of British conquest and of the British monarchy. When we visited the VM we couldn't enter and missed regrettably the Calcutta Gallery with its paintings, documents and photographs of old Calcutta and the Independence struggle. We did manage to see, however, the formal gardens and water features. Like many of the Raj monuments and buildings throughout India, the subplot is often one of 'shock and awe' – monumental edifices that are designed to convey power, authority, permanence and subservience. St Paul's Cathedral, where we had a picnic lunch in the shade of its numerous trees, must have provided similar bewilderment to the locals when it was opened around 1847.

Of less imperial significance but no less impressive is Howrah Bridge across the River Hooghly in north Calcutta which we crossed in the bus on our way to the Botanic Garden. This 750-metre single cantilever bridge was built by the British in 1943 to facilitate access to Burma during the Second World War. The traffic jam on the bridge is infamous as was the case on our crossing; it is said to be the busiest bridge in the world in terms of foot passengers. Apparently and difficult to believe, some two million cross it daily. Beneath the Bridge on the muddy grassed banks of the river are a busy collection of barbers, masseurs, cloth sellers, sleepers, people washing, buffalo grazing and rickshaws. The Botanic Garden founded in 1787 by the East India Company had seen better days and was in desperate need of support and toilets. It was nevertheless a welcome spot of calm and space in a city famous for its frenzy.

Equally restful were visits to the Maidan, the vast 1,283-acre open parkland in the heart of Calcutta incorporating several football stadia, the Kolkata Race Course and the famous cricket ground of Eden Park. Begun by the British in the mid-1750s, great tracts of jungle were cleared for military purposes and the creation of Fort William. Busts of Lenin and well marshalled demonstrations with hundreds of waving red flags with their hammer and sickle welcomed us as we strolled around the park.

I was in India during then British Prime Minister David Cameron's visit to India in February 2013. Little was made in the Indian newspapers of the economic agenda underpinning the visit or the biggest-ever delegation of business people accompanying Cameron. Space was provided for the expression of regret by the Prime Minister for the Jallianwala Bagh massacre of 1919 in Amritsar in which at least 400 unarmed Indian men, women and children were killed by British soldiers. Cameron remarked to the press in India that, "I think there is an enormous amount to be proud of in what the British Empire did and was responsible for. But of course there were bad events as well as good events. The bad events we should learn from and the good events we should celebrate." Always a smooth talker that masked a lack of substance to his politics, Cameron managed to smaltz his way through the India visit. Three years later, the political chancer gambled once too often and, in an attempt to quell the grumblings of the pesky reactionary wing within the Conservative Party, took Britain out of Europe.

For many British people and most of their daily national newspapers, there is little doubt of the benefits accruing from British imperial activities. The British historian Andrew Roberts for example wrote in the *Daily Express* that for "the vast majority of its half millennia-long history, the British empire was an exemplary good... the British gave up their Empire largely without bloodshed, after having tried to educate their successor governments in the ways of democracy and representative institutions." In another British newspaper – the *Daily Telegraph* – John Keegan argued that "the empire became in its last years highly benevolent and moralistic." The Victorians "set out to bring civilization and good government to their colonies and to leave when they were no longer welcome. In almost every country, once coloured red on the map, they stick to their resolve." A similar view was expressed in the *Daily Mail* newspaper. After berated Prime Minister Cameron's "exaggerated humility" on his 2013 visit to India, Dominic Sandbrook then outlines the reasons "why modern-day India... is a success story built on sturdy Anglo-Saxon foundations... The Raj survived not at the point of a bayonet, but thanks to the enthusiastic cooperation of ordinary Indians, who relished the order that their colonial partners had brought to a subcontinent torn apart by religious and ethnic conflict... It was no accident that when Union Jacks were lowered in Asia and Africa, there was a feeling of friendship and goodwill."

By way of contrast George Monbiot in another British newspaper – *The Guardian* – wrote that, "The story of benign imperialism, whose overriding purpose was not to seize land, labour and commodities but to teach the natives English, table manners and double-entry bookkeeping, is a myth that has been carefully propagated by the right-wing press. But it draws its power from a remarkable ability to airbrush and disregard our past."

Strongly opposed views about Britain's time in India are not difficult to find. The subject of 'The Empire' keeps appearing at regular intervals in the press in Britain but it is very much a partial, truncated and, for most of the daily press, a celebratory story of the benefits given to far-off countries by the British. By way of contrast, there are other complaints about the absence of the Empire from our views and understandings of who we as British are, where we came from and until very recently the extent of our involvement in other parts of the world. Moni Mohsin for example, who was brought up in Pakistan, had an article in *The Guardian* at the end of 2016 entitled, "Empire shaped the world. There is an abyss at the heart of dishonest history textbooks". Writing after the 'Brexit' vote where Britain decided to leave the European Union, her article reflects the present-day worries of British people of colour and ethnic difference with "the ugly xenophobia," as she puts it, unleashed by the vote. Reflecting on her daughters' (both born in London) educational experience at "a fantastic school", there was nevertheless this absent, missing element to their education. "Despite the range and candour of their education," writes Moni, "they haven't once encountered Britain's colonial past in school." One way or another, 'our' Empire keeps rearing its relevance and pertinence in a variety of ways.

Post-colonial understandings

I was interested in how my small group of Western tourists to India understood and related to the historical experiences of the British presence in the country. I asked a few questions along this line from my small sample and, not surprisingly, obtained views that reflected the ambiguities and hesitations that characterise the whole British colonial Indian experience. In the case of Sany from France for example, it had been school in Paris that first put India on the map. "It started at school when we started learning about Indian Independence and I said, oh, I'm interested – very interested. Jewish slaughter, Gandhi and Indian Independence, segregation in the States and apartheid in South Africa." Later on in the discussion Sany returned to the topic. Rather defensively knowing that I was from England, she continued, "England made excellent things such as the railway network. There was a peaceful struggle and India got its country back. *Gandhi* [the film released in 1982 and directed by Richard Attenborough] which I saw with the school connected me quite strongly to India. It had a great impact."

Pauline, who had grown up with Indian artefacts in her home in England as a result of her parents having been in the army in India, was interested to some extent in this history. "I'm not historically inclined but you can't miss what the British did and what was built. I remember talking to these two old men outside the Gandhi museum. One was a healer and the other was the curator of the museum. I said, I was 'ashamed because of what we did to your people.' The curator said, 'No, you shouldn't be ashamed. It was part of our history – to get to democracy. You should see it more as a trajectory to get where we are now.'" Pauline did admit that the two men might have been too polite to give her their real views but nevertheless hinted that she was of a similar view. It was the Partition of the Indian Empire which led to the creation of Pakistan on 14th August 1947 and India a day later that most interested Pauline. "The thing that made the most impression on me was the Partition. Horror – what people can do to each other. You see it always – how quickly things can blow up. We see in Serbia, Bosnia – neighbours living next door to each other and then doing these most horrific things. What human beings are capable of is terrifying. And it's possible today in India – it's definitely possible for these things to happen.

There is this underlying anger that is not shown."

Sheila too mentioned the Partition of the country. "Partition was unforgivable," she said. "But I don't know enough about how much we took from India. In England there are a lot of grand buildings built on the wealth not only of India but from the Commonwealth. It's amazing that so many were ruled by so few in India. Why didn't they do something about it? We must have ruled very well by dividing the ruled."

The word 'embarrassment' too is used by Steven. "Yes, the British in India does interest me a lot. I have watched a lot of TV documentaries (in the UK) on India and our colonial past. I am quite embarrassed about this past... our previous exploitation of the country as a colonial power. We weren't interested in the well-being of the Indian people. We wanted to force them to buy cloth made in the mills of Bradford. Obviously Mahatma Gandhi came in at that point. So I find our colonial past slightly worrying. The whole issue of Partition in particular. I had read that book *Indian Summer: The Secret History of the End of an Empire* by Alex Von Tunzelmann, about Mountbatten's relationship with Jinnah and so on. And the Emergency as well. There's that book *A Fine Balance* by Rohinton Mistry which is a novel set in the times of the Emergency. It really is a must-read but is difficult to get hold of. It really is a powerful work of literature. I was deeply affected by it. But in general, I try and keep up to date with developments since Independence."

I guess it is not that surprising that the British in India seems to be an issue that generally interests and, in some cases, continues to engage these frequent travellers to the country. I think that most visitors from the 'West' to the country, first-timers or those on package arrangements would have a vague working knowledge of this history – it's a global story full of drama, tragedy, mystery and big personalities. Arguably it can be seen as one of the defining significant historical stories of the twentieth century ranking, as Sany pointed out above, with the Holocaust and the apartheid struggles in South Africa. And it is one that refuses to fade away into the background as the heated media discussions around David Cameron's 2013 visit to India or the 70th anniversary celebrations of Independence in 2017 indicate. For Britain, this is perhaps understandable. Few countries if any value and parade their historical involvement abroad to the same extent as Britain. The Empire materially and ideologically shaped who we are and how we chose to be seen. In doing so these experiences also prevented or blocked other potentially 'modernising' initiatives and socio-economic developments over the last hundred and fifty years. Britain's militaristic history, its rigid class structure, its limited understandings and practice of 'democracy', its education system and economic dominance of the financial sector are only a few examples of the socio-political anomalies that can be traced to the adventures abroad. The deeply conservative nature of its institutions together with the failure to develop an alternative radical strategy to this dominant imperial story is partly explained by the compromises we made with the bounty and notions of superiority resulting from the Empire. It's a history of ourselves that continues to haunt us today. While the rest of the world may be surprised and bewildered at the dominance of one particular fee-paying private school Eton, in the make-up of the recent ruling Conservative Party's Cabinet, we from Britain are not. Our social elite, or should that be ruling class or maybe oligarchy, have not been swept away. Instead they have emerged stronger and more powerful from the upheavals, wars and political convulsions of the twentieth century. In fact, many of Britain's great aristocratic families owe their history, wealth, prestige and political influence to their participation in the country's imperial adventures – especially slavery – around the world. India was an important part of this story. It was after all only very recently that Britain began to withdraw from this imperial past with "our colonial partners" and with "a feeling of goodwill and friendship" and "largely without bloodshed", according to some of our newspapers. Ignoring the more nationalistic and xenophobic overtones of many contributions and in a spirit of generosity, so historically recent has been this withdrawal that it is perhaps too early to critically evaluate these defining experiences. Nevertheless, the Empire and India in particular will continue to figure prominently in Britain's national discussions, debates and reflections.

So what were the British doing in India?

Visiting any of the great Indian metropolises inevitably raises questions not only of the impact of the British in India but also as mentioned above of the impact back in Britain of this relationship. As William Dalrymple noted in a 2015 newspaper article, "For better or worse, the British Empire was the most important thing the British ever did. It altered the course of history across the globe and shaped the modern world. It also led to the huge enrichment of Britain." India was one of the biggest losers in this transformation together with the hundreds of thousands of slaves from Africa sent to work on the American plantations. In India's case, the fall was catastrophic – from a position of a global manufacturing power before the arrival of the British to impoverishment when the British left. Although receiving little attention in Britain, an Indian Congress Party member and writer Shashi Tharoor argued in a debate at Oxford University in 2015 that Britain owed India a huge amount of financial reparations for the damage inflicted while in India. The video of his speech went viral with three million views within three weeks. In the British press, it barely registered as a footnote.

There is a very obvious British footprint to many aspects of Indian cities, culture and political life. If we return to South Park Street Cemetery in Calcutta for example, there are clues to this interrelationship beyond the shady gardens, masonry and architecture. Buried here were the colonial elite of a part of the Empire 'at work' – civil servants, businessmen, military officers and assorted family members. This was the graveyard of that strangely disappeared, today unacknowledged key to British domination in India – the Governor and Company of Merchants of London Trading into the East Indies, more commonly known as the British East India Company. Calcutta was the company town of the East India Company and South Park Cemetery documents the contributions of many of its employees together with the military personnel that ensured its spectacular success. Today, many of those subjugated to its rule remember the Company, but in Britain, it seems to have been airbrushed from history. Nick Robins, author of the recent book *The Corporation that Changed the World: How the East India Company Shaped the Modern Multinational* mentions his search in London for any monument or plaque at the location of the Company. In a 'heritage' dominated country, he finds nothing. On the original site of the Company in Leadenhall Street, London instead there is the architecturally-famed Lloyd's Bank Building. This is strange, for the East India Company was no ordinary company. When the Company arrived in India as a trading enterprise in 1660, Britain's share of the world's Gross Domestic Product (GDP) was around 2%, India's was around 22%. When the British left India in 1947, its national income was 50% higher than India's. This was some reversal and the East India Company played a major role in this reversal. Yet still no plaque for this mother of the modern transnational company. Perhaps part of the reason for this amnesia today is the ambiguous attitude or even political embarrassment towards the Company today from a country that prides itself on its practice of 'cutting-edge' capitalism. After all, this was a company that began as a humble trading enterprise started by a few individuals (although with a trading monopoly granted by Elizabeth I) eager to share in the trade of silk, dye, sugar, spices and cloth from a sophisticated economy and in 'partnership' with the Mughal emperors. It ended up as a restructured shareholder company which through its own military resources conquered the country and ushered in a period of domination, oppression and economic exploitation. Gone and defeated were the Mughals, the French, the Portuguese and the Dutch. One of the key episodes in this transformation (and in the history of India) was the 1757 Battle of Plassey on the banks of the Hugli river, outside Calcutta in the state of Bengal. As many British schoolchildren with a smattering of history can testify, Robert Clive – Clive of India – is a name to be remembered and cherished. His victory at the village of Plassey on the banks of the Hugli River over the Nawab of Bengal in 1757 against overwhelming numbers ensured the ascendancy of the East India Company, the British against the French, of Clive himself as master of Bengal and, in the longer term, to the establishment of British rule in India. Although not mentioned in the history books, it was a victory, writes William Dalrymple, "that owed more to treachery, forged contracts, bankers and bribes than military prowess." The breakthrough of Plassey was that Clive was recognised by the enfeebled Mughal Empire and began raising huge revenues through taxation – the oil that greased the mechanisms of domination and exploitation. The East India Company through the military violence of Clive was now financially able to increase trade, raise and pay for an army of considerable strength, make wars and threaten those opposing its ambitions. The Company by now was second only to the Bank of England in importance. Clive returned to England a millionaire. Bengal was as Clive described it, "an inexhaustible fund of riches" and bled dry. Within three decades after Plassey, the Company was now a ruler increasingly concerned with issues of 'governance' and the raising of finances to fund this rule, an imperial power in its own right. And still, no plaque.

William Dalrymple in a 2015 article in *The Guardian* newspaper describes the East India Company as "the original corporate raider". It's a wonderful article. As he reminds us, "It was not the British government that seized India at the end of the

18th century, but a dangerously unregulated private company headquartered in one small office, five windows wide, in London, and managed in India by a sociopath – Clive." Dalrymple goes on to characterise the East India Company as "almost certainly" the best example of what "remains the supreme act of corporate violence in world history. For all the power wielded today by the world's largest corporations – whether ExxonMobil, Walmart or Google – they are tame beasts compared to the ravaging territorial appetites of the militarised East India Company."

So, at the beginning of the nineteenth century, the British through the East India Company had established a military dominance that enabled them to subdue all remaining important Indian states, either through conquest or through the creation of subordinate rulers. At its peak, it ruled the subcontinent, created countries such as Singapore and initiated forced production of the lucrative opium which was smuggled into China. Victory at Plassey was followed by victories over the Marathas in 1818, the Sikhs in 1848 and the annexation of Awadh in 1856. Huge armies were created largely involving local Indian conscripts to defend the Company's territories and assets, and to 'persuade' and crush any internal dissent and resistance. The export, import and manufacture of goods moved directly or indirectly from independent Indian merchants to the East India Company.

Around the middle of the nineteenth century, however, the Company was finished. The 1857 Indian Mutiny, as the British history books describe it, began as a mutiny of Sepoys in the Company's army. Quickly the revolt spread to numerous areas throughout the country. Also known as India's First War of Independence, the Indian Mutiny, the Sepoy Mutiny or the Uprising of 1857, the rebellion took on a popular patriotic revolt against the European domination of the country. The Uprising has exercised a powerful fixation for British opinion and history ever since. The roots of the revolt go back some time but the common understanding is of soldiers of the Bengal army revolting against their British officers and marching on Delhi. Their revolt encouraged rebellions by civilians, peasants and Indian soldiers across north and central India. British women and children were killed together with thousands of Indians by the avenging British armies. Retribution was savage and widespread. The mutiny, however, had lasting consequences and marked the transition from company rule to crown rule. In 1858 authority was transferred from the company to the monarch and in 1877 Queen Victoria was declared Empress of India. The need to keep remittances flowing through to London remained paramount irrespective of changes at the top.

The conquests in India by the Company were never agreed to in Britain. However, increasing British concern over the activities of the Company coupled with the Company's financial problems stemming from the huge military expenditures resulted in greater Parliamentary control over the Company in 1873 and the introduction of Governor General rule in India. Thus began the period of the British Raj with direct governing by the Crown. There seems little doubt that the 1857 Indian Mutiny had greatly unsettled the political powers back 'home'. In 1885, the East India Company was dissolved.

For almost 200 years there had been a systematic transfer of wealth from India to Europe and mainly to Britain. Central to this imperial looting was this East India Company. The booty from India and later other colonial adventures in Africa coincided with or perhaps provided an essential basis for the world's first industrial capitalist state – Britain. British banks used the Indian capital to fund industry in the US and elsewhere. The Industrial Revolution and development of modern capitalism was based on the Empire and principally India.

It was not only an unrelenting need for remittances from India by the British state that was needed. It was also a range of products and, in particular, food. It was food that underpinned a more notorious episode in the history of Bengal – the Famine of 1943. Madhusree Mukherjee's recent study (2010) entitled "Churchill's Secret War: The British Empire and the Ravaging of India during World War II" painstakingly outlines the gruesome details of this episode which today continues to provoke acrimonious debate and rancour. Japan had invaded neighbouring Burma – the War was not going well for Churchill. As Burma was important in supplying rice to India, Churchill stockpiled food for soldiers and workers, prices increased, distribution channels were blocked and transport vehicles (boats, bullock carts) destroyed in Bengal to prevent them from falling into the hands of a possible Japanese invasion of India. Rice was scarce and worsening hunger was spreading throughout the villages. As the *Times of India* wrote, "Emaciated masses drifted into Calcutta, where eyewitnesses described men fighting over foul scraps and skeletal mothers dying in the streets... The 'man-made' famine has long been one of the darkest chapters of the British Raj." About 3 million people died of starvation in Bengal. The causes of this devastation have always been disputed but after a seven-year study of original documents and Cabinet Papers, Mukherjee concluded that in the main Churchill was responsible for the great famine, often overruling close advisors, Viceroy Linlithgow in India and his own War Cabinet. Most of the official reasons for the famine are discredited in the book, such as the absence of requisite shipping to bring in food supplies and the absence of sufficient grain (despite a surplus of grain in Australia). Appointed as Viceroy of India in 1943, Archibald Wavell informed London that the famine "was one of the greatest disasters that has befallen any people under British rule." Incredibly, the famine occurred at a time when, in 1943, 2.5 million Indians were fighting alongside the Allies. As two Cambridge University historians pointed out, "It was Indian soldiers, civilian labourers and businessmen who made possible the victory in 1945." Their price was to be the independence of their country, despite the desires and efforts of Churchill. As an editorial in the Indian online site *Tehelka* mentions, "The Bengal Famine of 1943–44 must rank as the greatest disaster in the subcontinent in the 20th century. Nearly 4 million Indians died because of an artificial famine created by the British government, and yet it gets little more than passing mention in Indian history books." In Britain, perhaps unsurprisingly, it doesn't even merit a 'passing mention'. Similarly, the earlier Bengal famines of the 1760s – the 'paradise of earth' according to the Mughals and "an inexhaustible fund of riches" by Clive – receives little historical attention in Britain today although it remains a raw issue in India. Ravaged by war, disease and famine, a third of the population died of hunger. Historical narratives are, it seems, a very selective process.

However, there was another issue that was not only forgotten but never appeared in the reckonings today of the Raj and India. Poppies. It was Governor-General Warren Hastings that came up with the idea, in 1780, of exporting opium to China in order to resolve the huge balance of payment problems with China. In an interview with Amitav Ghosh on the BBC News Channel, the celebrated Indian novelist was discussing his historical novel, *Sea of Poppies*. "I had no idea," he said, "that India was the largest opium exporter (to China) for centuries. I had no idea that opium was essentially the commodity which financed the British Raj in India... Opium steadily accounted for about 17–20% of Indian revenues... Opium was the fundamental undergirding of our economy for centuries. It is strange that even for someone like me who studied history and knew a fair amount about Indian history, I was completely unaware of it." Today, the 'Opium Wars' figure vaguely in the British collective memory. Most people have heard of it but are not sure of the details or context.

Has India always been poor? The economic debate

Opium then was a fundamental characteristic of the Indian

economy under the British. At a more general level and of news to me and probably most tourists is that, historically, India has not always been associated with poverty and hunger. In order to unravel this story, we have to step back into a little more history and, inevitably when discussing India, into more controversies.

As mentioned in Chapter 3, India under the Mughals – especially Akbar – was one of the world's great powers. From the late 16th century through to the mid-18th century India together with China dominated world trade. As Mihir Bose wrote, "Even in 1750, 167 years after Elizabeth's begging letter, India had 24.5% of the world's manufacturing output – with China leading the field with 32.8% while the United Kingdom was barely visible with 1.9%." 1750 is not that long ago! Bose also points out that it was another seven years before Clive's victory over the Nawab of Bengal at Plassey in 1757 that "converted the British from traders to rulers and changed everything." Numerous very famous Western commentators on India such as Adam Smith, Montesquieu, James Mill, Karl Marx and Max Weber depicted India at the time of the British contact with the country as stagnant, without any known history, autocratic darkness, unchanged for a thousand years etc, etc. Most of course had never visited the country. The appalling condition of India in the 19th century was simply extended back in time. Recent scholarship largely from Indian scholars have contested such easy and erroneous but influential generalisations. Economic historians such as Prasannan Parthasarathi and Amiya Kumar Bagchi for example have demonstrated an India legendary for its immense wealth and wisdom prior to the arrival of the British. Vibrant production of cotton textiles for export resulted in a sizeable inflow of gold and silver which fuelled other commercial production. From 1600 through to 1800 Mughal India boasted a trading sector with well-functioning institutions, effective and integrated markets and pockets of highly skilled and internationally competitive artisans and workers. Agricultural production was efficient and characterised by investment and innovation. In the run-up to the Industrial Revolution in Britain and Europe, India it is argued was not profoundly different in its economic institutions.

What went wrong? Why did India not 'take off'? Why today is poverty such a strong image associated with India? So what made India poor, "indeed, one of the poorest countries in the world?" ask Jean Dréze and Amartya Sen in their recent book, *An Uncertain Glory: India and its Contradictions*. In common with the other commentators mentioned above, Dréze and Sen argue that before the arrival of the British via the East India Company in the mid-eighteenth century, the economy was seen generally as a trade-based, comparatively thriving economy with a number of towns and cities trading with other countries. Commentators from the Greeks and Romans through to the British economist Adam Smith identified a variety of factors that accounted for the success of the economy. Industrial exports, especially textiles from Bengal, were valued by Europeans and others. Merchants from Portugal, the Netherlands, France, Denmark, Prussia and other European countries were busy establishing trade links, write Dréze and Sen. Despite the weakness of available data, they suggest that wages of Indian labour were similar or higher when compared with other European workers. And as they say, "Just as it is unnecessary to invent some imaginary golden age to acknowledge the relative prosperity of pre-colonial India, one does not have to be an aggressive nationalist to recount the rapid decline of the relative position of the Indian economy during the British Raj." Economic decline appeared to be continuing throughout the nineteenth century. For long periods under British rule, per capita actually declined. The economy was largely stagnant; around the time of Independence, living conditions were appalling. Dréze and Sen quote Angus Deaton who argued that the deprivation facing Indian children born in the mid-twentieth century: "was (possibly) as severe as any large group in history, all the way back to the Neolithic Revolution and the hunter-gathers that preceded them. Life expectancy in India in 1931 was 27." This damning indictment of British rule makes even more remarkable the progress achieved since Independence. Not mentioned then by the triumphalist British press was this systematic impoverishment of India by British rule. So huge, purposeful, continuous and brutal was this decline that surely it must rank up there as one of the most barbaric episodes of modern times.

This question of India's comparative prosperity and then subsequent decline with the arrival of the British is, as I have discovered, a central part of a wider scholarly debate known as the 'Great Divergence between the West and the Rest'. There has long been a background rumble to these issues in the past but they seem to have gathered momentum in the last decade or so. Given the context of the disputes – millions dying of starvation, military domination and violence and distorted societal development – an anger and passion and, sometimes, crude partisanship often underpins the disagreements. Academic contributions from a variety of disciplines have enriched the often-dense discussions and reams of statistical data. There is no easy summary of these debates even for those steeped in the literature and history, but the drift of the consensus seems clear; namely, that the aim of colonial rule was to deliver a financial surplus to the ruling country. Most other activities – socially, politically or administratively – were geared towards this overriding objective or else were of secondary importance. Bagchi's figures in his recent book *Colonialism and Indian Economy* are persuasive. For example, he illustrates how the financial drain from India was critical in the rise and construction of Britain's Empire. It helped pay for British military expenditures in their century-long war against the French. Victory paved the way for British hegemony in Europe and elsewhere in the crucial period 1765–1812. Later, the financial drain from India during 1870–1915 was so large it could have financed anywhere between 75%–95% of British foreign investment worldwide. As Servaas Storm writes in his review, "Colonial rule over India was therefore an integral element of British capitalist accumulation, both as a source of funds and a sink for cheap Lancashire cottons." It was an export-led *exploitation* rather than export-led *growth*. This surplus was possible as a result of a variety of 'economic reforms', such as dispossession of lands and the deindustrialisation of manufacturing, especially in the textile sector. The cotton-weaving and spinning industries were wiped out and this was in a country that accounted for nearly a quarter of the world's manufactured output around 1750.

Without doubt, the 'Divergence Debate' will continue. Although difficult and complex to grasp, it is an important endeavour. India and Britain today are what they are because of their interrelated past and for both countries their historical involvement with each other are seminal, defining experiences.

For the Indian economy today, however, these 'costs' of British rule have been high. All countries that have emerged from colonialism exhibit particular characteristics that were shaped and moulded by this occupying experience. These countries today might well be industrialised, capitalist economies but they will demonstrate particular and distinct features that reflect particular and distinct historical experiences. India's manufacturing industry, for example, illustrates this historical 'deformation'. Since Independence of course it has crept up as a contribution to the country's growth in parallel to agriculture's decline. But so severe was the destruction of Indian manufacturing under the British that the growth has been nothing like it should have been. Instead it is the service sector which has benefited from this history. Largely as a result of British rule, the modern Indian economy has a most unusual, almost unique structure – economic development without a driving, expanding manufacturing sector. Moreover, as Surajit Mazumdar has argued, this comparatively small manufacturing sector until recently exhibited a limited capacity for the self-development of technology. Instead, it depended on its financial muscle to buy international companies to boost its international competitiveness. The country's trade pattern reflects the historical weak industrial base – namely, low manufacturing exports with significant volumes of imports. Trade balances are rescued by the very high volume of its services or, more particularly, its information technology (IT) and IT enabled services.

The East India Company together with the subsequent activities of the Raj might have been a long time ago but they continue to shape, direct and influence modern economic development.

Some good, some bad

When looking at the issue of the British Empire in India, there seems to be a consensus or a dominant narrative of Britain's time in the country – there were some good aspects and some aspects that were not so good. The Indian Civil Service, which administered the country as a colony from 1858 until 1947, is often cited as a good aspect, for example. Mostly staffed by Englishmen from private schools back in Britain, the Indian Civil Service was described in 1935 by David Lloyd George, a former Prime Minister, as "the steel frame on which the whole structure of our government and of our administration in India rests." Nehru on the other hand when writing about the Indian Civil Service saw it famously: "as neither Indian, nor civil, nor a service." Despite this polite difference of opinion, Prime Minister Nehru retained the organisation which today has around 6.5 million employees. The Civil Service after Independence was seen as an important contributor towards developing national unity and cohesion and today continues to be politically modelled on the British example. Overall then, it was a 'good legacy' from the British.

A similar story surrounds India's state-owned rail system. Begun in 1853 with the short link between Bombay to Thane (today, a suburb of Bombay), India has one of the world's largest networks (115,000 kilometres) with some 7,500 stations. The Bombay to Calcutta line across the northern plains of the country was completed in 1864. The rail system usually is identified as another of the 'good things' left to India by the British. Situated within the context of the British Raj and earlier, the East India Company, however, might provide a more nuanced appreciation. Economic and military motives dominated the beginnings of this wonderful system, not passenger or tourist travel.

And then, there is New Delhi. Wandering around Lutyens' Delhi there remains today a continuing sense of awe and bewilderment. The vast scale of the design, architecture, tree-lined boulevards and grandiose constructions remains breathtaking. Sipping coffee in the commercial centre Connaught Square (and politely fending off the numerous offers of shopping assistance from the locals) begins to reveal the extent of the enterprise but also to raise numerous questions. It was George V, King of England and Emperor of India, who announced at the Delhi Durbar in 1911 that Delhi would replace Calcutta as the new capital of the British Indian Empire; India would be easier to govern from New Delhi rather than the north-east coast of the country. The Raj was on the move. Edwin Lutyens and Herbert Baker were the architects charged with the design of the new imperial centre. Work started after the First World War and was completed in 1931. The splendour of New Delhi continues today to attract attention from visitors around the world and scholars from a variety of disciplines. Connaught Place, the India Gate war memorial, the royal mall Rajpath lined with trees and fountains, and the Secretariat Building are but a few of the sites which are known to a wider global audience.

The more one sees of this New Delhi, however, the more questions begin to arise. What sort of country and political class could imagine, never mind complete such a grandiose project? The First World War of inter-imperial rivalry had just finished with millions dead; Britain's economic and global dominance was on the wane and a restless nationalist movement in India was on the rise. Despite this wider context, construction began on the new capital. Not just any old capital, but a capital that was designed and constructed to last a millennium, forever and ever. Irrespective of the elegance of the architecture, Lutyens' Delhi embodied raw political power reinforcing the divide between the rulers and the ruled. It symbolised, similar to other empires and religions, a sense of impotence, obedience and wonderment. A foretaste of this arrogance and blind faith in the military might and, therefore, the future of the British state was evident in the photographs and numerous video clips available on the Internet of the 1911 Delhi Durbar. The vast pageant resplendent with elephants, jewels and, no doubt, 'grateful locals and dignitaries' not only centred on power but also on monarchy, Christianity and 'whiteness'. An interesting account of the Durbar is provided in January's edition of *The Caravan*, the excellent Indian cultural magazine. Some 84,000 Europeans and Indians were brought from different parts of the country to 233 camps covering 40 square kilometres under 16 square kilometres of canvas. 35,000 troops were in attendance. From the spring of 1911 onwards, some 20,000 people had been at work on these camps. Sixty-four kilometres of new roads were constructed, 80 kilometres of water mains and 48 kilometres of water pipes were laid. Farms with herds of cows and dairies, and markets for meat and vegetables were established. It must have been a good day out for everyone.

Thirty-six years later, Britain left India in a hasty, bloody, murderous and undignified exit.

However, it is not the East India Company, the network of rail or Lutyens' Delhi that automatically spring to mind when the British Raj is remembered. Other episodes and characters periodically filter through to the outside world. In 2015 for example, if you looked carefully, you could find some mention and discussion of the contribution made by an undivided India to the 1914–1918 First World War during the centenary commemorations. Careful examination of the media coverage, exhibitions and extensive documentation made available for the anniversary revealed a footnote on the Indian contribution. Over one million Indians were sent overseas to fight as combatants and non-combatants on behalf of the British in places as diverse as France, Egypt and Palestine. As one wounded soldier recovering in England put it, "Do not think that this is war. This is not war. It is the ending of the world. This is just such a war as was related in the *Mahabharata* about our forefathers." Many of these Indian troops saw action in some of the fiercest battles of the War – Ypres, Givenchy, Loos – suffering traumatic losses and injuries and, yet, they remained almost invisible in the centenarian activities. Given the absence of written documentation or records that reflected this experience, the British Library attempted to remedy these deficiencies by making available the censored letters home by Indians involved in the War, together with a collection of photographs. There have been a small number of academic texts available on the 'Sepoys in the trenches' but much remains invisible and unresearched. Despite valuable efforts like that of the British Library, the full heroic story and horror of the Indian experience remains today undiscovered and untold. *Dunkirk*, the big budget, blockbuster film success from the summer of 2017, managed to portray an almost totally white experience in this supposedly historical portrayal. Absent from the Dunkirk beaches were the Royal Indian Army Service Corps together with the large number of non-white faces in the marine evacuation – plucky Brits again saving the day.

In contrast to the semi-official version of the paternalistic, racialised, benign character of British rule, the British Empire responded to any challenges (anywhere) with ferocious repression. It is the great historical 'set pieces' and personalities that tend to be scrutinised and discussed but everyday life in the imperial enterprise too is usually underpinned by a degree and threat of violence. Such a view, however, has been overwhelmed by a popular consensus of Britain's concerns and ideals of 'justice' and 'fair play'. At times, the eulogies sounded almost 'cuddly'. Within such a perspective, Indians were seen as passive, static and almost welcoming of their subjugation and conquest. Occasionally an alternative view breaks through such as the study by Elizabeth Kolsky in *Colonial Justice in British India: White Violence and the Rule of Law*. Underpinning this economic extraction and military violence, however, was systemic racism. As Elizabeth Kolsky notes, "the unsettling picture that emerges from our investigation of white violence and its handling in the colonial courts should not be brushed off as a list of exceptions, an epiphenomenal sideshow to the main stage of Pax Britannica." Critical studies such as these, however, are the exception. Much more common are accounts of everyday life alongside records of major events which accept uncritically the perspectives and assumptions handed down from on high.

As was announced and proclaimed many times, it was the duty of the British to lead by example, display their moral and cultural superiority and provide good government on behalf of peoples for whom a free government was impossible. At the end of the day though, and underpinning the later Partition horrors, was a blunt truth. The Indian Empire was and had always been about the British economy and Britain's wider Empire. The need to keep remittances flowing to London remained central and most reforms centred around this imperative. Land revenue remained the largest source of income although politically difficult to collect. Exports grew rapidly in the second half of the nineteenth century. Coinciding with a growing independence struggle, export values increased fivefold between 1870 and 1914. Jute, cotton and tea went to Europe, and rice and opium went East. India was absorbing increasing volumes of manufactured goods from Britain, growing from 8% to 13% during the same period.

India was the most important market in the empire with Britain supplying 85% of India's imports in the 1890s. As the British historian Eric Hobsbawm put it, "India was the 'brightest jewel in the imperial crown' and the core of British strategic thinking precisely because of her very real importance to the British economy... (T)he international balance of payments hinged on the payments surplus which India provided." Each reform appeared to be agreed when no further options were available. While there was a historically strong sense of paternalism by the British towards their subjects, at the end of the day it was an exercise in naked plunder.

Partition and Britain's secrets

As some of the comments from the frequent travellers to India interviewed earlier in this chapter suggest, there is one particular episode from Indian history, or rather the Raj, that is better known not only in Britain but throughout the world. The Partition of the country and the Independence of India continue to resonate with tourists today. This is not perhaps surprising as it must be one of the dramatic, bloodiest and seminal events of the twentieth century. The subject of numerous academic studies, polemics, novels and films the division of the country together with the withdrawal of the British from India continues to arouse fierce passions and deeply-felt personal tragedies – not from the British leaving India but from the way and the consequences of how it was done. The barebones of Partition are generally known. Given that British rule in India never had more than 50,000 troops and depended on the co-option of Indians themselves, once that involvement was withdrawn the days of the Raj were numbered. The struggle for independence after the First World War indicated that this time had come. The founding earlier of the Indian National Congress created in 1885 to increase the involvement of Indians in government resulted in as Michael Wood puts it, "the greatest anti-colonial movement in history." By the 1930s it was clear that the end was in sight. It was clear that the united secular India championed by the Congress Party was not possible. A Hindu-Muslim unity was rapidly overtaken by events, fears, rumours, personal ambition, accident and mistakes. As the talks over power sharing involving the Indian Congress Party, the Muslim League and the British colonial government began to falter, partition seemed to be the only way forward. The last British Viceroy in India, Lord Mountbatten of Burma only appointed on 21st February 1947, quickly realised that if Britain was not going to be involved in an increasingly likely civil war, he needed to act quickly on both a partition and on an exit from the country. On the 3rd of June 1947, Mountbatten announced among other measures that partition of the country would be voted upon, a boundary commission was to be established should partition be the chosen way forward and India would be independent by 15th August – a few months away. The Quit India Movement launched in August 1942 was only subdued through massive repression: "by far the most serious rebellion since that of 1857 (the great Rebellion), the gravity and extent of which we have so far concealed from the world for reasons of military security," wrote Viceroy Linlithgow to Prime Minister Winston Churchill. Amid increasing mutinies, communal conflict especially in Calcutta, the formation of an interim government under Jawaharlal Nehru, an increasingly confident Muslim League under Muhammad Ali Jinnah and a post-war exhausted and bankrupt Britain, the British Parliament passed the Indian Independence Act on 18 July 1947 that finalised the arrangements for Partition, abandoning control over hundreds of princely states.

The 15th August 1947 Independence celebrations overseen by Viceroy Lord Louis Mountbatten and Jawaharlal Nehru of the Congress Party masked experiences that would remain and scar indelibly the new states of India and Pakistan from then through to today. Following the Radcliffe decision to partition Punjab and Bengal in the creation of the two new states – India and Pakistan – millions of people throughout the country discovered that they no longer belonged to their places of birth and livelihood. They might have also been of the wrong religion. In the months following the mid-August celebrations, some 20 million people would be on the move, 'religiously cleansed' and leaving all behind them forever. Up to a million and a half people died. Military action from each of the three communities – Hindus, Sikhs and Muslims – began enforcing the separation. The figures of those seeking safety were staggering. Once the lines of partition had been established, about twenty million people crossed the borders to a perceived religious and physical security – arguably the largest mass migration ever seen. Searing images of communal violence and slaughter remain today among those that participated and for the world at large. The birth of India and Pakistan from the ashes of the Empire was characterised by a terrible violence and resulted in a harvest and bitterness for further conflict. Four armed conflicts between the beneficiaries of Partition so far have taken place, with both countries remaining on almost permanent war alert with regards to each other; war and famine accompanied the creation of Bangladesh from East Pakistan in the early 1970s and a continuing low intensity conflict simmers in Kashmir.

It was, however, through this struggle for Indian independence that there emerged two of the iconoclastic figures of the twentieth century – the saintly Mahatma Gandhi and Jawaharlal Nehru. Despite its recent dramatic decline today, the Indian Congress Party is one of the great political parties of the modern world. As is well reported and accepted, this is the party that led the fight for independence, the party that united India and brought people of different religions and different languages into a single political project. It was above all Gandhi, on his return in 1915 from South Africa, that provided the depth, organisation and legitimacy to the party over the next two decades or so. Establishing a presence in rural areas, involving peasants and women, using languages other than English and campaigning to abolish Untouchability addressed weaknesses within the Congress Party as well as deepened and broadened its appeal. Peasants would play a significant role in the Non-Cooperation Movement of the 1920s and in the civil disobedience campaign of the 1930s. In recent years, there has emerged a more critical appreciation of the events and personalities of the organisation and struggle for independence. These weaknesses and shortcomings – such as the marginalisation of Dalits and Muslims together with the influence of Hindu conservatives – have reopened the examination of the Independence period. The achievements of the Indian Congress Party in 1947, however, provided an inspiration for many other subsequent anti-colonial struggles in the twentieth century.

It was the increasingly politically turbulent events of the decades preceding Independence that forced the hasty exit of Britain from the country. This was no dignified handing over of power. Until the very last moment, it seems that the powers in India never saw the writing on the wall. Events were spiralling out of control with a real risk of Britain being enveloped in a bitter civil war. Mountbatten's timetable suggests panic and, certainly, gross irresponsibility. Despite attempts today to absolve Britain from the chaos, suffering and carnage of the Partition, Britain was the central actor and power in a series of activities and decisions that continue to resonate today. The world was changing dramatically in the first half of the twentieth century and Britain had failed to grasp and understand these changes. Instead it attempted to preserve, contain and reverse what were irreversible trends.

Not surprisingly, the partition of the continent and Britain's subsequent hurried withdrawal remains today a topic of major contestation, literature and research. For one of the seminal events of the twentieth century, it continues to arouse bafflement, debate, study and incredulity. The magnitude of the Partition events and experiences helped to explain the outcry in 2015 when it was revealed that thousands of documents detailing some of the most shameful acts and crimes committed during the final years of the British empire were systematically destroyed to prevent them falling into the hands of post-independent governments, reported *The Guardian*, in April 2012. The archive came to light after a group of Kenyans, detained and allegedly tortured during the Mau Mau rebellion, won the right to sue the British government. The government promised to release 8,800 files filling some 200 metres of shelving from 37 former colonies. Many of the most sensitive files, however, were not hidden away but destroyed under instructions from the government in 1961. Dummy files were created and inserted to replace individual destroyed files. These 8,800 colonial files are a small part of the 1.2 million files occupying around two kilometres of shelving, the secret 'Special Collections'. Historical scholars from Britain have described their feelings and revelations as "scandalous", "wholly inappropriate", "very angry" and "staggering".

No doubt in the decades ahead, documents relating to the British in India will be forthcoming. Detail well might be shone on 'everyday' issues and events but also on continuing controversies over some of the big episodes, such as the Partition of the British Indian Empire.

Post-colonial dilemmas

"The moral balance sheet of the British Empire is a chaotic mixture of black and red. So it is understandable that people today, trying to evaluate this momentous episode in our island history, are confused," suggests Piers Brendon in the magazine *History Today*.

India – its history, culture, cricket, politics – continues to provide an enduring presence within British cultural life in the twenty-first century. India and Britain seem to go together; it is difficult to imagine India without imagining the Raj. It should be true the other way around and it is but in a peculiar, partial and distorted manner. The violence, racism and economic robbery that characterised much of the British presence in India is airbrushed to one of a benevolent gifting of railways, cricket and a civil service to those who didn't know better. The economic strength of India today opens a few cracks in this widespread historical amnesia of our imperial past, as for example when Prime Minister David Cameron apologised recently for the Amritsar massacre. It is far easier for 'our' history to focus on the evils of Nazi Germany or Belgian Congo experiences in Africa than our own imperial legacy.

And yet, there is that connection. Little incidents even in Britain today continue to remind us of this history. In 2015 for example, it was reported that a museum and library will be built in London to honour the life and work of the Indian campaigner, Dr Bhimrao Ramji Ambedkar. Ambedkar was a Dalit or 'untouchable' who drafted most of the Indian Constitution and tirelessly campaigned (largely unsuccessfully it must be said) for the rights of Dalits. He warned of the perniciousness of the caste system, and controversially in India then and even today associated the caste system with Hinduism. He remains a revered figure among India's 200 million Dalits with his portraits commonly available throughout the country. Ambedkar studied in London in 1921–22 and eventually qualified as a barrister in London. He was India's first Law Minister in the Independent Government of 1947.

Another example of the links between the two countries was the erection of the Gandhi statue on Parliament Square in London in 2015. Making the announcement in Parliament after returning from India with $300 plus million contracts for the British-made Eurofighter Typhoon jet airplane, British Foreign Secretary William Hague praised Gandhi's commitment to non-violence as "a legacy that is as relevant today as it was during his life."

Of course, as many commentators have made clear, the ending of Britain's imperial role together with the ending of the neat securities of 'goodies' and 'baddies' associated with the Cold War have resulted in a confusing and bewildering loss of purpose. Britain's 'greatness' is no more, and the global, international presence of yesteryear is an embarrassing irrelevance. Things aren't what they were. As the Scot Tom Nairn put it when talking about Britain, "The empire may have gone politically, but it has bequeathed a formidable psycho-social inheritance focusing naturally upon the question of Englishness. English identity was for so long over-extended by the needs of empire that it was bound to experience problems of contraction." Constructions and understandings of 'who we are' today are inseparable from understandings of 'Empire'. Britain was transformed by empire. It shaped even the identity and nature of the emerging British working class – from revolt to incorporation – and legitimated the rise of elite social institutions – Oxbridge.

This awareness must be true for all citizens from imperial powers visiting former colonies, but I think that the British together with the French have had the most difficulties in coming to grips with this imperial past. Maybe it is simply a case of these pasts being so recent. All post-colonial countries today struggle to a greater or lesser extent with the presentation of their past history to a general public. Whether Spain, Portugal, the Netherlands, Germany, Britain or any of the other colonial powers, they face similar ambiguities and decisions. Inevitably perhaps, they come down on the side of pride and sometimes 'glory'. For Britain, this seems more acute than most other powers given the recent nature, importance and breadth of 'its' Empire. In the main the principal vehicle for coping with such dilemmas is selection; that is, emphasising certain perspectives and episodes at the expense of diluting or forgetting others. It seems to work, politically anyway, as British politicians have demonstrated in recent years. Historically, culturally and materially, India remains as a positive and, even, sometimes glorious episode of the Empire. That Britain benefited materially so substantially at the expense of its overseas adventures simply complicates and further confuses any reckoning of its imperial past. Perhaps not surprisingly is the realisation that we in Britain do not yet have a developed and agreed account of our colonial experiences. Our history is too turbulent and unsettled. Instead a contradictory, self-defensive tone is in evidence when our political representatives visit India, Jamaica or Africa. For Britain today, their time in India remains both controversial and contradictory. It elicits a widespread range of emotions – sometimes pride, sometimes shame, sometimes guilt and sometimes nostalgia. As Rajnarayan Chandavarkar perceptively notes, the British Raj "is not merely a relic of the past but a vibrant, self-generating, living myth. Its collective memory, images and symbols have proved indispensable to the definition of Englishness, or perhaps Britishness."

In the light of the 2016 Brexit vote in Britain, it is probable that Chandavarkar's insights on Englishness and the place of India within that are likely to remain a source of consternation and fascination for many years to come.

Chapter 6

The 'Uncertain Glory': poverty and riches

Searching for that key

"We don't understand much as tourists," remarked Janet when I asked her about everyday life in India. Later during the same conversation, however, she let slip that "it makes you realise that it's the same for everyone – people want their children to be fed, to go to school, to get a job. There are the same needs." More than anyone else I talked to, Janet and Mike had travelled the most throughout India from the far north-east and north-west, along the eastern coast and throughout the south. While most aspects of people's lives are beyond our understanding "as tourists", they had experienced enough to have perhaps an inkling of some aspects of daily life. As a general category, tourists to any part of the world are not likely to be that interested in the culture and lives of their 'hosts'. After all, they have come for a tour of a city, a visit to a number of famous monuments or maybe a hot two weeks on the beach under the palm trees. Next year they might return but, more likely, they will take in another country. By contrast, more frequent visitors to the same country especially those that travel around are likely to be a little familiar with some aspects of Indian life and culture. Even if they remained puzzled or bewildered it would be interesting, I thought, simply to know what issues and aspects of local life interested them.

Nevertheless, Janet's observation that "we don't understand much as tourists" still holds. We don't. Worse still, most of us don't *want* to 'understand much'. However, a few of the people I had interviewed had developed quite a detailed understanding of particular aspects of Indian life. Helle from Denmark for example had not only immersed herself in Indian cinema over the last twenty years or so, but actually made two films in India.

Sany from France had lived and studied in Indian centres of religion and classical music. Jeff had augmented his passion for cricket 'back home' by visiting stadia and watching matches around India over the last decade or so.

However, language, culture, colour, power, gender, religion and history are a few of the filters and obstacles that minimise these understandings for all us foreigners and probably too are the sources of many misunderstandings. The variety and complexity of Indian life and culture is both an attraction of visiting tourists and also a source of frustration. Taken-for-granted assumptions don't work in India which is why most of the people interviewed mention 'observation' or 'just looking' as important activities. Just watching street life or visiting local eating places or taking a local bus trip assume significant sociological importance. That doesn't mean some visitors from abroad especially regular returners are not interested in issues such as poverty or education or health. Indeed they spend much time discussing these topics in an attempt to understand and make sense of people's well-being, livelihoods and ambitions.

Part of the difficulties in these discussions is identifying 'which India' is being discussed. It seems that for any particular example or perspective there is a contrary example or perspective that can be suggested. The complexity of the country's history, social structure, economy and culture are so great that it threatens to overwhelm efforts to understand. Even for those living in the country, the difficulties are great. Those Indians living in the northern states for example have little in common with those from the south. Sometimes, without the use of English, they cannot even communicate with each other. Different histories, climate, religions, music and languages are only some of the obstacles of 'being an Indian'.

A second difficulty is the absence of some overarching narrative that integrates India into some global context. The only story today that seems to provide the reference point for any report or journalistic account of the country is the economic growth rates over the last two decades. This is the 'handle' that the rest of the world seems to need in order to make sense of any developments within the country. Even this angle, until recently anyway, runs secondary to stories about China's economic growth rate. The difficulties we from the West have in discussing India is in knowing and grasping how its past shapes and remains visible in its present and likely future. The recent prominence of stories in the Western media about violence involving 'gau raksha' gangs or cow vigilantes patrolling roads in their attempt 'to save cows' is a more difficult narrative to situate in understandings of modern India. Our largely accepted linear perspective on the advance of modernity in the West doesn't hold for India or many other non-European countries. Important aspects of the 'modernity' story such as the break with tradition, the rise of secularism and of capitalism raise very uncomfortable issues for important sections of the population, and for India's place and status within the global community. In fact I wonder whether the very notion of 'modernity' is that helpful in seeking to make sense of India today. While the term is commonly used in the West as a shorthand for this transition from the traditional to the modern, it also implies new experiences and understandings of the world around us. Above all, the term suggests the making anew of social and economic arrangements and relationships through the active and conscious intervention of actors. New understandings of the self and the collective emerge within a framework that is both exhilarating, exciting and enabling – liberating as well as alienating. As the sociologists put it, a new 'subjectivity' is made possible with the self as a conscious and purposeful agent. Analytically useful as the term might be in diagnosing the transition from medievalism to capitalism in the West, 'modernity' has less use as an interpretative prism outside this particular historical and geographical experience. It is too crude, blunt and ideologically specific a term to do justice to the social fabric and complicated historical developments in India. So what is the key conceptually to opening up these puzzles? I don't know – which is one of the reasons why I enjoy returning to the country year after year. It's not all done and dusted.

I do like though the notion of 'citizenship'. This term, I feel, is a useful vehicle for interpreting, situating and discussing changes occurring within the wider socio-political environment. It provides space, for example, for exploring and rethinking the relationships between governance and agency and also the quality and patterns of social institutions within particular political arrangements. Active participation by citizens – socially, economically and politically – are prioritised. 'Active' as opposed to 'passive' are qualities that I think are important and which interest me. A focus on citizenship moreover can be seen as a useful framework for those interested in wider yet more particular issues such as environmental or gender issues. Here, previously accepted assumptions and relationships of power, sexuality and equity are the focus of critical inquiry. More generally, citizenship concerns (or should that be 'democratic citizenship' or 'active citizenship'?) raise issues such as social inclusion, access, participation, belonging and equity – again, issues which I think are important.

Citizenship doesn't figure that strongly in my readings and discussions about India. Interestingly though, Edward Luce in his recent book *In Spite of the Gods: The Strange Rise of Modern India* concludes his readable account of modern India by noting "a lack... of genuine citizenship." As he rightly notes, "Most people who sample Indian food, music, dancing, literature, architecture and philosophy acquire a lifelong taste for all things Indian. If world trade were to be conducted purely in cultural products then India would have a thumping annual surplus." However, this lack of 'genuine citizenship' is largely because it is "presumed to be a reality. But in practice India falls far short of the claims it makes." This absence of 'genuine citizenship practice' he argues imposes a high moral cost on the country. An examination of poverty, gender, religion or nationalism today illustrates some of these contradictions and 'moral costs'. The crushing weight of poverty for substantial sections of the population, the position and role of women, child marriage, the perseverance of caste, the unequal access to education and health all contribute towards an uneven and distorted ability to play an active part in society. Active citizenship – the belonging and the participating – falls short in most societies and not only India. As such, the idea provides a critical prism through which to examine important societal features. In India this can be a cruel exercise. The contrast between its rich cultural diversity and ever-present histories with participation in civil society based on mutual respect and societal rights falls short, big time.

For us as tourists who as Janet correctly points out, "don't understand much", grasping aspects of this reality is difficult. 'Being in India' offers glimpses, however inadequate, of this citizenship subtext just as much as the Taj Mahal, the Himalayas or the beach does.

The shock of the everyday

Puzzlement and amazement by travellers are normal reactions to any attempt at making sense of perceived everyday life in the host country. Integrating these largely visual experiences with prior understandings and stereotypes is a complex and often contradictory process. Things don't add up, appear bizarre, overtly friendly, rude or unintelligible. Unsettling experiences are matched by displays of friendliness, warmth, generosity and of a genuine sense of welcoming. Poverty, homeless families living on the pavements of Indian cities and emaciated portraits of children are, however, the popular, global images from India that keep flashing around the world. So entrenched are these images and views of India that many overseas tourists refrain from visiting the country. "I don't think I could cope," is a popular response. However, a walk around any of India's cities might suggest another perspective – trendy, affluent, modern, urbane, coffee-drinking busy people. Most of the popular press seems to promote such a perspective. Once again, we return to the difficulties of trying to encapsulate the complexity and richness of the country that is called 'India'. It is baffling as is any shorthand attempt to generalise about any country. In the case of India, however, these two bland, seemingly contradictory views of wealth and poverty preface many print discussions of modern India. As the Indian magazine *Outlook*, for example, recently put it, "is India doing marvellously well, or is it failing miserably?" For most of the world though, it is the images of poverty that most commonly are associated with the country. The issue of poverty in India is a real and pressing concern. It does have an indelible and lasting impact on visitors to the country and raises myriad questions and concerns. Sending spaceships up into the skies and building Formula One racetracks don't sit comfortably with outsiders and probably also a lot of people in India. Many of the regular visitors to the country involve themselves in some form of giving and charity even though they are aware that their efforts are not going to resolve the problems. It's a way of coping. Less open and understood by the traveller is how people in general 'get by'. How do they earn their living, what do they get paid if anything, how many hours a day do they work, how did they get their job? Sometimes, it's as basic as simply wanting to know, "What are they doing?" Most people are interested in this 'work' gossip because they have participated in some version of this back home. And of course, there are glimmers of an answer around them in the streets, not only in India but any city. Wandering around London for example, there are the expensive cars and houses, people begging, posh hotels next to churches that shelter the homeless at night and a 'tourist' architecture that reflects a narcissistic glory and power of its past. The economic and political structures that support and define these scenes and livelihoods, however, are harder to decipher. The newspapers as usual provide clues as do conversations with the 'locals'. But sitting on the buses or trains raises more questions than answers. For my Japanese friends regularly visiting the north of England, the highlight of their stay is always having access and photograph opportunities to the sheep that populate the hills and fells of the north. Fields with cattle are not entered – too dangerous. Different cultures lead to different priorities and highlights.

The same is true for visitors to India. For those from the West, it is as intense and bewildering as it would be for Indians visiting Britain. There would be a general awareness of India's recent history as it is a heroic global story recounted in many schools from around the world. There would also be a recognition of the recent economic success of the country, and its likelihood of becoming a global economic power on a par with China in the decades ahead. But perhaps above all, there would an awareness of poverty and the numbers of poor in the country. Not that long ago, the issue of poverty was the dominant image associated with the country; today, it is more confused and contradictory. There are poor people but there is also a record of economic growth and success that Western countries can only envy.

"Friends said they would love to come to India but said they wouldn't be able to handle the poverty, but I said, 'Forget about the poverty – just go'," said Sany from France when I asked her about the poor in India. "Poverty is happening all over the world. India hits you bigger – your emotions, it's so quick." She continues getting quite animated, "How can they keep smiling – no legs, begging. They're just not smiling, they are shining, radiant peace. It's an inner something. For sure, it's to do with their religion. In this country, if they stopped believing in karma there would be a massive riot. Resignation, not screaming. It's the karma that keeps them quiet."

"It's part of the culture shock," said Stephen. "There are so many poor people in the streets, you can't help everyone. When I first arrived in Mumbai, it was terrible – a massive shock. It is so great a problem that whatever we do we can't make a difference."

Janet and Mike from Colorado too had pondered on this issue. "My understanding is that India has nearly 300 million graduates which is nearly the population of the US and yet they have all these poor people. What's so amazing is their spirit. These people have little but the kids seem generally happy – playing, chasing, smiling. They seem to be happy even though they had insufficient food last night. It makes you realise that it is the same for all humans; you want your children to be fed, to be educated, to be safe, all the same needs." This characteristic of resilience and seeming fortitude in face of acutely difficult material circumstances was mentioned by most of the people I interviewed.

For any outsider travelling in India, the poor and poverty in general is a difficult issue. You are aware of it before you arrive. You have chosen to come despite the poverty. No one visits India without being aware of 'the starving children' images. Many no doubt chose not to come. "I do whatever makes me happy," explains Sheila when I raised the issue of coping with the poverty. "I say no, then look, and it's a deserving case. Some say you should give, others say no, so I do whatever makes me feel OK. It's the only way to do it because inevitably you are going to disappoint. Some local people give, others don't. I remember on a train, I saw these men kicking a poor beggar boy. I was on the top bunk and came down like a bat out of hell I was so angry. They were shocked and contrite. I thought afterwards I shouldn't have done it like that, but I just reacted instinctively. It was because he was sitting in a seat in the compartment. No one was sitting there. Before I got off the train, I went over and shook hands with the men, but you don't know what goes on."

"You have to work it out," says Gina. "That's part of being in

India." She's right. Everyone has to work it out and come up with a solution that's acceptable to them. It might be a pragmatic, on the spot decision – to give or not to give; it might be more radical, involving changes in one's own life and activities based on new understandings or it might just be a case of ignoring the poor. In Gina's case, she and Mick have for many years been involved with an indigenous humanitarian NGO in Mumbai that focuses on street orphans, HIV awareness programmes and feeding programmes. "We send bits and pieces, have visited them and support them. They teach kids and give them a meal a day."

Everyone, locals and foreign tourists, responds to the plight of the poor usually in a generous and spontaneous manner. The worry though are responses that marginalise or eliminate thinking about the conditions or structural reasons relating to 'why there is this poverty'. Why in most parts of the world is there entrenched and growing poverty? Yes, there might be baddy politicians and rampant corruption in particular countries, and there might also be global economic policies that benefit us in the affluent countries and which we are keen to politically support but which play a part in this poverty elsewhere. In other words, enjoying our Western lifestyles might be dependent on maintaining poverty levels elsewhere.

A further issue underpinning this stereotypical view of 'poverty' and 'India' is its ahistorical perspective. India hasn't always been associated with poverty, famine or starving children. As was mentioned in the previous chapter, India has had trading routes stretching back thousands of years and Adam Smith in his *The Wealth of Nations* (1776) detailed some of the reasons for India's comparative prosperity. With the arrival of the East India Company, the British government saw the industry and exports from India as a threat and went as far as prohibiting the wearing of Indian textiles. As the British journalist and author Ian Jack reminded us recently, we the British flooded the Indian markets with cheap fabrics after cutting off the fingers of the

Bengali artisans and breaking their looms. "India still grew cotton, but Bengal no longer spun or wove much of it. Weavers became beggars." As in other regions of the world, there is the persuasive tale of Britain deliberately impoverishing India. A little bit of history sometimes helps when considering 'the poor'.

A third danger of a focus by visiting tourists or the global media on India's poor is a distraction from what is happening in the rich countries' own back yard. The charity organisation Oxfam announced in 2014 that it was now opening UK programmes to tackle poverty. Its report "A Tale of Two Britains" in the same year detailed how five of the richest families in Britain now own more wealth and financial assets than 12.6 million Britons put together. The 'austerity' drive by the Conservative governments has resulted for the first time of more *working* families in poverty than non-working ones. As in other late capitalist economies, the most vulnerable and poorest section of the population is bearing the brunt and costs of the 'Great Recession' of 2008–2009. Obviously this poverty is of a different character and nature to that in India but the 'poor' are not only to be found in poor countries. Poverty and inequality seem to follow neoliberal policies everywhere as the riots and looting in London and Athens in 2013 indicated.

However, poverty in the case of India has taken a bit of a back seat over the last decade or so. It is being replaced by stories of its booming economy in recent years and is being widely documented. Expanding at an average of 6% per year since 1991 India today is seen as a 'global economic power'. Nevertheless, poverty remains very much a part of modern India. Despite the numerous debates about the definition of 'poverty', there is a broad consensus that around one-quarter of India's population or 350 million people live in poverty. More shocking is the statistic that about one-third of the *global* poor live in India. These desperate figures are based on an official poverty line of 32 rupees (around 30 pence in Sterling) per person per day in urban areas and 26 rupees in rural areas. Beyond the bland figures, though, is the pain, powerlessness, despair and resignation that often accompany destitution and poverty. And nowhere in India has this 'qualitative' aspect of poverty been more clearly outlined and detailed than in Katherine Boo's remarkable study of life in a Mumbai slum in *Behind the Beautiful Forevers: Life, Death, and Hope in a Mumbai Undercity*. Together with Suketu Mehta's *Maximum City* and Sonia Faleiro's *Beautiful Thing*, Katherine Boo's study joins a growing list of non-fiction writing that helps illuminate aspects of daily life so difficult for 'us tourists' to grasp. The detailed, painfully moving account of the life and dreams of the slum dwellers of Annawadi is a remarkable study. Situated beside the luxury hotels surrounding the new Mumbai international airport, Annawadi is 'home' to a collection of rag pickers and migrant wanderers in search of work, safety and security. Devoid of sentimentality and condescension, Boo has managed to convey the drama, pain and brutality that characterises the most marginalised of the poor in the city. It's a very difficult read.

Most tourists walking around any city in India or spending some nights in the city will have witnessed the homeless and poor. As in London, New York or Paris, there seem to be areas which are safer or more attractive to the homeless than other areas of the city. Close to rail stations or alongside waterways or near to public parks are favourite spots. In the small areas of Bombay that I am familiar with I know a number of these 'addresses'. Bed rolls are kept neatly rolled and placed behind tree trunks or atop pavement walls. A sack of cooking utensils is usually close to hand and small children play on 'their' pavement. Quieter streets have blankets spread out permanently on the roadside where a number of families seem to live. It's not uncommon to see some form of paid work being performed on the blankets such as vegetable peeling or plucking chickens for, I assume, some local restaurant or hotel. Pedestrians politely move on to the road in order to circumvent the blankets or plastic sheets. In addition to the pavements, the large cavernous halls in city rail stations are usually home at night to many hundreds of people. A walk around the city late at night – and outside the monsoon season – reveals a completely different perspective from that available during the day. Largely hidden in the shadowy minor roads are sleeping the millions of homeless city 'dwellers'. Any space and shelter will do. Given that each city has millions of homeless there seems to be a relaxed attitude by the authorities towards the sleepers. On the other hand most buildings and residences in downtown areas have the ubiquitous security guards ensuring perhaps that their premises are not on the list of hospitable night stops. For the tuc-tuc taxi drivers, home is more assured, i.e. sleeping in their cabs as an early morning walk in the city indicates.

The plight of the poor in India is not the result of an absence of policy formulation. Every government since Independence has placed poverty more or less centre stage. The succession of Five Year Development Plans have all shown a concern with the poor. The problem remains one of implementation and, more importantly, of the structural and political characteristics of the Indian state. Important features of the problem – such as agrarian reform and land distribution – have never really been followed through apart, to some extent, in Kerala and West Bengal. These rural areas incidentally remain more invisible to us tourists than urban centres. The vast majority of India's poor are landless, exploited people. Today the situation in the rural areas is possibly worse than it has ever been. Roughly 750,000 million people continue to live in the country's 680,000 villages. Anti-poverty policies targeted at the urban and rural poor is not the problem. As Mari Marcel Thekaekara argues on the website, *infochange*, "We have the most brilliant legislation in the world; we have pro-poor policies spelt out in the most moving rhetoric. Yet, implementation of these plans and strategies was ignored, circumvented and in many cases deliberately prevented. There has to be a will to eradicate poverty."

This 'problem' of poverty and this "will to eradicate poverty" has been a dominant theme in the work and writings of India's most celebrated philosopher and economist Amartya Sen, winner of the Nobel Prize in Economics in 1998. In a number of publications, often in collaboration with Jean Dréze, he has inquired, analysed and advocated a variety of measures aimed at confronting and tackling poverty. Dréze and Sen's recent publication *An Uncertain Glory: India and its Contradictions* (2013) is a wonderful detailed, critical and authoritative analysis of contemporary India. Much of the analysis in this chapter heavily relies on their empirical data and arguments.

In a public lecture in London in 2014, Sen discussed a question that has bewildered overseas tourists and also those with a passing interest in India – namely, how can such levels of suffering linked to poverty seemingly be tolerated. Sen reminded the audience that "no country in the world is free from poverty" and that "'blaming the victims' is as common today as it was in the era of Britain's Poor Law" (1800s). Certainly, 'blaming the poor' is the dominant perspective in Britain and elsewhere in the aftermath of the 2008–2009 Great Recession. However, tolerance of mass destitution "demands explanation," argued Sen and Dréze. Two common explanations – of ignorance and of inevitability – are unsatisfactory. In the case of India it was more a case of "skewed priorities," argued Sen. India's growing middle class is an infatuation of the national media. Poverty and deprivation has been "crowded out of discussion," he suggested. Great progress in alleviating and reducing poverty has been achieved in other countries, most noticeably in China. There is nothing inevitable about poverty. In order to break the prevailing character of the Indian poor, Sen and Dréze focus on the importance of 'human capabilities' and 'democratic participation' – not dissimilar to notions of democratic citizenship. By 'capability', the authors mean the capability to have a healthy life, to have an educated life, to have a secure and safe life, having the capability to read and write for both girls and boys. Economic growth is important but a sole concern with growth is part of the problem. Expanding and safeguarding human capabilities is not only a route pursued by other Asian countries such as Japan, South Korea, Singapore, Hong Kong and Taiwan; it is a pathway that in India is linked to the quality and extent of its democratic system. As Dréze and Sen argue, "Development is not... merely the rise in the GDP (or in personal incomes); nor is it some general transformation of the world around us, such as industrialisation, or technological advance, or social modernisation. Development is ultimately the progress of human freedom and capability to lead the kind of lives that people have reason to value."

"Tolerance of the intolerable"

All countries have poor people, as Dréze and Sen point out. But as mentioned above, poverty and India are synonymous for many people throughout the world. This is perhaps less so today with a growing story about economic success but it retains its strong association. However, and perhaps surprisingly, it remains difficult to gauge the extent of poverty in the country. There have been in India over the last few decades numerous debates about its nature and extent. As mentioned above, from mid-2011 the official poverty line was seen as 32 rupees a day in urban areas and 26 rupees in rural areas. Commentators pointed out angrily that it is simply not possible to live on such low rates. As an article in *The Hindu* daily newspaper in September 2011 pointed out, these "paltry sums" are meant to cover not only food costs but also clothing, footwear, cooking fuel, lighting, transport, education, medical costs and house rent. It continued to say that the poor do not 'live' in any true sense. Instead they are underweight, stunted, subject to high levels of sickness and without the means to obtain adequate food or medical treatment.

If the 2009–10 figures are used, the article continues, then at least 75% of the total population is in poverty i.e. around 975 million people. As Dréze and Sen argue, "What is really startling is not so much that the official poverty line is so low, *but even with this low benchmark*, so many people are below it – a full 30% of the population in 2009–10, or more than 350 million people." Historically, a more shocking picture emerges. Gross Domestic Product per person indicated that per capita income (in real terms) was about one-third lower in 1895–1900 than in 1794 – a staggering, absolute decline. Yet another measure of the cost of British occupation.

For many of those in the rural areas, conditions appear to be desperate. And we are talking about 600–700 million people still making their living from agriculture. One story above others which has highlighted this desperation and which is reported upon regularly in the Indian newspapers, but has now attracted global attention, is the issue of farmer suicides. Almost every 30 minutes, a farmer (invariably male) commits suicide. Since 1995 – the first year the government started keeping figures – some 300,000 farmers have taken their lives. In 2011 alone, government figures indicate that 14,000 farmers took their own lives. Academic articles suggest these terrible figures are a gross underestimation of the numbers due to official figures relying on police records. These suicide rates amongst farmers are around 50% higher than the national average. A number of states are of particular concern, namely Maharashtra, the new state of Telangana, Karnataka and Punjab. The reasons behind these appalling tragedies are varied – failure of crops, mounting debts, economic problems, personal shame and humiliation, failure to fund a dowry and so on. Hanging, drowning or drinking pesticides are the most common methods of suicide.

However, and perhaps of greater concern, is that these rural suicides when compared to other employment sectors are not unusual. Although media attention and government reports in

India have focused on farmer suicides, the rates are higher in other jobs. The main concern, reports a recent study, should be suicide rates among young adults joining the workforce or getting married. Social pressures is the main driver of high suicide rates not farming, states the report.

Whatever the real figures are, the numbers of those living in poverty are huge. A United Nations report of 2006 calculated that 80% of the Indian population was living on less than $2 per day. Claims by the government in 2014 (with a general election around the corner) that it had presided over the largest percentage fall of poverty ever – down to 270 million – were treated with disdain. What does seem to be acknowledged is that one in three children of the world's malnourished children live in India – a truly shocking figure.

Harrowing statistics could be multiplied many times over. When doing so, the individual and collective human struggles and stories of mere survival behind the figures become less and less apparent. The key concern is, as Amartya Sen puts it, the persistence of the poor. It is, he argues, "the tolerance of the intolerable." The poor rarely are the focus of media attention. There is, Dréze and Sen argue, "a powerful bias in public discussions towards focussing on the lives and concerns of the relatively privileged." And later when reflecting on the last decade or so, they suggest that, "The history of world development offers few other examples, if any, of an economy growing so fast for so long with such limited results in terms of reducing human deprivations."

Something is going wrong big time in India – something "defective" as Dréze and Sen put it. Using a range of various social indicators from the health, education, nutrition and the economic sectors, they demonstrate that India is falling behind every other Southeast Asian country apart from Pakistan. Bangladesh, Nepal, Bhutan and Sri Lanka are all doing better than India in these important areas. This is shocking. Even though

India has a 60% higher per capita income than Bangladesh, Bangladesh has *overtaken* India in areas such as life expectancy, child survival, immunisation rates, reduced fertility rates and even some educational indicators. Comparisons with troubled Nepal are even more damaging to India.

Tolerating the intolerable in India though doesn't mean that policy initiatives are absent. As agreed by all political actors and parties, health and education policies that work would have a transformative effect on India's poor. Similarly, providing income support for those in poverty has long been the subject of discussion and policy initiatives.

Abolishing hunger?

On my various visits to India, I began slowly to realise that there had been, or are currently, a number of national, state and regional policies focussing on addressing poverty concerns. The daily newspapers mentioned their acronyms frequently, and subsequent discussions with local people helped me understand these initiatives in a little more detail. Potentially more powerful and beneficial than individual charitable efforts, I felt that knowing more about these developments should be part of the 'tourist experience'. It was another interesting and surprising journey!

I came across for example a 'targeting scheme' called the 2005 Mahatma Gandhi National Rural Employment Guarantee Act (NREGA, renamed MGNREGA). This act provides for every rural resident above the age of 18 years the 'right to work' by guaranteeing 100 days of work, minimum wage rates, payment within 15 days and essential worksite facilities. Moreover, the legislation was seen as building on social objectives such empowering women – working outside of the house, earning their own income, opening up a bank account, learning to defend their rights. As Dréze and Sen conclude, despite the shortfalls and weaknesses of the NREGA, the enactment was a very significant development in many ways, especially in the areas of poverty reduction and social equity. As well as its social ambitions, it was an attempt to introduce new principles and practices in rural governance, significantly expand rural public works programmes, introduce changes in wage relationships in the countryside and provide an opportunity for the marginalised to 'get a foot in the door'. Official figures indicate that around 50 million households have been participating in NREGA every year since 2008 with an average employment level of around 40 person-days per household. Half of the participants are women and half belong to the poorest section of the population, the scheduled-castes. It was only after the introduction of NREGA in 2006 that rural wages began to rise especially for women, from a point of about zero growth in the early 2000s. The peak period for the programme was 2009–2010, when more than 2.8 billion days of employment were provided to members of 54 million rural households. Even at its peak, the programme amounted to only 0.8% of GDP, but nevertheless still making it probably the most efficient employment programme ever.

Since 2010, however, the NREGA has been in decline as a result of cuts in funding to the states by central government. Even though the scheme was available to all those who requested it, today it is financially capped. Payment to workers has been delayed with large and growing arrears in payments and days are rationed. In short, states Jayati Ghosh, "central government has been slowly trying to kill this programme by starving it of essential funds." This was begun by the Congress-led government that introduced the scheme but has gathered pace by the current Modi BJP government. As Ghosh puts it, "the NREGA came into being not because of a benevolent government, but because of pressure from social movements and rural workers. Much more pressure will now be needed to save it."

The debates and performance of NREGA laid bare the ideological divisions that continue to consume India today.

However, from the evaluation studies that are regularly undertaken, it seems clear that corruption within the scheme is not as widespread as feared and is decreasing, and secondly, that the value of the completed projects is not as wasteful as some have argued. Despite the need for more evidence, Dréze and Sen conclude that the available evidence does suggest that, "NREGA has a great deal of productive potential, provided that adequate structures, including technical support, are in place."

Apart from NREGA, the other large programme of economic support for those in most need that is mentioned frequently in the media is the Public Distribution System (PDS). The PDS is a food security programme which distributes subsidised food (such as wheat, sugar and rice) and non-food (such as kerosene) to India's poor through a network of public distribution shops. There are some 478,000 'ration shops' across the country. Under this scheme, each family below the poverty line who has a ration card is entitled to 35 kilograms of rice or wheat every month. The equivalent figure for the poor just above the poverty line is 25kg. Widespread stories and examples of corruption, erratic distribution of food and the narrow coverage with the early scheme seem to have been addressed in newer versions of the PDS in the mid-2000s, although quality will vary from state to state. Corruption and a lack of transparency continues to be a problem in what is a very expensive scheme – about 1% of India's gross domestic product or $14 billion dollars a year.

Larger issues, however, underpin the efforts of getting food to those who most need it. Encouraged by a generous system of financial subsidies and of technical developments in the agriculture sector, India has a surplus of grains and a bigger stockpile than any country apart from China. Produce is exported to other countries. Political debates in India over the last five years or so point out that no one need go hungry, provided that a reform of existing programmes is undertaken so as to include more people and eliminate 'leakages', as corruption is euphemistically labelled. The World Bank estimated that less than 50% of the grain collected by the states from the federal warehouses reached those it was supposed to benefit.

However, something clearly is not working with the PDS – a continuing 21% of India's 1.3 billion population remain undernourished, a proportion that has not changed much over the last two decades despite a 50% increase in food production. Again, a number of horror stories appeared on a regular basis in the newspapers documenting the shortcomings of the PDS. These included the large number of people mistakenly excluded from the scheme, erratic supply and poor quality of the food and, above all, the massive corruption by the numerous 'middlemen' and those along the chain from warehouse to shop. Some people were unable to obtain the ration card as they were unable to pay the requisite bribe.

However, so great have been the improvements in the last year or so that commentators are referring to the 'old' and the 'new' food security system. New reforms encompassed within the 2013 National Food Security Act proposed doubling the number of eligible participants, increasing the quantities of food that could be bought, providing more choice and building new silos for the storage of grain. New technology would be used to track food and ensure most people obtained their ration cards.

The delivery and operation of the PDS differ obviously on a state by state basis. But as Dréze and Sen point out, great improvements are clearly becoming visible. In Tamil Nadu for example, PDS is universal, regular and relatively corruption-free. The big example of what was possible, however, was in the state of Chhattisgarh, traditionally seen as almost ungovernable and characterised by massive corruption. A range of statistical tables is available demonstrating the turnaround of the state in the efficiency and inclusiveness of the reforms. Massive 'leakages' have been reduced. That is not to argue that all is well with the 'new' improved PDS as Dréze and Sen explain and document in their book. Lurid stories in the newspapers in early 2015 for example documented the PDS scam in Chhattisgarh involving several high-level state officials. Corruption continues to plague the system despite the improvements in structural features.

A third policy initiative that I came across and which focusses on India's poor is the 2013 National Food Security Act (also known as the Right to Food Act). As one local commentator put it, "After vacillating for four years, India's United Progressive Alliance (under the Congress Party) finally did something worthy and had the National Food Security Bill passed." Seen as a 'pet project' of Sonia Gandhi, President of the Congress Party and introduced just before the 2014 general election, the Act was seen as a controversial development. It was, said Sonia Gandhi, India's chance "to make history" by abolishing hunger. The aim of the legislation is to provide subsidised foodgrain to about two-thirds of India's 1.2 billion people – 75% of the rural population and 50% of those in urban areas. Beneficiaries will be able to purchase 5kg of grain per month at a rate of 3 rupees per kg, 2 rupees for wheat and millet at 1 rupee per kg. Critics alleged that the costs of the programme will be prohibitive (3% of gross domestic product), increase price inflation, squeeze out the private sector, reduce competition and promote cereal production at the expense of fruit and vegetables. For some critics such as Vivek Kaul, the programme is a disaster – "the passage of the Food Security Bill might turn out to be our biggest mistake (since Independence)." By way of contrast, Jean Dréze (of the Dréze and Sen book) who was closely associated with the legislation, wrote that: "the Bill is a form of investment in human capital. It will bring some security in people's lives and make it easier for them to meet their basic needs, protect their health, educate their children, and take risks." Others stated that the legislation did not go far enough; Right to Food campaigners wanted 35kg a month instead of the agreed five.

The success or fate of the National Food Security Act will

depend on the Bharatiya Janata (BJP) government, elected by a landslide in the 2014 general elections. It is clear, however, that historically there have been a number of policy initiatives – some of them very expensive – which have attempted to engage with and ultimately reduce the country's appalling levels of poverty. Equally clear is that the promised 'transformative' claims of such initiatives are not working although many millions will be grateful for any supplements to meagre diets. Lack of food is obviously the most important feature of 'being poor'; but as the central message of Dréze and Sen's *An Uncertain Glory* hammers home chapter after chapter, the poor in India are poor because of numerous interrelated reasons as is explored below.

If a wider, more global perspective is taken, it isn't all bad news. As the United Nations (UN) reported in 2015 at the conclusion of its Millennium Development Goals (MDGs) campaign, one billion people worldwide had been lifted out of extreme poverty in "the most successful anti-poverty movement in history." In the previous 15 years the MDGs had pushed to meet 8 goals – on poverty, education, gender equality, child mortality, maternal health, disease, the environment and global partnership – and had delivered some impressive results. The number of people for example who lived on less than $1.25 a day has fallen from just under 2 billion to 836 million in 2015. Between 1990–2015, the proportion of undernourished fell from 24% to 13% or around 800 million chronically malnourished people today. Child mortality has declined by more than half over the past 25 years. In other areas, the results have not been not so impressive – for example, in maternal mortality rates and HIV/Aids. As was noted, nearly 60% of extremely poor people live in five countries – India, Nigeria, China, Bangladesh and the Democratic Republic of Congo.

Successful examples from Brazil with its Zero Hunger programme, Bolivia, Nicaragua and Ecuador illustrate what can be achieved with a concerted political campaigning from grassroot organisations together with legal reforms. In the case of India, these battles on the streets and in the courts are what resulted in the National Food Security Act of 2013.

Working, India style

Any policy discussion today of 'poverty eradication' will usually be coupled with 'sustainable livelihoods'. The latter is the new buzzword and is strongly associated with global heavyweights such as the United Nations and their various branches (such as the United Nation Conference on Environment and Development, UNCED, or the various world conferences on women). These global summits, reports and conferences are largely invisible to most people but do provide a small political space within which activists can seek to move forward their agendas. As was mentioned, the recently concluded Millennium Development Goals (and their replacement by the Sustainable Goals programme) demonstrated selectively what could be done with a concerted push, financial support and political will. (They also illustrated valuable lessons in what not to do!)

This notion of 'livelihoods' is a difficult one to grasp for visitors to India although it is an issue that interests many of us. How people obtain their food, what health care is available, safe and secure housing, how work or labour is understood and structured are all examples of 'tourist invisibility' for us. We know that most people do not 'work' in the sense we understand. Yes, there are trade unions and employers' organisations, campaigns for better wages and workplace health and safety just as in the Western economies. This is the organised sector and what most overseas tourists are familiar with. Within this organised sector, around two-thirds are national and regional government employees – some 21 million. What characterises Indian 'livelihoods', however, is the informal sector – some 90% of the working population. As an Indian colleague patiently explained to me, this unorganised or informal workforce covers a wide variety of jobs from working in households, small enterprise units, night watchmen, sweepers, farm or agricultural workers, working from home or on construction sites, and domestic work. For the overwhelming majority of people in India (or other countries in the developing world), having an employer, a workplace or wage is not a reality. Instead as the excellent website *InfochangeIndia* details, most 'workers' have to create diverse and complex strategies to survive economically, especially in rural areas. India might be the pin-up global economy and destined for greater economic success in the years ahead, but it seems unable to provide the most basic of employment rights for the vast majority of its working population. The country's unmatchable growth rates continue to exclude most of the poor yet is constructed on the backs of the poor – an 'economic law' that characterises most economies from around the world.

Replacing the notion of 'work' by 'sustainable livelihoods', it is argued by the UN, helps address some of these anomalous issues that have been ignored and provides a better understanding of all the complex means by which people make a living, or simply survive. A focus on 'sustainable livelihoods' in other words provides a better framework for poverty reduction strategies.

Sensible as all this sounds, there are problems. There are for example numerous different understandings of what is meant by 'livelihoods'. Many of the current definitions leave untouched the causes of poverty, of why there is such a huge number of people living in desperately poor conditions. Untouched also is the basic truth that improving the material conditions of most of the poor requires wealthy executives in the West (in the coffee, tea or grain businesses for example) acknowledging that their fat salaries and bonuses are dependent on keeping 'livelihoods' as little as possible.

The big footwear companies in the West for example have been cited in recent years for their use of 'cheap labour' in the production of trainers and sport footwear. India is the second largest global producer of footwear, accounting for over 13% of the world's production, is valued at around $35 billion and provides around 2 million jobs. 70% of the workforce is in the unorganised sector. It is the home-based, exploitative nature of the sector that underpins the entire industry. For every factory-based worker in the sector there are ten home-based workers existing on piece rates. Homeworkers are not covered by minimum pay legislation, have insecure employment, no safety or health coverage, no sick pay or any other entitlements. Unknown to most tourists on their way to the Taj Mahal in Agra are some 4,500 home-based units in this footwear capital of North India – all invisible workers in the supply chain of the footwear industry. Specialising in one of the five major shoe production activities – cutting, upper stitching, upper closing, pasting and finishing – these homeworkers symbolise the artisan-based, low technology oriented manufacturing that characterises much Indian industry. And because of their invisibility, trade unions have been unable to reach these workers. Other organisations, however, have evolved to involve homeworkers, to press for ethical solutions such as 'fair trade' agreements and to raise awareness of transparency, human rights and ethical supply chains.

Many other examples or case studies could be identified which reproduce similar or worse conditions of employment than the shoemakers of Agra. A recent report of 2011 entitled "Captured by Cotton" for example documents the interwoven context of garment manufacturing in Tamil Nadu with dowry payments, unacceptable working conditions, bonded labour and child labour.

Any understanding of 'sustainable livelihoods' must therefore be situated in contexts that address issues of inequity, of global exploitation of poor countries by rich countries and of tackling structural privileges. If the inequality facing Dalits in India is to be addressed, for example, this will involve reducing the power and influence of the upper castes. However, the opening up of the Indian economy in the 1990s and their acceleration under the current Modi government has reinforced the marginalization of the poor in favour of big business. Numerous stories make it through to the press of the disastrous change in policies and practices flowing from the pursuit of short-term, market-driven policies over the last 2–3 decades – of the switch from rice to prawn cultivation or the decimation of small textile weavers as 'their' industry was 'modernised' through subsidies, inducements and tax breaks that favoured big business and technology intensive 'solutions'. Hundreds of thousands of poor and vulnerable weavers had their 'livelihoods' destroyed in the name of progress and national interest.

Poverty wages have a variety of knock-on effects such as fuelling a modern slave trade. It is estimated that there are around 5–10 million children working in semi-slave conditions throughout India. Figures are difficult to collect but it has been estimated that many of this total of around 10 million child labourers are 'employed' by third parties in carpet making (around Varanasi), cigarette making and match making. Strong laws against trafficking, child labour and bonded labour exist but are enforced spasmodically. School truancy rates are estimated to be around 40 million. Semi-slavery in India persists because it is remains profitable and is enmeshed in a web of corruption and bribery involving the police and traffickers, says Kailash Satyarthi. Over 100,000 children are employed as domestic servants in Delhi alone.

In 2014, Kailash Satyarthi from Delhi was awarded the Nobel Peace Prize together with Malala Yousafzai, the teenage girl from Pakistan. Satyarthi received the award because of his lifelong work around the rights of children. His activities have included rescuing dozens of children from the trafficking of boys from the state of Bihar through to exposing the trade in girls from the tea estates in Assam. Satyarthi's recognition and work are symbolic of what is not working in India. It's the tip of the proverbial iceberg. The contrast of wealth and economic success for the few with continuing and desperate levels of poverty for the vast majority is difficult to grasp. The textbook story of development – gradual economic growth involving more and more people – seems to have failed. Maybe today, this development paradigm is exhausted.

"The monster that crosses your path"

For us tourists wandering around city centres, visible dimensions of India's gross economic inequality are clear and stark. While this is true for most grand cities in the world, the contrast in India's case is extreme and therefore more visible. Less visible to us, however, is the social differentiation that is as pernicious as the economic divisions; in fact it is largely invisible to us but very visible in thousands of ways to Indians. Central to an understanding of this social world and therefore to dimensions of inequality – whether of an economic, political, gender or class-based nature – is the issue of caste. We as visitors to the country together with most people around the world associate caste with India but have only a flimsy grasp of the nature and consequences of these divisions. Even this flimsiness, however, provokes bewilderment and astonishment.

The complexities surrounding the historical nature, evolution and status today of castes provides a continuing debate in India, as evidenced by contemporary studies and commentary in the media and elsewhere. Caste permeates every pore of Indian society but usually in hidden and insidious ways. Put at its most simple, castes are ranked, named and endogamous (permitting marriage only within the group), and where membership is gained only through birth. As the prominent India sociologist Andre Beteille puts it, "In the old order the hierarchical relations between men and women were expressed in the ritual idiom of purity and pollution, perhaps the most compelling idiom devised by human ingenuity for keeping a social hierarchy in place. While the idiom of purity and pollution was all pervasive, it bore most heavily on the weaker sections, notably untouchables and women."

Modern India is often marketed as a land of opportunities but those opportunities are structured and filtered by caste. Caste remains as a powerful regulator of these economic opportunities. Although of ancient origin, caste today has adapted and reproduced itself in the fast-growing Indian capitalist economy. There are thousands of castes and subcastes which are linked to occupational specialisations, are usually locally based but also connect to complex networks across the region and country. For many sociologists, the caste system is seen as an intricate division of labour and method of exercising social control and maintaining social order – in other words, knowing one's place. Its power, as Thekaekara reports in the *New Internationalist*, is that the caste system is underpinned and legitimated by religious beliefs originating thousands of years ago, the Laws of Manu. According to these 'laws', society has four broad social orders or varnas. At the top were the Brahmins, the priestly class and most 'pure' group. Beneath the Brahmins came the Kshatriyas (the warriors and rulers), then the Vaishyas (the traders), and finally, the Sudras, the lowest caste whose purpose in life was to serve the other varnas. Apart from the four broad social orders, there are over 3,000 subcastes, or jatis. Below these four varnas are the 'Untouchables' or Dalits as they are called today, so unclean and impure that they were not included in the Manu system.

There are some 180 million Dalits today in India and, on a wide variety of measures, are substantially worse off when compared with the rest of the population; less than a third are literate, just under 50% exist on less than $2 a day and infant mortality rates much higher. There are another 60 million Dalits around the world who continue to face discrimination to a greater or lesser degree. *CasteWatch UK* for example was recently formed to confront the spreading influence of caste in Britain. In India Dalits confront total social exclusion especially in rural areas on a daily basis. For example, eating out often includes sitting outside, eating at a distance from other customers, drinking from special 'Untouchable' cups and poured from a non-polluting distance. After drinking, the cup must be washed by the Dalit and placed on the Dalit cup shelf outside the cafe.

Entrenched systems of privilege anywhere diminish the quality of life and democracy for all. In Britain we are familiar with the upper echelons of the military, the judiciary, the media, the civil service and our political parties being dominated by the minority from a fee-paying educational background. Although different in nature, origin and outcome both systems socially and politically exclude and divide. In India, the violence, oppression and social brutality of caste continues for around one quarter of the population. Examples and reports almost on a weekly basis of caste violence in the media are not uncommon. A recent article in the Indian *Economic and Political Weekly* journal analyses in painful detail the ransacking and torching of 268 Dalit homes in three villages in Tamil Nadu's Dharmapuri district. Tamil Nadu is a state with a record of many progressive reforms in recent years and home to major anti-caste organisations yet is witnessing rising violence against Dalits. In 2011, 890 Dalit women were murdered, 40% of them in caste honour killings. A nongovernment organisation in Madurai, Tamil Nadu has recorded 144 murders, 18 of which were women and 336 cases of atrocities against Dalits.

Numerous other reports and stories of atrocities suffered by Dalits today could be identified. In the British *Guardian* newspaper of October 2014, for example, there is an article entitled "Lynching of boy underlines how the curse of caste still blights India". The report details the burning alive of Sai Ram aged 15, a goat herder whose goats strayed on to the land of a higher landowning caste in a village south of Patna in the state of Bihar. Sai Ram was just one of 17,000 Dalits to fall victim to caste violence in Bihar. Earlier that month, five Dalit women were allegedly gang-raped by upper caste men. Of the 17,000 pending trials in Bihar involving charges of violence against Dalits, only a tenth were dealt with in 2013.

Lowest on the caste demarcations are the 800,000 or so toilet cleaners. Thekaekara reports on an interview with a toilet cleaner from Gujarat which illustrates the humiliation, suffering and stoicism of one particular occupational grouping. "In the rainy season," the woman said, "it is really bad. Water mixes with the shit and when we carry it (on our heads) it drips from the basket, onto our clothes, our bodies, our faces. When I return home I find it difficult to eat food sometimes. The smell never gets out of my clothes, my hair. But this is our fate. To feed my children I have no option but to do this work." 'Fate' is the key word in these comments from the toilet cleaner. 'Fate' for many Dalits is seen as an incontestable consequence of a religiously ordered and structured social system; a system that is characterised by its extreme inequality, labour and sexual exploitation (semi-slavery in some cases), powerlessness and degradation. What started out as medieval occupational divisions were cemented structurally by a set of powerful social and cultural rules. The origins of caste are disputed. For some, the nature of this 'fate' for most people is underpinned and legitimated by powerful 3,000-year-old Indian Hindu texts, scriptures and spiritual claims. Occasionally, a dissenting view can be found. An article in daily newspaper *The Hindu* from 2001 challenges the religious orthodoxy underpinning casteism. The Rig Vedic scriptures, it argues, not only repudiated the birth-based caste system but advocated a Varna system based on Talent, Action and Aptitude (Guna, Karma and Svabhava). The article continues by stating, "that scriptural legitimacy had to be invented for caste... as it could not have been justified or legitimated in other way... In point of fact, caste is a post-Vedic invention meant to perpetuate the religious, social and economic domination of a few over the rest." More recent studies on the origins of caste stress the colonial experience of the British as crucial in persisting with and codifying understandings and practices of caste. It was a useful and convenient administrative tool for arranging and governing the myriad complex communities.

Irrespective of the origins of caste, more worrying is the spread of caste in more recent times to other religions that admit converts from Hinduism such as Islam, Christianity and Buddhism. Even Sikhism the great reforming religion launched some 300 years ago is not exempt from aspects of casteism. If the euphoric birth of Independent India was expected to wash away caste, the opposite has happened. A narrow and intolerant form of Hinduism has begun to assert itself in the country over the last two or three decades. "The major institutions of our society and culture of our society are being ideologically colonised. Policies and priorities are being tilted in favour of the upper castes and to the disadvantage of the dalits and minorities. The rights and guarantees enshrined in the Constitution are being eroded," argues *The Hindu* article. And this was written in 2001, before the Saffron march and the landslide national election of Narendra Modi and the BJP in 2014.

Any discussion of caste and necessary reforms inevitably throws up the name of Bhimrao Ramji Ambedkar, seen as one of India's foremost crusaders for dignity and human rights – and from a Dalit background. Traditionally recognised by all as the architect of India's Constitution as mentioned in the previous chapter, Ambedkar has nevertheless suffered in much historical and intellectual appraisals of the country's struggles for Independence and in post-India developments. An informative article by Namit Arora in monthly Indian journal *The Caravan* from 2013 explores this neglect and draws parallels between Ambedkar's life with that of Martin Luther King, Jr. in the United States. While opposing British colonialism, Ambedkar didn't join the Congress Party which was leading the struggle against the British. In contrast to both Nehru and Gandhi, Ambedkar understood, "that India's deeply entrenched social inequities and caste loyalties were serious obstacles to democratic participation and a shared sense of citizenship and nationhood," suggests Arora. Focussing on political democracy while doing little to achieve social democracy, wrote Ambedkar, was "to build a palace on a dung heap." It was Ambedkar's political struggles with Nehru and, above all, Gandhi over advancing the situation of 'the depressed classes' (through reservations) in the proposed new independent India that led to his invisibility or at least marginality, in the chronicles of India's struggles in the last century. Additionally, he sought to ban polygamy and advance the rights of women, especially upper caste women. His democratic socialist ambitions, however, clashed with the sanitised 'correct' nationalist, Hindu version of what officially happened; that is, a Congress-led struggle largely populated by upper caste men. Leading a mass conversion to Buddhism which he argued was better adapted to the modern age than Hinduism added to the antipathy he faced from the dominant class.

Today, however, as Arora documents, there is a renewed interest, re-examination and celebration, over the last decade or so, of Ambedkar's activities and writings. New studies, films, articles in popular outlets, websites and numerous new statues testify to this growing mainstream interest. Arora sees this growth as being fuelled by the growing politicisation of the lower castes and growth of low-caste political parties together with the emergence of a small group of educated and self-confident Dalit scholars, activists and artists. However, as he concludes in his article, Ambedkar's critique of India, "rooted in a worldly, inclusive, scrupulously reasoned, secular and radical egalitarianism, coupled with bracing civil rights talk of social justice and dignity still hasn't received its due in mainstream scholarship and opinion."

Any discussion about caste is complex. Andre Beteille has pointed out in many recent articles that there has been a steady and continuous decline in practices associated with purity and pollution both in inter-caste relations and in the relations between men and women. "Untouchability has also declined," he argues. The reason for this decline he suggests is the rise and social and cultural ascendancy of the middle class. Behaviour determined by rituals of purity and pollution are "inconsistent with the functional requirements" of a modern society. The rise of the Indian middle class has not led to the elimination of inequality "but it has rendered obsolete some of its most oppressive and odious forms." While I am sure that Beteille is correct especially in urban areas, it is in the political sphere that caste is seen as getting stronger rather than weaker. In a contradictory and recent development, the phenomenon of caste has emerged in certain areas as more important today than in the past. Indian political parties have always played caste politics. 'Vote banks', where social groups such as lower caste groups are 'persuaded' to vote a particular way, have always been a feature of electoral politics in India. Local landowners, industrialists and moneylenders for example have always used their dependents – tenants and labourers – as vote banks. But as Christophe Jaffrelot points out in *The Caravan* from 2012, in the 1980s and 1990s this system began to disintegrate. Local low-caste parties began to emerge in a number of states. The growing political clout of these parties has resulted in a number of important consequences. First, an increased turnout of voters. India is probably unique in having a higher vote amongst the poor when compared to the wealthy. Secondly, there has been growing rejection of elite idioms, most notably away from English as the main language. Thirdly, there has been the growing influence and power of state legislatures at the expense of the centre. But in this case, small is not necessarily beautiful. This fragmentation along party lines has not always led to a deepening of democracy as will be later examined.

Even where the caste system has lost some of its earlier brutality and barbarity, it continues to be an important instrument of power throughout Indian society, argue Dréze and Sen. They list a number of key social institutions – such as universities, reporters, police officers, trade unions, legal bodies and artists – where around 75% of the top posts are shared by upper caste groups. And this is in places where the upper caste groups make up only 20% of the population. Other recent stories in the media detail the suicides of Dalit students in elite universities due to caste prejudice and discrimination. In 2016 *Outlook* magazine outlined the spreading boycotts and demonstrations across Mumbai, Pune, Delhi and Hyderabad by Dalit students, provoked to action by the rising and confident Hindutva student movement. 'Anti-nationals' as non-Hindutva students are described are being purged. The hanged Dalit student at Hyderabad University was another gruesome statistic of Dalit deaths. Armed confrontational incidents along inter-caste lines in Bihar over the last few years have fuelled fears of further bloodshed.

In the success stories of India today, most would have assumed a dissolving and disappearing of caste beliefs and rituals. Inter-caste marriages are on the rise, laws prohibiting caste are in place, positive discrimination or quotas to ensure Dalit participation are promoted but, it seems, caste practices persist. Six decades of illegality but still today caste persists. It is the great embarrassment that is not mentioned. It is not only not mentioned in polite company, but until recently was not recorded or included in survey data.

Being poor, being socially marginalised and humbled as well as being powerless point towards understandings and experiences of injustice. While there is evidence available of the improvements achieved in addressing those conditions contributing towards these socio-political injustices over the last few decades, there has been no 'breakthrough'. Change for the better, studies suggest, has been incremental. The evidence still suggests instead a perniciousness that is a result of a network of the mutually reinforcing of severe inequalities that result in an oppressive social system, as Dréze and Sen relentlessly demonstrate in page after page in their *An Uncertain Glory*. Those at the bottom of these multiple disadvantages, they illustrate, "live in conditions of severe disempowerment."

Caste has a peculiar role in India that separates the country from all others. Being poor, however, is more than the caste system, important as it is in understanding poverty. There is probably no single bullet that unlocks or changes these circumstances. However, in discussions with friends and from general reading, something becomes clearer. There is one factor that seems to come closest to being 'the magic bullet' – to carry a greater weight than other issues. This magical ingredient is the role and contribution of women.

Women and the 'new' India

Poverty at the end of the day is a political issue. It can be eliminated or exacerbated through political action and programmes. Any welfare initiatives directed towards alleviating poverty as outlined above are to be welcomed. Any institutional reform in this direction is important. Crucial to the success of these reforms though is the role of women. Reinforcing the grip of caste on social injustice and inequalities is the issue of gender. "Gender inequality," demonstrate Dréze and Sen, "is among the social disparities that keep large numbers of people on the margin of the 'new India'."

As noted earlier, the authors compare the progress towards poverty alleviation in India with a number of its neighbours. India does not fare well. In particular they look at Bangladesh, a very poor country that only gained independence in 1971. Despite calamities from cyclones, famine and civil war in the 1970s, the country remains one of the poorest in the world but has made rapid progress on a number of social fronts and in living standards over the last couple of decades. As Dréze and Sen indicate, it has overtaken India in crucial areas of social development even given its much lower growth rate. Despite the 'democratic problems' in Bangladesh, there are "also features of astonishing achievement... that cannot but excite interest, curiosity and engagement," they argue. "The most important clue (to these astonishing achievements) is a pattern of sustained positive change in gender relations." On a wide variety of gender indicators – such as participation in the workforce, literacy and education, health education, breastfeeding, hygiene facilities – Bangladesh has overtaken India. Although not fully yet understanding all the changes underway in Bangladesh, the authors feel that it is the crucial participation and activity of Bangladeshi women that accounts for the difference.

By way of contrast, Dréze and Sen examine a number of social indicators in India to illustrate the marginalisation of women – this "truly shocking" picture, as they put it. Their analysis is wide ranging in their attempt to illustrate the absence of women as significant actors – socially, economically and politically. The issues that they identify contribute towards the low-status and marginalised nature of women especially from the lower castes.

First is the pain behind the figure of there being 37 million more men than women in the country. As Sunny Hundal summarises the consequences flowing from this figure, "A social time-bomb is now setting off... with terrifying consequences." Most of these 'surplus' men are at a marriageable age. The state of Punjab is seen to have the worst ratio – 300 girls per 1,000 boys. For India to have a 'natural' sex ratio similar to the rest of the world, India would need to have another 23 million women. Adding this total to the earlier 37 million results in a 60 million 'missing' women from the population of India. A large cause of these skewed ratios and the missing millions are the rise of sex-selective abortions due to availability of ultrasound technology. Boys are preferred for a number of reasons. Dowry payments for example, although illegal for many decades, are a major reason. Daughters impose a considerable financial cost on their parents. 'Pay now, save later' warn some of the unlawful marketing hoardings. Far from decreasing, the practice of dowry has spread to now involve communities previously without a dowry tradition. Secondly, women's workforce participation rates are extremely low – 15% – and for those with work, they are likely to get considerably less pay than men. Thirdly, women are less likely to be able to read or write when compared to men – 47% of rural women and 70% of urban women are literate. The corresponding figures for men are 66% and 82% respectively. Fourthly, there is a long history of official indifference to claims of rape by women. In the vast majority of cases, rape crimes are committed against women from lower castes. Victim blaming and a slow bureaucratic justice system result in a massive under-reporting of rape – some estimates calculate that only 10% of cases are reported. Fifthly, the low status of women is seen as contributing to this gender inequality. The child malnutrition rate in India is nearly double that of sub-Saharan Africa but nearly a quarter of Indians are born with low birth weights which are 40% higher than in sub-Saharan Africa. Why this discrepancy? Because Indian boys receive more attention and preference at meals than girls, who eat later and less than their brothers. In some of the country's poorest states, annual surveys indicate that girls are going missing not so much because of foeticide but from infanticide. Sixthly, this persuasive patriarchal form of social and cultural relations works itself out in varied ways. Property inheritance is strongly patrilineal and post-marital residence remains overwhelmingly patrilineal. Freedom of movement is curtailed. Over 40% of child marriages in the world take place in India. There are over a 1,000 'honour killings' a year in India, happening in big cities as well as rural areas. Most of the perpetrators were family members and represented a culture of honour, patriarchal authority and violence for the transgression of the perceived value of 'respect'. Jason Burke from *The Guardian* quotes Prem Chowdhry, "The social situation is very volatile. The marriage market is very tight and that causes huge problems... leaving more than a third of lower caste men without wives."

Unsurprisingly, India is ranked 116 out of 130 in the global gender gap index. The horrific rape and killing of the student in Delhi in 2012 resulted in demonstrations, political attention and outpourings not previously seen in such cases. After all, there had only been one conviction from the 635 cases of rape reported in Delhi between January and November in 2012. There might well be something specific about Delhi. The city after all has a record of rape that is nine times worse than Calcutta and much higher than other large Indian cities. As the press reports demonstrated over the next couple of years after the notorious 2012 rape, India, and Delhi in particular, is a very tough place to be a woman.

Rape and sexual violence of course are not particular to India. Survey evidence in Britain and various other European countries indicated the wide occurrence of violence against women – two women a week are murdered by their current or former partner in Britain, and we have the lowest conviction rate – 6.5% – of all 33 European countries. Here as in India and elsewhere, there is nothing inevitable about violence against women. Nor is it a case of 'happening out there' and not here. The protests and demonstrations from around the world in solidarity with those in Delhi and other Indian cities indicated the widespread anger at this latest example of patriarchal violence.

As mentioned in the opening paragraphs to this chapter, it *is* a difficult task for outsiders to make sense of or understand everyday life in cultures different from our own. Visual representations are available and provide clues as well as provoke further consternation. Being poor constitutes a collection of images and experiences that risk overwhelming what we can cope with and what we can absorb. We might not be clear on the origins or reasons for this poverty, but the evidence is clear. No one visiting the country will forget the images. It is difficult to not contrast these images with the economic success stories dominating popular coverage of the country, locally and globally. It doesn't add up. It's a puzzle. It's bewildering. And sometimes, we realise that it doesn't need to be like this.

The final words in this chapter should be those of Dréze and Sen. I have benefited enormously from their 2014 publication and quoted from it liberally throughout the text. Although far from a bedtime read, its closely argued and statistically supported analysis provides a passionate and authoritative dissection of India's "great achievements" since Independence as well as its "deeply uncertain" future. I doubt the authors ever saw their book as a 'tourist publication'; but for me, it has opened many closed and, even, invisible doors and avenues. It has helped in outlining and clarifying many issues and topics that were for me as an outsider and occasional interloper mysterious and difficult to experience. The questions and answers raised provide an unsettling read but, importantly, contribute towards a more nuanced understanding 'of being a tourist'.

Chapter 7

"The nearest thing to another planet"

Contradictory tourists

It's funny being a tourist. You think you are a regular, everyday person simply wandering around the city centre, temple, church or whatever. Often you are invisible – not identifiable as 'a tourist' – until you open your mouth. At other times, you are very visible and from the looks you get, remember that you are a tourist – different to those around you. Sometimes, as when in Japan for example, this obvious difference results in the opposite – being invisible. Physically and culturally you are different but cultural politeness from local shoppers or bus passengers means they do not acknowledge this difference. To do so would be considered rude or impolite – no eye contact, no greetings, nothing. It's very weird. Stopping someone and asking for help is another matter; no effort, time or patience is too much trouble. The important difference of course is that you initiated this changed relationship and so indicated a desire to interact.

After all, we all know what a 'tourist' is. We use the word frequently. The people I interviewed and myself are all tourists in India. It's not too difficult to recognise other types of tourists – namely, white Western tourists. Other tourists are more difficult to recognise. So already 'being a tourist' is getting a little more complicated – maybe, after all, we don't all know what a 'tourist' is. In fact the more I considered the term, the more befuddled I became. As questioned in Chapter 2, is 'being a tourist' that different from 'being a traveller' or 'being on holiday' or 'being on a leisure trip'? Yes, there are technical definitions of being a tourist but they are so broad and general as to be of little value. It is easier to talk of 'tourism' rather than being a tourist. In the case of 'tourism', we are probably referring to flows of

211

people, infrastructure, revenue streams, transport systems, visa regulations and like matters. People talk of the 'tourist industry' or 'sector'. In contrast, 'the tourist' is more complex. For those who study tourism or are involved in the planning or policy aspects of tourism, it is obviously important to be clear on the nature of being 'a tourist'. There have been frequent and continuing attempts to clarify the nature of this particular experience or activity or effort, as was touched upon in the earlier chapter. Trying to describe, explain or account for all the various aspects associated with this type of activity is not easy. Any attempt to be more precise about what is meant by 'being a tourist' (or any other general social experience) inevitably will be contested, and views range from those that agree with the proposed typology to those that reject it. The very nature of any conceptual work comes with debate, controversy, sometimes acrimony, but hopefully also insights and clarification. The payoff for any progress can be significant for various 'stakeholders'. These intellectual efforts focus mainly on trying to distinguish what is particular to the touristic experience as opposed to other types of experiences. Issues such as permanency, distance, purpose of trip, temporary escape from home routines and self-discovery are some of the avenues explored in studies over the years. These distinctions and characteristics then allow a differentiation of different tourist types and experiences. There are different categories of 'being a tourist', in other words. One of the earliest and more influential typologies is Erik Cohen's 1979 study. At one end of his spectrum is the 'recreational' mode, followed by the 'diversionary' tourist, then the 'experiential' mode, the 'experimental' tourist and, finally, the 'existential' mode of tourism. Different types of tourists might be distinguished as doing different things – lengths of time away, flexibility of the journey, destinations, accommodation, spending power and so on. More ambitiously, psychological features might be attached to these different types of tourists. Their views of their own society, their motivations for travel, general political views or their general outlook on life might be distinguished along the spectrum. Then there are other attempts to understand 'tourists' by concentrating more on the experiences, meanings and attitudes of the tourist themselves – a more subjective focus. This line of thinking allows for the identification of 'anti-tourists' – I might be a tourist but I'm not like those other tourists who only want to tick boxes. OK, then comes the rejoinder – but do you know that some types of tourists define what they do in opposition to what they understand 'tourists do'? And so it continues. While there appears to be no easy consensus to these studies and efforts, it does at least clarify particular aspects of 'being a tourist' as well as demonstrating the complexity of the seemingly simple activity of being on holiday or doing a little sightseeing.

This book is about travelling in India and about a small number of people from outside the country who enjoy travelling in India and have returned a number of times to the country. However, a number of things do hit me when I think about this group and the nature of 'being a tourist'. For example, they combine or integrate a number of different 'experiences' in their visits – exploration, visiting attractions, independently organised, distrusting of 'authenticity', aware of being an 'outsider' and accepting of the inevitable constraints and limitations associated with tourism. Above all they attempt to engage to a greater or limited extent with the cultures, peoples and environment of where they are within India. Our scholarly friends probably refer to these qualities as 'agency' – not passive consumers of attractions, cultures or everyday life but instead as actors engaged in attempting, however pathetically, to understand and make sense of their surroundings. Could they even, heaven forbid, be examples of 'anti-tourists', mentioned above? To some extent I think they do fit this description. While recognising the huge differences between themselves and the local indigenous population, relationships of trust, intimacy and warmth have developed between these 'frequent returners' and particular families and villages. Shared histories characterise these relationships. Small children of long ago are today getting married, others are leaving school to find work, while illness and death take their toll – and they are all shared between the outsiders and the locals. Hurried visits are arranged for the celebrations and for the sadnesses. The visitors remain 'tourists' and as such are limited and curtailed by a variety of powerful constraints. They still go 'sightseeing' and travelling around the country, still take the trains to go trekking and still go watch and follow the fortunes of various football or cricket teams. Amazing. Yet at the end of the day, it can never really be 'shared histories'. Although unacknowledged and displayed, the relationships involving the outside tourist are ultimately defined by their power and affluence – it is an unequal relationship. Despite these structural constraints it is difficult not to be warmed by the intimacy of these relationships. Yes, these are tourists but particular types of tourists.

In this chapter, I explore and discuss aspects of this 'agency' or 'engagement' by focussing on two of the areas popularly associated with India – namely, Indian cinema and cricket. It didn't have to be these two subject areas. It could have been Indian cuisine or classical Indian music or Indian wildlife. It happened to be cinema and cricket because two of the small group I talked to were interested in these topics. Both examples I think illustrate the quirkiness and richness of the experiences of India thrown up by this random, small group of people I interviewed. Before I do this I discuss whether the numerous visits to India by some members of the interviewee group had any lasting impact on their lives 'back home'. I would imagine that all holidays or visits especially abroad would have some lasting influence even though it might be difficult to capture or measure. But what of a group who had made numerous visits to the same country? At the very least, the answers to this question from this group would provide clues about the nature of their tourist experience.

"Clothes, ganeshas and bangles" back home

As I mentioned above, one of the areas I was interested in exploring with the informal interviews I did in 2013 with the regular visitors to India was whether 'India had changed them'. The obvious answer I knew would probably be 'yes' but I was interested in hearing about the extent and nature of that change. Much of the general international tourist experience is after all about limiting or closely managing that interrelationship between engagement and experience especially in poor countries. Negotiations take place, at many different levels and in many different ways. Quite a few visitors to faraway, 'other' countries seem content to never leave the hotel complex (if on the beach) or without the chaperoning influence of guides and air-conditioned transport. Above all, the best way of getting around – local buses – should never be considered; too dangerous, unsafe or unclean we are told!

I expected the stories from my interviewees to be different. As might be anticipated, a strong theme that emerged from a number of respondents was a greater critical reflection on their own cultural and material lives 'back home'. Janet and Mike from America for example talked about their own children and their friends having "been given too much without having to work too hard." They came "to expect things" and weren't "too appreciative or grateful" for what they had. In general they felt that: "kids are too isolated and not aware of what is going on in the world. They should see these kids over here," they continued, "swapping school uniforms every other day so that they can go to school. Our kids should see this and know that education is a privilege. They should want to learn." Being here in India has "certainly given me a better outlook on life," remarked Janet. "Those who have nothing are still so friendly and are still smiling." Mike agreed adding, "It is really amazing that given the poverty, there is no hostility. I really want our children to travel so that they can put things in perspective. It would make them better people if they could see different cultures."

Andy, the hospital and care home worker back in England, also picked up on this theme of India leading to re-evaluating things back home. "I appreciate simplicity in life more I think. I seem to be more tolerant here and more patient. I guess you have to be or else you get frustrated and angry." Given Andy's developing interest in Buddhism and spirituality in general since coming to India, it wasn't surprising that the increasing materiality of life in rich countries and also in parts of India worried him. "I have become increasingly aware that Western societies don't have all the answers. People smile a lot here even when they haven't got much. I don't know why."

Gina, the part-time employee in the post office in England, and who with her partner Mick at first couldn't decide whether to visit India or Africa, seemed astounded that I could ask whether visiting India had changed them at all. She then began telling me in great detail about her continuing involvement with the Goan family and the villagers over the last decade or so even when back in England. "The politics of the extended family here is unbelievable," she said, pausing for breath. "No, no, no – I never switch off from India. My front room back home is like an Indian restaurant with all those table and chairs. I've got ganeshas on the wall, drapes on the wall and elephants throughout the house. India brings you up with a jolt; not Goa – you have to travel throughout India. It has a very powerful impact. When invited I give talks in the local school back home. The last talk I gave was in the granddaughter's infant junior school. The topic was on India and I took in these photographs, terra cotta pots filled with spices, clothes, ganeshas and bangles. The kids sat there riveted. They thought it was brilliant."

For Pauline and Sjoerd from the Netherlands, their visits to and experiences of India had changed over time. "When we first came here, we wanted to make a difference, to do things to help," they said. "When we did, we found out that it wasn't as good as we thought it was." I think but am not sure that Pauline was referring to involvement and work with elderly Indian widowed women. "You always think you understand but you never do. You always only have a partial view, especially of village life. Now we seem to be retreating more and more. We are not as involved as much. We are just trying not to leave footprints. The more you try and do something and involve people, the more it seems to backfire." It appeared to me during the interviews that both Pauline and Sjoerd had thought hard and discussed previously this issue of themselves and India. "Maybe it's old age," Pauline continued. "But this place has had a deep impact on me. Before coming to this country I had to make big changes in my life. Everything you thought you had sussed is confronted here and you have to deal with things at a much deeper level. It made me think of changes in my own life. And over here it's the extremities of having to deal with things. It made me think about the changes in my and our lives. If you have a weak point, you will be confronted by it and have to deal with it. You can't get round it." A little later in the interview I returned to this theme of change. "It almost as though India forces you to confront things you have been putting off," observed Pauline. "And it's true of other people that I've spoken to. Being in India forces you to place or order things in your life. And some of these things are difficult. Something fundamental changes in you. A lot of things begin to add up – not on the surface but on a much deeper, deeper level. I don't mean this on a political level. It's a more spiritual thing and has nothing to do with religion." At the conclusion of our discussion, both Pauline and Sjoerd agreed that, "India does have this incredible effect on people especially young people. We see and talk to young backpackers and even those that have been in Africa or South America. It hits them when they reach India."

Common to these reflections from this sample interestingly is not the difference, the darkness, the dangers or the exotica of India but the impact individually and socially on themselves. Being a tourist, it seems from their responses, is about being inquisitive and has this self-revealing quality. There is this quest for immersion in aspects of Indian life and culture together through personal experience. There isn't this experienced commodification of places and cultural practices. It isn't the marketing industry that defines what is distinctive, unusual, striking and extraordinary, not to the same extent anyway. These frequent travellers to India instead seek to move beyond the latest 'destination branding' efforts of the tourist industry. And from some of the comments above, the explorations and discoveries while in India – irrespective of their success or otherwise – seem sometimes to be of a qualitative and lasting nature, as the examples below of Helle and Jeff suggest.

Bollywood and the land of the mad hatter

The Regal Cinema in Mumbai is a famous and well-known landmark in the city. Located in the Colaba district adjacent to the huge roundabout (Mukherjee Chowk) and opposite the Prince of Wales Museum, the 1930s art deco yellowish building was India's first cinema with air conditioning and an underground car park. There is only one screen and the velvet-lined seats and curtains are situated within large curved balconies. Hopefully, its days are not numbered despite its image of faded glory. Certainly, it is no match for the shiny new all singing and dancing multiplexes that arrived in the mid-1990s with their improved seating, sound and locations (and increased prices). The single screen venues are kept going apparently by the poor who cannot afford admission prices to the multiplexes as well as by interested overseas tourists. I have passed the Regal many times and also the similar art deco Eros Cinema in Churchgate, almost opposite the station. I've not watched a film in either cinema as they appeared closed whenever we passed them.

It is difficult, however, for outside tourists to appreciate the hold and importance of cinema in Indian culture (and the economy). 2013 was the official hundredth anniversary of Indian cinema. From its first showing of the Lumiére Brothers' world tour of cinema demonstrations in Bombay in 1896 to showing its first Indian feature film *Raja Harishchandra* in 1913, Indian cinema today is the biggest film industry in the world. Nowhere else does cinema impact on people's lives to the extent it does in India. And Indian cinema is a growing popularity – from Hong Kong through to the Middle East and parts of Africa. It's mainly Europe and the Americas that have not witnessed (yet, perhaps) the explosive growth within 'mainstream' cinema seen elsewhere.

My local cinema in Leeds, UK shows Indian films every Sunday and some multiplexes have a regular 'Bollywood' choice. The National Media Museum in Bradford, ten miles from Leeds, celebrated the anniversary of Indian cinema with a series of films (including *Mother India*, *Silsila* and *Mughal-E-Azam*) and a display of rare and some hand-painted Indian film posters. As I wandered around the exhibition I kept thinking of Helle whom I had interviewed back in Goa in 2013. It was an extraordinary discussion and, in a way, epitomised the surprises, knowledge, expertise and quirkiness of the small group of people from one small homestay in India that I interviewed.

Helle is from Denmark. She was in the room next to mine. I used to see her quite often sitting in her balcony overlooking the garden. I had never met her before although she had been coming to India for around eighteen years and often stayed at this same village homestay. Helle was an elderly woman and deeply suntanned. She described herself as a yoga teacher. We greeted each other frequently but never really chatted. She always seemed so busy running around, chain-smoking, grumbling about this and that, and always out somewhere. I eventually plucked up enough courage to get talking to her and asked her for an interview.

Helle talked very quickly in her particular form of 'Danish English'. I didn't always manage to understand everything she said and I was a little hesitant (and afraid) to stop her when she was in full flight. After explaining what I was after in the interview, Helle responded immediately, "You will not get a good love story (of India) from my side – far from it."

She talks very passionately, waves her hands around a lot and gets angry quickly. "I am a film director. I make movies in Denmark and have made two documentaries here in India. Back in the 1990s I went to see a film (in India) because I am a film person. And these Indian films, everyone knows they are real bad – all that singing and dancing. So I went to the cinema. I thought, 'What is this?' It was really good – good mainstream cinema. I didn't understand what they said but it was good. I then went three times to the cinema. Then I bought a film magazine. I completely went mad. This is completely fantastic. Films are god in this country – films and cricket. In the West we are so ignorant. We don't have a clue. They must make a lot of good films here and crap too, just like we do." Helle watched these first films while in Bombay trying to sort out her visa. "I know Bombay. I have spent more than two and half years in Bombay, not all at one go. Bombay is hard I can tell you. I have never, never liked Bombay. But the colour and music of the films, I love it but hate all the rest. The money, money aspect of things – I don't like that but I love the films they do. The way they go about their films… They just do things that we don't have the nerve to do. That's why I have been to India so many times."

I wanted to get Helle talking about her India films and, after a number of miserable failed attempts, got her back to the mid-nineties where she had just seen her first Indian films. "So after all my hassles getting the visa in Bombay, I came down to Goa.

Then I went to Margao [Goa's second city and not far from where Helle was staying]. I asked around, 'Where can I find films?' I was near the market and someone told me to go up to the second floor of this dirty, old building. Along the corridor was a small film shop in a dirty little cubby hole, a couple of metres wide. There was this man and after a while he realised I was serious and gave me ten films to watch. These are good he said and told me something about the directors. So I was here (in this homestay where the interview was taking place) for a couple of months just watching films. Went back and got some other films. That's how it all started.

I then went back to Denmark. It must have been around 1997. I went to get some money, and research into the industry. It took me three years to get the money together, bits and pieces from all over. Also, it took me a long time to get into the film industry in Bombay. I kept going back and forward from Denmark and Bombay to watch, research and learn. I wanted to put this documentary together. I wanted to do it on my own just with a camera. These men wanted to do it with computers and all that stuff. They wouldn't listen." So what was this documentary that you made, I asked. "I met this man in Rajasthan. He just knows everybody. I have been with guides in Rajasthan and I've been there on my own. I shot the cow film myself. I didn't search for money. I edited it myself. I met this cow and followed him around filming him and then he was joined by four other cows and I followed them around too. It was shown back in Denmark on television."

And that was all I got from Helle about the 'cow documentary', which a year later I found out was released in 2006 and was called *Nandini*. It was filmed in Udaipur, Rajasthan and was an hour in length. On returning to England, I eventually found Helle's website. "What do cows do all day?" reads the blurb. "Where do they go? What is it with Hinduism and cows? *Nandini is* about cows in the city. It follows one and then a few others from early morning to late evening... *Nandini* is a portrait of a society and culture which is different from ours and where humans and cows are living side by side... still."

It's a wonderful idea for a documentary and the sort of film that I would go to a cinema to watch or stay in to see on television. It sounds a very imaginative idea and also intriguing – how do you fill an hour on cows wandering round a city? "It's full of music, colours and lively city life," concludes the blurb. It must have been a good documentary as Helle mentioned that the British Broadcasting Corporation (BBC) wanted to buy it but also to add English commentary. Typical Helle – she refused saying it would destroy the coherency of the film!

Nandini was released in 2006. What puzzled me when I listened to the interview some six months later was that Helle almost ignored telling me about her earlier Indian film called *Larger Than Life*, released in 2003. This was the film that took three years of fundraising back in Denmark which Helle referred to earlier in the discussion. Her website describes the film as "communicating what Indian cinema is all about... In *Larger Than Life* the director undertakes a journey into the spirit and soul of Indian cinema. Indian cinema is epic, grand scale, glamour, singing, dancing, drama. It's fantasy and bone hard realism. It's everything. The film goes to the core of India film culture, sensualism – how India film culture does not let anything go untold but without the sex scenes... The film is also... about letting one be inspired by what is different." And that's the sum total of what I can find out about *Larger Than Life*. I assume it was a studio production, made in Bombay and must have been shot in the early 2000s. Again, it sounds an exciting and innovative idea for a film targeted at a Western audience. I don't know whether it 'worked', found a distributor or even was ever shown.

It was strange that Helle said so little about the film especially when you see the cast list. The two principal leads were Shah Rukh Khan and Manisha Koirala. Unfortunately, my ignorance of Indian cinema didn't allow me to pick up on the names when Helle mentioned them and later in the interview told me a little more about Shah Rukh Khan. These are today mega powerful, rich, global stars especially Shah Rukh Khan, as their Wikipedia entries indicate. Back in England I had to do a number of double checks to make sure that I had the right people.

Shah Rukh Khan, also known simply as SRK, is today the second richest actor in the world with a net worth of around $600 million. Referred to in the media as the 'King of Bollywood' or 'King Khan', he has appeared in over 80 Hindi films, won numerous national and international awards (including a Legion of Honour from France), is Chairman of the film production company Red Chillies Entertainment, has been honoured for his charitable work by UNESCO, been described by the *Los Angeles Times* as perhaps the world's biggest movie star and, perhaps in his spare time, is co-owner of the Kolkata (Calcutta) Knight Riders – one of the cricket franchises in the Indian Cricket League (IPL). Phew! What the Wikipedia entry didn't mention was that he had the lead role in Helle's *Larger Than Life* film!

And what of Manisha Koirala? Born into a long-established political family from Nepal, Manisha is a well-known actress in both India and Nepal and has appeared in numerous Nepali, Tamil, Telugu and Malayalam films. She has been awarded a number of national awards and is a UN Goodwill Ambassador. Described as a 'social activist' because of her work and activities promoting women's rights, violence against women and trafficking of Nepali girls for prostitution, Manisha was announced as Woman of the Year by the magazine *India Today* in 2014.

Not a bad cast list for your first Indian film!

Towards the end of the interview, Helle said a little more about getting entry into Bollywood. "My way of India is through films," she said. "Through the films I got to know the people and parts of the country. I can handle Mumbai. I can handle that fucking city. I know it very well. But working as a white woman is a problem. When you are inside, it's not a problem anymore; it's over but it can't really, really ever be over because of the whole attitude to women. I got into the studio in Mumbai because of an Indian woman. She phoned up and made the introductions to the studio saying I was a Danish director who wanted to come over to the studios. We were stopped at the gate in the rickshaw. 'Can't go in.' Once we were in it was a very nice place. Filming and people were busy in the courtyard. The Indian woman introduced me and then left. They sat there looking at me. 'So you have come to put us down.' 'What?' I said. 'No, sir, I have not. Why on earth would I want to do that!' I told them I was trying to do this documentary. Then I got angry when they said, 'Yeh, yeh, yeh.' I said, 'Do you want me to leave?' This man said, 'Sit down over there.' So I hung around there until they had finished. Then at eleven at night I said that I had to catch the train to Churchgate from Bandra back to Colaba where I was staying. 'Can I come back tomorrow?' Yes, they said. I went back the next day. Rukh Khan was there. He was the one I wanted. At first I couldn't get close to him. He was always completely surrounded. Next day I went back. This man said, 'Have you recovered from my outburst the other day?' That was quite nice. I said, 'Yes.' He said, 'OK.' Anyway, they were now shooting a scene where Shah Rukh Khan was involved. A double was involved in the scene. I watched and then suddenly, Khan was alone, sat in a chair. I went up to him and said, 'Hello. My name is Helle Ryslinge.' And that's how I met him. It was around 1988."

An amazing story and very typically Helle. Gatecrashing Bollywood studios, no bureaucracy or long drawn-out formalities, confronting the gendered and patronising attitudes and eventually getting her man! "With Bollywood, everything is money, money, money. Money is first and last. Except Shah Khan. He is a big, big star. He did all those things for me and never wanted money."

The imperial game

The Indian film industry obviously has reflected and engaged with the wider societal context within which it is situated. Given the difficulties which we from the West have in understanding India, it is not surprising that we have difficulties in relating to its cinema. Helle seemed to grasp this point. Its mainstream 'language' – songs, dance, fights – are rooted in a different aesthetic tradition from ours. Its legitimacy and appeal is not based very deliberatively in claims of 'authenticity'. Instead they have their own heroes and villains and it is this 'unreality' that allows the millions of viewers to enjoy, understand and relate the stories to their own very different situations or 'realities'. Historically, a central preoccupation of Indian cinema has been the Indian state, both in pre- and post-independent cinema. As Sunera Thobani mentioned, "Popular Indian cinema has been a rich site for the study of the processes that help constitute particular forms of nationality, including common language, culture and identity." In short, cinema has been a central pillar in the politics of 'national belonging' and of raising or omitting issues such as class, caste, gender and communal violence.

Given the mass basis of film audiences in India and this link between cinema and politics, it is surprising that greater attention is not given to Indian cinema in mainstream commentary in the West. One of the other great institutional spectacles of India – cricket – generates more column inches in the press but within a largely depoliticised context unless the discussion is focused on money and finances. Cricket like Indian cinema can be seen as an example of 'affirmative action' – largely based on ability that ignores caste, class and religion. Muslims can also be selected to play in the national team. And similar to Indian cinema, cricket has this connection to 'identity politics', to what it means to be an Indian. The wild jubilant celebrations throughout the country when India won the World Cup in April 1983 testified to the deep embeddedness of this sport within Indian political culture.

Bollywood too recognised the distinctiveness of cricket and India. While there have been numerous films about cricket, it is the film *Lagaan* that has been the most commercially successful. Released in 2002 the film is set in India during the time of the British Raj and focusses on a group of poor villagers who beat their British rulers at cricket. As a number of commentators have pointed out, cricket in India only makes sense when situated within this wider historical and socio-political context.

I like cricket. I realise that it is an acquired taste for many, mysterious beyond comprehension to others and like watching paint dry for others, but I like cricket. I am a member of the Yorkshire County Cricket Club and, only a few days ago, was looking at a photograph exhibition at the Club of some of the famous overseas players who have played for Yorkshire. And there was a picture of a young, chubby-faced Sachin Tendulkar. As most people know Tendulkar was, before he retired, probably the most famous sportsman in the world and in India has a god-like presence. No other batsman in the world has scored so many Test Match centuries and runs. His twenty-four-year cricket career seemed to epitomise the resurging, confident new India. The boy from Mumbai made good and yet has always seemed to retain a modesty and decency that is in contrast to the brash, corrupt, money spinning, administratively incompetent regimes that direct cricket in India and internationally today.

Anyway, there I was in September 2015 looking at this photograph of Sachin Tendulkar in the display stand at Headingley, Yorkshire. It wasn't that picture of him dressed in a Yorkshire Cricket Club cagoule, bat in one hand, a pint of beer in the other and wearing a flat cloth cap, but it should have been – a most unlikely alliance. "One of the greatest four and half months I have spent in my life," was how Sachin described his summer of 1992 as Yorkshire's first overseas player and first non-white player. I guess this quote can be interpreted in different ways, as Yorkshire would not have been the most hospitable club to play for, nor did West Yorkshire have too many similarities to Bombay but I'm sure he made these comments in a complimentary manner. Many Yorkshire members today can still recount stories of the 'Little Master's' time with the club as a nineteen year old. He not only rewrote the history books of the cricket club but also was the first batsman to reach a thousand runs in that season. He changed Yorkshire cricket forever but he very nearly didn't come. The Australian cricketer Craig McDermott was the Club's first choice as their overseas player for that year but was injured just before the start of the season. Yorkshire was in South Africa playing a number of warm-up games when news of McDermott's withdrawal was announced. Against the background of the referendum in South Africa to determine whether power-sharing would replace the apartheid system, Yorkshire Committee members were in a panic – who was available at this late stage to be their first overseas player. The phone lines between Headingley, Leeds and South Africa must have been steaming. Eventually with the help of Solly Adam, a captain of a local Yorkshire Bradford League club and with wonderful contacts in Indian cricket, Tendulkar was identified and via conversations with Tendulkar's mentor, the wonderful Sunil Gavaskar, was persuaded to sign on the dotted line. The young Tendulkar had become an honorary Tyke.

As mentioned earlier I have spent many hours sitting in the shade at the Oval Maidan in Bombay watching the various games of cricket going on around me. When Susan and I visited Calcutta, we made a pilgrimage to Eden Gardens (home incidentally of the Kolkata Knight Riders co-owned by Shah Rukh Khan, as mentioned above). I have childhood television memories of seeing a packed Eden Gardens with the cameras largely focussed on the hundreds of 'spectators' precariously perching from the branches of the surrounding trees, cheering their idols on. Built by the British in 1864 alongside Fort William and beside the wonderful Hooghly River, Eden Gardens is one of the iconic cricket grounds in world cricket. Unfortunately, there was no match in progress the day we visited so we missed the famous vociferous crowds. Most of the trees seemed to have disappeared, and the new floodlighting introduced in the 2011 stadium renovation for the Cricket World Cup appeared as giant engineering sculptures astride the stadium. The new roofing and seating arrangements has transformed the stadium, as well as reducing the numbers from around 100,000 to 60,000.

Once we had found an open entrance gate, a bored but kindly security guard allowed us to wander around the stadium, up to the top seats and then down to the pitch where I walked for a few minutes along the boundary grass. I was paying my respects. It was quite spooky, all alone in the giant stadium with my childhood memories of the frenzied spectators.

I had the same 'spooky' feeling at another famous cricket stadium in India. This was at the Brabourne Stadium in Churchgate, Bombay in February 2013 where India was hosting the tenth Women's Cricket World Cup. It's a lovely old colonial ground, built around 1936 with the three public stands and their huge overhanging roofs, all facing the clubhouse. It was built on land reclaimed from the sea and is situated alongside Marine Drive, perhaps the most famous thoroughfare in Bombay. I knew the World Cup was happening – I had been reading about it back in England before my arrival. There was, however, no bunting or flags welcoming participants from around the world at the airport when I arrived, no banners in the streets and no fanfare at the Brabourne Stadium which I walked around trying to find an office to buy tickets. A kindly woman, probably a participant, eventually helped, telling me to turn up at a particular gate and walk in. Entrance was free. As my hotel was just across the dual carriageway from the Stadium, I had a very pleasant week watching various matches in between rests in the hotel room when escaping the heat.

As a spectator watching the cricket in the middle, however, I was almost alone in this vast cavernous stadium – very spooky. The opening game involved the Indian team. Groups of young schoolchildren were enjoying themselves, running around between the empty seats and above all trying to catch the attention of the match camera. Apart from the schoolkids, there were few other spectators. The next game involved the English team – no schoolkids and a smattering of spectators, maybe a dozen in all. In a country which is fanatical about cricket like no other country, I was a little surprised. Maybe things picked up somewhat later in the tournament. I got talking to an Indian man sitting along from me. He had nipped out from work for an hour or two to watch the action. No, he said, it was not that surprising that so few people were interested. This was women's cricket, he reminded me and had received little coverage or excitement in the city or nationwide. He was aware that things were slowly getting better in England and hoped that India too would begin to support women's cricket with more money, media coverage, grassroot initiatives and organisation but he was not too hopeful. My new friend's pessimism was echoed in an article the following year on *cricinfo* – the cricket Internet site – that detailed how Indian women's cricket continues to lag behind other countries, both on and off the field. We grumbled to each other for a while and then he had to get back to work leaving me with no one within thousands of empty seats to chat with; good cricket though.

Memories of my 2013 visit to the Brabourne Stadium flooded back when I read that the English cricket team were using the Stadium for practice in November 2016 before the start of their five Test Match series against the Indian team. How I wish I was back there.

Jeff was one of the travellers that I interviewed back in 2013 and he is mad keen on cricket. He has visited India around twelve times. His first visit was in 1997. "I first came simply because I had heard from friends over the years what a fascinating place this was. It was. It was the nearest thing to another planet compared to what I had been brought up with," he said. Although from England, Jeff works as a freelance tourist guide in Munich, Germany and is able to plan his time and visits to India. He tends to stay around five weeks on each visit although he might combine these visits with trips to other countries. He has been all over India and has twice followed the cricket involving England around the country. "Originally, it's taken me to places I might not have got to like Chandigarh (high up in north-west India close to the Pakistan border) and Allahabad (up north, mid-country in the Ganges plain). I went to the World Cup two years ago. That took me up to Jaipur and I stopped off in Hyderabad on my way down to Bangalore.

The things I tend to remember," he continued, "are simply those things that are so different to what I was used to. But I am changing. I used to like cities, especially Calcutta. Now I'm less tolerant of the noise and rubbish. I'm getting older! I've been to all the big cities – Bombay, Delhi, Calcutta, Madras, Bangalore, Hyderabad. I used to love the madness and chaos."

Throughout our conversation, Jeff kept up with a steady stream of anecdotes and stories. It seemed to me that for him India and cricket were fused, an interrelated whole. Maybe it was my questions as he was also keen on his Indian cuisine but it is cricket that I most associate with Jeff. "The first time I went I flew from Delhi to Chandigarh where there was this Test Match. December never really gets warm. The sun was out for a few hours and it was only a few months after 9/11 so security was kind of top alert. Lighters and cigarettes weren't allowed in the ground so everyone put them under their hats to get in. It worked every time. The young kids at the match were very boisterous. In fact the forty year olds were very boisterous as well. Being a Test Match, it wasn't that well supported as with the one-dayers which is a great shame. It's a completely different experience from watching a game in the UK – very noisy and boisterous.

There's usually around 60–70 English supporters in the crowd. This was this one time when it was a dry period (no alcohol) in Chandigarh because of the elections. We were in this place outside the cricket ground. I was actually caught with a beer in a metal beaker, trying to disguise it. I hadn't noticed these two police. All the staff scarpered and they came over. I ended up in the police station for about three hours. The police made up a statement for us and told us that we were to stay in our hotel, come back tomorrow and in half an hour all the formalities will be done. We can then have our passports back. It actually took six hours with endless cups of chai. We were very polite to him. Kumar Patel was his name I think."

I was impressed with Jeff's memory. His overall grasp of detail from long ago was excellent. Some things though are that epic at least for cricket lovers, that it is easy to recall. "The first game I saw in India was at Chennai. India was playing Australia. This was the long-awaited confrontation between Sachin Tendulkar and Shane Warne. Warne took a wicket with the fifth ball of his first over, caught at first slip by Mark Taylor. India were two wickets down and the there was this huge roar which meant that Sachin was coming in. The first ball he received from Warne, he cover drove for four. Tell a lie, Tendulkar played a few defensive shots and the last ball Warne got him. In the second innings, he smashed 164 not out which was great."

And it was cricket that resulted in Jeff visiting Pakistan. "In 2005 I was in Pakistan. It was not at all dangerous. I first watched a game in Islamabad and then afterwards in Lahore. I had a day or two before the game so I went to the Murree Brewery – the one and only in the country. Very drinkable beer." I had never heard of this brewery or beer but soon was engrossed in the long, colourful history of Pakistan's only major alcohol producer and "oldest continuing enterprise in Pakistan." Established in 1860 by the British to quench the thirst of its army, it has survived (just) hairy historical episodes such as the creation of the new country and, later, the total alcohol prohibition in 1977 (later amended) and the military government of General Zia-ul-Haq. In addition to beer, the brewery also produces varieties of gin, vodka and, above all, malt whiskies. Few countries like their whiskies more than Pakistan and India.

Why cricket and why India?

Indian cricket today has moved a long way from its colonial days. As Ramachandra Guha quotes in his wonderful *A Corner of a Foreign Field: The Indian History of a British Sport*, an account of a game in 1850 noted that Indians: "were rather apt to look on a cricket match as proof of the lunatic propensities of their masters the sahibs, and to wonder what possible enjoyment they could find in running about in the sun all day after a leather ball."

No more, not by a long shot, no more. India today sits astride world cricket, calling the shots and making all the plays. Although unrecognised at the time, it was 1983 that signalled the beginnings of far-reaching changes in the power and finance of world cricket. On the 28th June 1983, India won the World Cup at Lord's, London under the leadership of the wonderful Kapil Dev. As Debanjan Chakrabarti recalls from that day, "Indian cricket, egged on by the full-throated chant of almost a billion fans, surged ahead whose apt culmination (or nadir, depending on your perspective) was the Indian Premier League – IPL for short – an orgy of fast-forward cricket laced with Bollywood razzmatazz, draped with oomphy cheerleaders in skimpy outfits, making the show every marketing person's wet dream." Today it is the Indian IPL that provides the bedrock for the funding and direction of world cricket, and all under the control (at the time of writing) of the cement magnate Narayanaswami Srinivasan – President of the Board of Control for Cricket in India (BCCI), owner of the IPL's Chennai Super Kings, and more importantly, President of the International Cricket Council (ICC). A wonderful article by Rahul Bhatia in *The Caravan* in 2014 provides a detailed portrayal – much of it unsavoury – of the murky financial world of Indian and international cricket today. The two other representatives from England and Australia on the ICC obediently follow India along. In an ironic historical twist, an elite English sport is today controlled by a former colony. For many of the fanatic Indian cricket fans, none of this murkiness matters. As Chakrabarti notes, for nearly two months every year, "a cricket addict nation goes on a booze-addled, fast-food fuelled binge of cricket every evening where the ratings of all other television channels apart from the IPL broadcaster Sony Entertainment plummet to zilch."

Cricket was above all the game associated most closely with the imperial empire of the British. A very credible and detailed analysis and understanding of India could be provided by tracing the development of this sport in the country. The great historical narratives of nationalism, communalism and political struggle are all present in the rise of Indian cricket and the domination today of world cricket by India. The Caribbean writer CLR James was the first to recognise cricket as a platform for political struggle many decades ago in perhaps the most important book ever written on the sport, *Beyond a Boundary*. But it wasn't only cricket. As a number of commentators have pointed out, in the training and practices of the British imperial class athleticism and imperialism were integrally part of the whole. Sport, any sport and competition was seen as integral to the 'civilising' mission of the Empire, as Fahad Mustafa points out in his analysis of cricket and globalisation. Embedded within nineteenth century institutions of British fee-paying education, elite universities, the clergy and the monarchy, competitive 'games' were seen as building sound character, moral fortitude and promoting good sense. It was cricket, however, that had pride of place in the development of imperial culture. It was cricket that provided the vehicle for the imperial masters in their search for an educating and civilising mission. Yet a hundred years later in a series of deliciously contradictory narratives, India is today master of the cricket world. Usurping those very claims of identity and nation state enthusiastically promoted by the imperial elite, India has successfully appropriated and commercialised global cricket. Asserting nationhood on the cricket fields for the benefits of a post-colonial India including its huge diaspora has proved a winning formula. The move from West to East in the twenty-first century has been complete and breathtaking. Global cricket has been transformed from 'a gentleman's game' to that of assertive ethnicity. The colonised have turned the tables on the colonisers. Today Southeast Asia is the home of cricket with India calling the shots.

I really enjoyed listening to Jeff and Helle's stories and experiences of visiting India. I remember chuckling a lot as they raced through their adventures and could have spent a lot more time quizzing them for greater detail. I have discovered a new interest – Bollywood – and hope soon to watch in India a Test Match with the all-conquering Indian team. On the other hand, their experiences did little to clarify my problem of understanding 'being a tourist'. Maybe Helle and Jeff were examples on being 'anti-tourists'; they do a lot of things that other tourists do but they do a lot more. But I don't know and maybe I'm not alone. I mentioned at the beginning of this chapter that there seemed to be a continuous effort by scholars to nail down this issue. I can't pretend to understand most of their thinking or conclusions but I found their formulations and insights suggestive. I also found it frustrating because, after all, they were discussing and arguing about me and Helle and Jeff and the others that I talked to.

One aspect though did emerge from these musings. A strong feature of Helle and Jeff's stories were sensory descriptions of their respective experiences. Smells, dirt and food for example came through strongly in my discussions with them. Helle as a filmmaker I guess would strongly relate to the sensory environment. I haven't seen her 'cow film' but I imagine that this element would be a strong theme. Thinking about their comments together with the other frequent visitors that I interviewed coupled with my difficulties about 'being a tourist', I began increasingly to notice mention being made to 'senses' and 'sensations'. This was often in conjunction with a wide range of cultural, artistic and creative activities such as photography, street life, dance or eating – in fact, nearly any aspect of everyday life. Instead of reading, visualising or thinking about the city or the Taj Mahal, we are invited to 'sense' the city or the Taj Mahal through the use of our taste, smell, touch as well as visual faculties. Experiencing something is more than a cognitive or intellectual activity seems to be the message. It is not a one-way process, however. The presentation of events, images or even of a country to the tourist market is similarly highly structured and arranged. Certain things are stressed while other things are omitted in an attempt to portray a particular perspective. Similarly, our senses are socially constructed and experienced differently in different cultures and at different historical periods. We usually fall for their messages but sometimes we resist. Yes, our senses are culturally grounded, are fragmentary and undeveloped but with a little bit of practice allow a more nuanced and critical appreciation of 'seeing' and 'experiencing' as a tourist. India in particular would seem a good place to experience as a 'sensoryscape'. As every guidebook points out, India is an 'assault upon the senses', unlike any other country. We only have a small capacity to appreciate the richness of this 'assault' due to our sensory impoverishment – we have forgotten in these modern times how to experience things 'bodily'. Our capacities are diminished for meaningful engagement with our environment. We are not very good with the smells, sights and sounds around us. But things are changing apparently. There are guided 'sensory walks' in some cities and talk of a 'new urban anthropology of the senses'. Some commentators are speculating on what town planning or an architecture informed by 'the sensorial revolution' might entail.

I am not a 'bodily' tourist but I am going to try harder on my next 'Colaba walk' as well as raise this issue with Helle next time we meet – never too old to learn.

Chapter 8

Getting richer and its problems

On the move

On the morning of Wednesday 9th November 2016, I remember sitting at my desk back in England flicking through the news channels on the computer. Two items were the subject of my searching and reading. First as the final voting results were announced, it was clear that Donald Trump was to be the new President of the United States of America. Against all expectations, expert opinion and polling evidence, he had defeated the favourite Hillary Clinton. The second item that I kept an eye on was the opening day of the first Test Match between India and England held in Rajkot. England was beginning a massive series of five Test Matches against India, the number one world-rated cricket team. England had a good opening day, batted first and the Yorkshireman (from down the road from where I was sitting) Joe Root was getting his century. Both stories rekindled thoughts and memories of when I was last in India. I wished I was there to listen to the reaction of the locals to the stunning and unexpected Trump victory and what it might mean for India, and also, to be watching some of those cricket matches around the country. Seeing and listening to the noise of the cricket fans screaming on their idols out on the pitch is one of my unfulfilled dreams. Maybe another time.

Thinking about the impact of future American trade policies on the Indian economy as well as about the world number one ranked Indian cricket team are reminders of how far India has travelled in so short a time. It is difficult not to see the changes. Wandering around the downtown areas of most big Indian cities is to witness the affluence and relaxed atmosphere of people confident about themselves, where they are currently and where things are going. And it's not only downtown – many of the suburban centres are the same. Most of these people seem to be young, returning from school or meeting with friends after work for a drink or gossip. Coffee and cake shops are popular. Large department stores are busy as are their cafes. The poor and homeless are not that visible. There are quieter, less harassed areas to make home than in posh downtown areas. The daily newspapers and especially the weekend press are full of fashion advice, the latest film reviews, and best places and restaurants to visit, just like everywhere else in the world. Numerous pages of course are given over to stories or interviews with this or that Bollywood film star. The numerous bookshops are busy. Prominent displays in their windows (or the plastic sheets on the pavements for copied versions) are given to the latest fiction and non-fiction titles from India and from around the world. The more popular television channels seem to reflect this ambience, affluence and relaxed lifestyle. Everywhere – in the home, in the countryside, in the cities – is spotlessly clean and modern in these programmes. Apart from the celebrities, the TV advertisements are not dissimilar to those from Europe, or probably anywhere else in the world. There seem to be more of them but the products advertised are familiar.

Occasionally, cracks are visible or can be found in these islands of calm if examined more closely. The hum or visibility of the electricity generator machines can often be heard or seen. The city buses have seen better days. The ubiquity of security guards outside many buildings and shops suggests a problem with intruders. The sheer volume of traffic on the roads occasionally merits a cough or two but the emissions tend to be hidden from sight and detection. The high metal fencing and locked gates around most public parks suggest a concern with exclusion rather than inclusion.

Every now and then, an event happens – for outsiders anyway – which encourages a re-examination of these taken-for-granted views and assumptions. Power cuts for example are common in most of India – irritating but not threatening for us tourists at least. Wait for a few minutes and back on it comes. In July 2012, however, it was more than an irritation. Half the country lost its electricity. Some 600 million people were without electricity. 200 million of this total didn't have access to any power in the first place but this aside, the country experienced what has been described as: "the largest blackout in human history." 21 of India's 28 states had been plunged into darkness. As William Dalrymple put it, the power failure resulted in international scrutiny of "the scandalous state of Indian infrastructure and the failure of the Indian state a full 65 years after Independence to provide even the basic necessities of modern life across most of the country." Since 2006 China has added about six times more power to its grid than India – 84 gigawatts compared to India's 14 gigawatts.

The same year, the country was engulfed by another outrage– this time, by rape and sexual violence against women. From then until today, India seems gripped by a series of brutal rape cases. International media reports seem suddenly to have discovered the extent and scale of violence to women in the country. The case of the Delhi bus gang-rape of the twenty-three-year-old student who was returning home after watching a film with a friend in December 2012 resulted in global attention. The death of the woman – popularly named Damini – also provoked thousands to take to the streets in many cities across the country, angry at the unchecked violence against women. In 2013, another story hit the international headlines. Thirteen men were detained after a Swiss tourist was gang-raped when she and her husband were camping in Gwalior, India. Many of the international reports seemed to imply that rape and violence, more generally against women, was a particular Indian problem. A small number of articles did in fact situate the Indian incidents against a backdrop of the situation in France, Britain or the US. It didn't make for comfortable reading.

Other cracks have become apparent over the last decade. The telecommunications scandal when the 2G telecom spectrum was corruptly undersold by government ministers – amounting to some $40 billion in lost government revenue – raised serious questions of governance. Then the botched and corrupt 2010 Commonwealth Games in Delhi, which many Indian commentators saw as a political and economic humiliation for the country. India appeared not to be 'shining'. Indeed, it was looking very tarnished.

'India Shining'

Before and during the 2004 general election, the slogan "India Shining" emerged as one of the defining moments characterising the period. Commissioned from an American marketing company, the marketing and campaign slogan was widely promoted but also aroused critical comment and negative appraisals. The slogan apparently was to highlight the rosy economic progress and future aspirations of the electorate. Today it is for most people viewed with a degree of mirth and ridicule. For others it is seen as encapsulating the unfaltering rise of a country over the last decade or so. Perhaps because of this controversy and debate, "India Shining" remains one of the more memorable slogans of recent years.

For some commentators today though, the 'shining' has returned after a dimming over the last few years. Most people are aware of the Indian economic success story of the last two decades. The popular narrative is that the change from Nehruvian socialist forces and other leftist influences, which dominated economic and intellectual life and village existence for so long, eventually embraced the new forces of the global economy. The so-called 'Hindu rate of growth' of around 3–4% per year that characterised the post-Partition economy was seen as sluggish, bureaucratic and unacceptable. Liberalisation and the "free play of market forces" came to the rescue in the early 1990s. The minority government of PV Narasimha Rao guided by the Finance Minister Dr Manmohan Singh opened the economy to foreign investment, trade and other 'liberalising' winds. The currency was devalued, import controls were dismantled, tax rates were reduced, the public sector weakened and the licensing system on private capital substantially reduced. As a result of the reforms, inflation in the mid-nineties came down from 15% to 6%, growth was around 7–8% and foreign reserves shot up. As Pavan K. Varma put it in one of his widely read books, "The year 1991 removed the stigma associated with the pursuit of wealth. It buried the need for hypocrisy about the aspiration to become rich. Most importantly, it made policies congruent with the temperament of the people... find ways to make money for themselves." This triumphant but rather nasty tone is not uncommon among commentators in India and elsewhere in the rush towards brave, new capitalism. The era of privatisation had arrived. Western products and 'brands' increasingly were available and replaced Indian import-substituted products. Financial credit was cheap. India's internal market of 1.2 billion consumers provided a tantalising glimpse into the future, especially for foreign investors.

This familiar narrative of poverty to prosperity and from tradition to modernity has been retold in a number of best-selling books in India and today continues to inform understandings in the daily newspapers. The Indian economy has trebled in size over the last decade and average incomes are set to double every ten years. Mobile phone usage has jumped from three million in 2000 to 100 million five years later and about a billion today. It is a persuasive story. Foremost alongside the graphs and figures describing the impressive national economic growth of the last two decades is the widespread acknowledgement of the country's information technology expertise. Bangalore is the city most often associated with this expertise with over 400 software companies and with customers from around the world. Over the last decade, some $50 billion has been generated by this sector alone, mostly in export revenues. Less well known but also important are Hyderabad, Chennai, Gurgaon and Pune.

Just as important – even more important – as the country's growth and expertise in IT is the country's role, nationally and globally, of reliable cheap medicines. Much less publicised than the IT sector, the pharmaceutical production of inexpensive medicines in India is a boost to the poor throughout the world. India today is the largest supplier of generic medicines.

India's economic and business elite had embraced enthusiastically the latest, new economic version of capitalism that had emerged in the Western economies in the 1970s–1980s. Neoliberalism as it is often called, and often collapsed into 'globalisation', saw the emergence of a different kind of economy with changed international rules. Currencies were floated, capital controls were abolished and policy experiments with deregulation, privatisation, marketisation, easily available credit and low personal and business taxes were the new magic bullets that would deliver the promised bounty. Growth rates in most countries did grow although the reasons behind this growth were disputed. Even after the financial failures in the Western economies around 2008, growth continued but at a slower rate. Above all, the new order was defined by soaring inequality, everywhere. Stated bluntly, the growth-inequality paradox of most economies in recent decades is simple: the wealth that has been impressively created in recent decades is being claimed by an increasingly small number of already wealthy people. Beyond occasional rhetorical flourishes that focused on 'the left behind', elections, budgets and policies relentlessly drove the brave new world of gross inequality and the accompanying social injustices. Little critical scrutiny is wasted in the media. Instead, in Western economies at least, there appears to be a general acceptance that the 'captains of industry' not only merit their gigantic rewards but also that those least able should pay for these rewards. Champions of this new economic wisdom have been the Anglo-American countries but the rest of Europe is following. In the case of India as the *Times of India* reported in 2014, "The net worth of India's billionaire community has soared 12-fold in 15 years – enough to eliminate absolute poverty twice over in the country." Today as Arundhati Roy points out, a number of corporations "run India". Mukesh Ambani for example is personally worth $20 billion. Reliance Industries Limited (RIL) of which Ambani has a majority controlling interest is valued at $47 billion and includes global interests that cover oil, natural gas, polyester fibre, fresh food retail, petrochemicals, high schools and stem cell storage services. RIL recently bought 95% of shares in Infotel, a TV consortium that controls 27 TV news and entertainment channels in nearly every regional language. Ambani also owns a cricket team.

A number of other corporations boast a dominant economic presence – Jindals, Vedanta, Infosys, Essar and Tata for example. The Tatas are well known in Britain having bought Jaguar and Land Rover, British Steel and Tetley tea. Their other acquisitions of over 100 companies in 80-odd countries include Daewoo, a chain of bookshops, the cosmetic giant Lakmé, the Taj hotel chain, mines, gas fields, broadband networks and entire townships.

It's not only economic influence and control that drives these mammoth organisations. Their marketing and commercial strategies include immersing themselves in a variety of cultural and artistic spheres. "(F)ilm, art installations and the rush of literary festivals have replaced the 1990s obsession with beauty contests," observes Roy. This interrelating of the economic with the culture is not particular to India, of course. Part of the neoliberal vision resulting from reduced public funds and the 'smaller state' is the involvement of private sponsorship and capital to run schools, hospitals and, in fact, anything and everything. As we all know, 'everything has a price'. So in London we have the ArcelorMittal *Orbit*, the UK's tallest sculpture designed by Anish Kapoor and constructed for the 2012 Olympic Games. Sponsored by Lakshmi N. Mittal, the Indian steel magnate and richest man in the world, the sculpture provided a defining and much discussed addition to the London skyline. I happen to like it but also to not like the intrusion of inevitable commercial contaminations into public spaces.

Anyway, the Indian economy since 2000 has continued to grow. 2005–2007 was just under 9% with a low point being 2013 where growth was 5%. In 2014–2015 the rate was 7.5, and in 2015–16, it is predicted to be around 8–8.5% making India the world's fastest growing economy. Between 1991 (the 'freeing' of the economy) and 2001, the Indian economy trebled in size and, it is worth repeating, average incomes are predicted to double every ten years – quite phenomenal. Comparatively and using a wide variety of indicators (such as ownership of mobile phones, the number of available TV channels, car ownership or foreign holidays), it is possible to grasp the extent of this change and it is breathtaking. For millions of people, the impact of these changes on their everyday lives has been staggering.

The context of this staggering impact on people's everyday lives, however, needs to be remembered. As was outlined in an earlier chapter, some 300–500 million people live in poverty depending on how 'poverty' is defined – a "tolerance of the intolerable", in Dréze and Sen's memorable phrase. Maternal mortality rates are higher than that of Sudan, Ethiopia or Bangladesh. Infant mortality in the state of Madhya Pradesh is higher than Senegal or Eritrea. Malnutrition in Gujarat, one of the richest states, is worse than the average level of malnutrition in sub-Saharan Africa. Structurally and politically, there are emerging 'rich' and 'poor' states with Gujarat, Maharashtra, Punjab and Haryana being winners, and Orissa, Bihar, Rajasthan, Madhya Pradesh, Tamil Nadu, Karnataka and Uttar Pradesh being amongst the losers. Andhra Pradesh and Kerala are rising stars. Key factors seen as dividing these states' well-being are the usual list of developments: that is, infrastructure progress (railways, electrification, power supplies, education enrolment, health facilities), and secondly, local state expenditure.

Today, India indeed does seem to be 'shining' but in particular and distinctive ways. The figures are impressive and life for millions of people has improved considerably in recent decades. There are, however, a number of historical structural features to the 'growth miracle' that sets apart the Indian economy. Perhaps the most important is a feature that rumbles away in the background discussions and debates. As many commentators have pointed out, the Indian economy has this peculiar, unique or 'strange' quality – the dominance of the service sector at the expense of the manufacturing sector. As pointed out in the earlier chapter, India has a lopsided unbalanced growth profile. Sustaining economic growth on the back of the service sector is not the usual pattern for future development. Generally speaking, industrial growth, a declining agricultural sector, productivity growth and technological advancement are seen as the necessary mix for economic development. Dependence on natural resources and agriculture diminishes. Yet India has not followed this path. This distinctive character of the Indian economy helps explain some of the differences between itself and China over the last 30 years or so. Indian manufacturing accounts for only 15% of GDP, while in China, it is 32%. In Thailand, it is 34%, the Philippines 31% and Malaysia 24%. India has yet to experience the economic transformation that has swept through China, a transformation that has been built on the expansion of manufacturing production from textiles, garments, toys, cars through to ships and electronics. If you want to prosper, you have to make things. The current Modi government's campaign to "Make in India" and to tackle 'business bottlenecks' are seen by many in the country as belated recognition of the need to focus on manufacturing. As one newspaper headline put it, "Can Modi

Turn Indian Manufacturing's Whimper Into A Roar?" There are though two important characteristics of India's manufacturing sector which are seen as limiting its effectiveness: first, it is small, and second, productivity is low due to the small scale of most manufacturing firms. Despite abundant, low-skilled and relatively cheap labour, the manufacturing sector is capital and skill intensive.

A further important element contributing towards this weak manufacturing sector is the country's infrastructure which has been an important focus in the new government's first years. Recognising that the infrastructure sector is crucial to future economic growth, the government has earmarked considerable funds for rail, roads, ports and the aviation industry. National highway development, roads to unconnected rural villages, new metro schemes in large cities, the development of 100 new 'smart cities', new ports and airports and monies set aside for rural infrastructure are some of the listed projects itemised in Modi's first two budgets. We shall see – the record is not a good one for such lists.

If manufacturing has traditionally been the way forward for developing economies, it is not so easy today for a country such as India. While the reasons behind the need for such an infrastructure and manufacturing 'catching up' is agreed by many commentators – the locking out the Indian economy from global trade and investment for some two hundred years by the British – the difficulties ahead are formidable. Moving from low-paid agricultural jobs into better paid urban employment is a little more complex today. It was always going to be difficult to mirror China's export-driven manufacturing strategy. The wobbles in the Chinese economy in mid-2015 have made this export-driven model even more difficult. Furthermore, manufacturing today is increasingly characterised by its technology rather than its labour content. Yes, India has the technological expertise, but it is too small a sector to absorb the millions of new entrants into the labour market each year. India will need to expand its manufacturing sector but not at the expense of its service expertise.

There is a further structural problem that weighs heavily on attempts to reform and address the peculiarities of the Indian economy. Any attempt to turn into reality the "Make in India" campaign of the current government or to regenerate the country's dilapidated infrastructure will need to deal with the crisis in the agriculture sector. This is where more than half the country works and lives – some 200–300 million people. Other estimates put the figure around 600 million. According to government figures, just over 60% of the population is designated as rural and dependent on agriculture.

Rural desperation

Outlook the popular Indian magazine seems to agree with Dréze and Sen's worries about the neglect of agriculture and rural development. In 2016, they ran a series of articles which warned that "many in New Delhi have not grasped the enormity of the rural crisis and how this could affect the India story." Unlike wandering around Indian cities, rural India is difficult for tourists to grasp or experience. Train windows on long journeys provide a romantic but distorted glimpse of events. Workers in the fields walk behind wooden ploughs pulled by bullocks, grasses and cereals are scythed and neatly tied together awaiting collection in the evening, and food and water breaks are taken under any shade available. In scenes such as these, as the guidebooks tell us, things seem to have changed little over the centuries. Along the wine-growing areas visible from the train on the route from Mumbai to Aurangabad on the other hand, the latest labour methods with the latest technology provide an oasis to the more common impoverished rural vistas. Neat, ordered vineyards with their accompanying 'Chateaus' would not look out of place in the Bordeaux region of France. Big money, high tech and a highly-skilled and trained workforce constitute something of a sudden shock to the traditional views from the carriage window.

Growth rates might be high and consumption goods might also be flying from the shopping malls in India's cities, but in the country's villages, a number of studies and reports seem to suggest, all is not well. And we are talking about a significant number of people here – about 160 million farming households. Around half of India's population live in rural areas – a faceless, politically weak and an increasingly desperate population. "By all accounts, large parts of rural India are bleeding," states the *Outlook* report. Discontent, suicides, resignation and poverty seem to characterise village life for many in the countryside. *Outlook* provides a graph which summarises the pain. 302 districts out of India's 676 are facing drought or some other natural calamity, 13 states out of 28 are facing drought and agricultural output is down by over 50% in 2015 compared to the previous year. Consumption of food, transport and implements are all significantly down. Growth in real wages have dropped from 18% in 2014 to under 4% in 2015. And so on. It's a bleak picture. Migration to the cities has increased, transferring poverty from the countryside to the urban streets. "It is a silent migration as we are not hearing anything about it," reports one specialist. Work in the villages and countryside is hard if impossible to get. With no sowing of crops, work is disappearing. Unsurprisingly, there has been a resurgence in claims for support under the National Rural Employment Guarantee Act (NREGA). Although under attack from the Government, NREGA provides 'guaranteed' at least 100 days of work.

Other indications of the rural desperation are evident. At the end of 2016, millions of marchers and demonstrators – mainly from the Maratha community, the landowning farmer caste – took to the streets in the western state of Maharashtra. "We want our farmers to be looked after and we will keep marching until they are," stated one participant. The silent protests are complex involving caste and anti-Dalit issues but at the centre are themes of the forgotten or ignored agricultural sector.

The droughts are identified as the main culprits behind the crisis. In mid-2016, some 330 million people were seen to be affected by these severe water shortages. The earlier than usual high summer temperatures added to the problems. Three consecutive weak monsoons were to blame. Media reports have been dominated by stories and case studies on the effect of drought on rural families and villages, with rationing of drinking water evident and wells that have dried up. Particularly hard hit has been the paddy production. Rice is a water-intensive crop requiring 2,500 litres of water to produce a single kilo of rice. Schools in Orissa were closed and protests around the country sought to draw attention to the problem. Doctor surgeries were reported closing due to insufficient water required to wash hands after medical activity. Stories of protests in Bangalore and across the state of Karnataka were reported over the sharing of 'their river waters' with the neighbouring state of Tamil Nadu. A High Court ruling in 2016 instructed the government to take action.

As usual, the situation on the ground is always more complex and often worse than the bald figures. The charitable trust based in Bangalore, the Foundation for Agrarian Studies, has provided a valuable and continuing source of data and perspectives on agricultural and rural development since 2003. Glancing through some of its studies and presentations begins to open up the hidden aspects of rural life. The 'feminisation of agriculture' for example is a process that has begun to reflect the movement of rural males from farm to nonfarm sectors. The growing confidence in these women groups is providing an opportunity to manage small and marginal farms. The lack of land and property rights together with low literacy rates has been identified as holding these women from further progress. Caste-based discrimination in access to water was highlighted in another detailed study of

11 villages from five states in India. A variety of socio-economic factors – size of landholding, occupation, income – were seen as determining access to drinking water. Dalit, Adivasi and Muslim households were seen as those most discriminated against in access to drinking water.

Numerous studies at a local village level are situated obviously against the wider context of the restructuring of the Indian economy. India has always been seen as the sleeping giant of global agriculture. It ranks as one of the world's leading producers of agricultural goods, but because of its hesitancy over integration into the global markets, it doesn't figure greatly in the international media. Until there is a crisis. Farming in India has always been seen to be somewhat of a gamble. Even when most things go well, many farmers find it difficult to make ends meet. The agricultural sector is contracting slowly both in terms of output and of jobs. But small, more optimistic changes are reported in some rural areas. A growth of blue-collar jobs in rural areas has taken up some of the slack, educational levels between urban and rural areas have closed, and wage differences (where work can be obtained) have narrowed. Whether this good news is the result of the recently arrived poor in the cities from the rural areas is unknown. Irrespective of these changes agricultural and rural lives will remain of significant importance in the country in the years ahead. Few other countries depend so much on its agricultural produce, and few other countries employ so many workers in the rural areas. And yes – the annual monsoons are critical to the well-being of the sector and to rural lives, but introducing crop insurance schemes as the current government has done comes nowhere near addressing the problems.

The new middle class. "We are coming, we are developing."

Any discussion of agriculture or the economy in general in India, especially in the decades ahead, usually includes mention of the rising 'new middle class'. Given the rapid growth and 'success' of the Indian economy over the last three decades, this new focus of media infatuation is perhaps not surprising. What is surprising is the consumer-driven focus of content. Even with online newspapers, you have to scroll down a significant way past the gossip and tittle-tattle to get to the news sections.

The structural changes occurring in India – the slow decline of the agriculture sector, service-led economic growth, rapid expansion of urbanisation and higher education – are seen generally as fuelling the rise of the middle class. The existence, nature and size of India's new 'middle class' is of course an important issue. It does impact on consumption patterns as the newspapers have discovered but it also has important wider implications which are the focus of excitable debates. Did the success of the BJP in the recent elections, for example, depend significantly on the middle class vote? Is the middle class more secular than other groups and does caste still maintain its grip with this group and, anyway, who are the middle class?

Conceptually there are numerous debates about understandings and definitions of social class, and especially the 'middle class'. The most often quoted data (from outside the scholarly literature) in the Indian media is from the *McKinsey Global Institute* which defines middle class as those with an annual disposable income between $3,500–$18,000. Using these figures India today has a middle class of around 200–250 million – huge in absolute numbers but only a small percentage of the population. This figure will more than double by 2025 to around 583 million. Any discussion of numbers is important here given the slippery nature of the subject matter. Credit Suisse for example quotes 23 million people instead of the oft quoted 260 million as being middle class in India. This lower figure is arrived at by looking at wealth rather than income. Despite these large differences in understandings, more considered opinion seems to concur that the Indian middle class is very diverse and is characterised by its differences and divisions, unlike the middle class in Europe or the USA. It is a group that has benefited substantially from the liberalisation reforms of the 1990s. Reflecting this change, it's common to read of the 'new' as opposed to the 'old' middle class. It is the 'new' middle class which replaced and did not integrate or blend into the 'old' middle class, which was seen as mainly coming from state institutions. This 'new' group for example is not a middle strata existing in some tension between the poor and the elite. In India the 'new' middle class merges into the elite because of its privileged position. Its influence comes not from its wealth but from its privileges. They are educated, English-speaking, mainly from the upper castes, have benefited from the increase in private sector jobs and are in better paid work, especially in the technology sector. What was 'new' was not only the background of its members but the production of a distinct social identity that has claimed the fruits of the 1990s liberalisation reforms. This new middle class, argues Gurcharan Das, "is different from the older bourgeois, which was tolerant, secular and ambiguous." Instead, money, drive and an ability to get things done are seen as characterising the new order. Rather than entrance being based on education, capability together with a liberal optimism, there is this emphasis on consumerism – "without social responsibility, let alone spiritual values" – that is seen as providing access. Das in his *India Unbound: From Independence to the Global Information Age* is an enthusiastic advocate for the rise of this new class although he laments the passing of his own class, the 'old' middle class. Instead of having one foot in India and the other in the West, the new class is constantly bemoaning the decline in our national character, he points out. He is surely right in locating the rise of the new middle class to more universal social changes associated with the rise and spread of capitalism and the relationships characterising this development. "It is," he continues, "free from the inhibitions that shackled the older bourgeois. It doesn't seek endorsements from the West; what works is good. It is non-ideological, pragmatic, result oriented." Cricket stars and, above all, Bollywood personalities are its only heroes. It accepts affirmative action for the lower castes and Hindu nationalism (with the accent on the BJP), says Das. For the older middle class, it is common and popular to grumble about the new wealthy upstarts. They lament the decline in commitment towards a more egalitarian society, the crippling ideological barrenness, naked self-interest and rampant consumerism.

Das' account is perceptive although a little uncritical. It sometimes blurs exactly what needs further exploration such as the 'non-ideological' or the 'bourgeois' nature of this new middle class. They seem to me very ideological views, and I'm unclear in what sense they constitute a 'bourgeois'. But he is right to see the arrival of this 'new middle class' as a significant development with important ramifications for India at all levels. Interestingly, Dréze and Sen have little time for "the new middle class". As scholars and campaigners steeped in statistical tables and graphs stretching back centuries, they avoid the shorthand descriptions of social change, preferring instead the painstaking accumulation of numbers and tentative conclusions. It makes for a less interesting and riveting read but, however tentative, its conclusions carry substantial weight. This is why their views of "the relative affluent" as they persist in labelling the new middle class are important. And they are not very flattering. Their ability to see themselves as 'the common people' – aam aadmi, in Hindi – is deceitful, manipulative and wrong, the authors seem to suggest. The complaints of the relative affluent they say, "are powerfully aired, and the perspectives of this easily mobilised group get the lion's share of the championing of the major political parties." The strength and great achievement of the new middle class it appears has been the imposition of its demands on the polity as a whole. It has captured the political agenda. Its influence, if this is correct, goes way beyond its tiny numbers. Poverty and hunger are no longer central agenda items – that was the 'old' middle class, well-educated and embedded in the public state structures. Instead, infrastructure issues such as electricity, roads and water are the new mainstream agenda issues. Disregarded in public policy and political programmes, for example, are the lamentable states of school education, health care and social security. The "biases of public policy towards privileged interests... (includes) the neglect of agriculture and rural development, the tolerance of environmental plunder for private gain" and the showering of public subsidies on already privileged groups.

The new middle class is arriving and the implications of this arrival is far reaching for all India. Although 'their agenda' might be dominating the media outlets, there are other stories that come and go. In the last year or so, it has been the weather that has emerged as an item of national concern – and with good reason. Droughts and water seem to be monopolising stories in the popular press. If it's not an absence of water, it is stories about too much water. Following the heaviest rainfall in over a century in November 2015, the Adyar River which flows through the middle of Chennai surged flooding the city with muddy waters and causing hundreds of deaths. The international airport was closed, power supplies were down and roads across the region were flooded. The elephant in the room – climate change – is a bigger problem than insurance schemes, the fate of NREGA, bigger even than floods and unpredictable monsoons. India has over the last few years struggled to cope with extremes of water availability (too much or too little), heat and with urban pollution. Climate change has begun to creep up the national policy agenda. While never being invisible it has now assumed greater importance. The crux of these problems in India and throughout most the world is the pact made between what resources are available and what we need. Our insatiable appetite for resources of a non-renewable nature has finally caught up with us.

India has a fast-growing economy, a national power shortage and the world's fifth largest coal reserves with little access to 'cleaner' fossil fuels such as gas. It also has some 400 million people with no access to electricity. 85% of the coal production is from opencast workings. Coal production is set to double by 2020. By 2030 coal use is predicted to be 2.5–3 times current levels, suggests a recent report. Much of the richest untapped reserves lie under heavily forested areas of Madhya Pradesh, Chhattisgarh and Jharkhand. As a government document dramatically put it, "It is estimated that more than half of India of 2030 is yet to be built." The country's admired economic success needs energy, desperately and a lot of it. "Coal has captured India," warns some of the press headlines. Development means more coal has to be mined, more ore extracted, more steel produced and more environmental damage.

Power cuts are almost a daily occurrence. As mentioned earlier, the most famous of these was "the largest power blackout in human history" in August 2012, which left 700 million people across 21 of India's 28 states in darkness. Traffic lights, air conditioning, cold storage, television – everything shut down. A major, maybe even dominant global economy cannot function in this way. It is estimated that even today, some 800 million people use traditional fuels – fuelwood, agricultural waste and biomass cakes – for cooking and general heating needs. All are inefficient sources of energy and release high levels of smoke. The World Health Organization calculates that some 300,000–400,000 Indian people die each year from indoor air pollution and carbon monoxide poisoning through use of traditional stoves using these traditional fuels. These chronic health problems are unlikely to decrease unless cheap electricity and clean burning fuels are made available and adopted in rural and poor urban areas. It is estimated that only 52% of rural households have access to electricity. Overall, some 35% of the population still live without electricity.

Coal and lignite remain the main source of electricity generation – 70% – but is of poor quality with a high ash content. Not surprisingly, India is the world's third largest greenhouse gas emitter. Despite government policy of focussing on developing alternative sources of energy such as nuclear, solar and wind energy in future years, progress is painfully slow and subject to a number of blockages and delays. Given that India is projected to be the second largest global energy consumer by 2035, it is unlikely that power failures and intermittent blackouts are a thing of the past.

Looking out for the environment

Finally and at long last, it has begun to be acknowledged in the country that any discussion of power and energy involves climate change considerations. It represents something of a breakthrough. After decades of campaigning by environmental groups and activists, climate change issues are emerging as important policy agenda matters. Surprisingly, Dréze and Sen in their *An Uncertain Glory* had very little to say on this topic. It was mentioned at various times but never figured as a major concern or focus in their publication. Anyway, in 2015 the Indian government finally submitted its climate change plan to the United Nations ahead of international discussions to agree on measures for tackling global warming in December 2015 at Paris. The government has committed to reduce its 'emissions intensity' up to 35% by 2030. Included in the submission is the focus on clean energy including solar power. It also prioritised the planting of more forests by 2030 to absorb carbon emissions. India also reminded the developed West that it "must take moral responsibility for the state of the world today", an important perspective which tends to be forgotten at such gatherings. India's submission was generally welcomed in the country although there were those who felt that more could be done, especially in the need to phase out HFCs which are used in air-conditioning units.

Coal is a problem for India, not only because of its poor polluting character but because of its abundance. It has the world's fifth-largest coal reserves and very few cleaner fossil fuels such as natural gas. Some 400 million tonnes of coal are imported. In the drive to force up economic growth rates, the BJP government is looking to double coal production by 2020. Over a six-month period, the government has given environmental clearance to 41 new mining projects. As the government minister boasted in 2015, "a new mine will be opened every month through till 2020." The government's determination over its current and future energy needs are continuingly expressed. "Energy requirements have to be met," stated the government minister. India has a "right to growth," stated Modi. It is the West who is responsible for reducing carbon emissions: "They must vacate the carbon space because we are coming. We are developing."

Despite the rather belligerent tone of the current government, they do have a point and it's a "scary point" as a campaigner for climate change in Delhi acknowledges. Even with India's projected population growth together with the dramatic growth in emissions from coal consumption by 2030, per capita carbon emissions in India will be 4 tonnes. By contrast it is 14 tonnes in China and the US. Yes – developing countries are increasing their carbon footprints, including India. But even with their projected increase in carbon emissions in the decades ahead, the major culprits remain the developed economies of the West. While their media continue to blame the likes of China and India as the 'baddies' for the climate change crisis, the current British government in 2015 set about ripping up most of their promises and financial commitments towards green energy as soon as they had won office.

And yet, and yet and yet? This same BJP government has

quintupled the 2020 targets for non-fossil energy set by the previous government – almost six times the current level.

Maybe this is all huff and puff. We'll see, but clearly global emissions are everyone's problem and concern, and those countries having the highest carbon emissions – the Western economies – can make an important contribution. Per capita usage rather than usage per country significantly alters the debates and indicates that the West should be cutting emissions by 10% or more as soon as possible.

As mentioned above, it was the Paris Climate Agreement of 2015 which brought to the world's attention India's energy plans and environmental concerns. Agreed by nearly 200 countries and operational from November 2016, the agreement commits these countries to keep global warming below 2°C. Despite President Trump's announcement in 2017 that the USA would be withdrawing from this Agreement, a long-term goal for zero carbon emissions, effectively phasing out fossil fuel, was agreed. Angry debate about the agreement continues to feature in the international media. As George Monbiot concluded, "By comparison to what it could have been, it's a miracle. By comparison to what it should have been, it's a disaster." A key focus in these debates was India and its ambitious plans for future energy production. When portrayed as the guilty partner in efforts to reduce greenhouse gas emissions, the country's politicians respond by citing the Western economies' historical responsibility for the current disastrous environmental situation. Figures are reeled out indicating that India is not a great consumer of energy-sapping goods – ownership of refrigerators and air conditioning is small compared to the Western economies. On a per capita basis, carbon dioxide emissions of the Indian population will remain well below those of Western economies, even in 2030. And the Modi government has surprised many doubters by its actions and plans for non-fossil energy. In the case of solar energy for example, production will rise from around 3GW to 100GW in seven years. As the journalist David Rose notes, "No country has ever built solar at anything approaching this pace, and it would leave India with three times as much solar capacity as Germany." Germany incidentally is Europe's leading producer of solar energy (at 38GW) – twice as much as in America. These are not figures to be sniffed at – India sees 15–20% of its energy needs coming from solar sources "in the very near future". Alongside the growing importance of solar energy is a recognition that the catastrophic pollution associated with earlier mining and power generation is unacceptable. Legal challenges and local campaigning groups are having some impact. Levies on mining royalties and payable to state governments are to be given to local communities, which could transform the well-being of those living in these districts. New pollution standards for coal plant technology – as strict as those anywhere – are in force, although with a worrying lack of enforcement.

As always though, any good news needs to be balanced with what is happening elsewhere. In an alarming development for India's environmentalists, the government in 2014 gave the go-ahead for a huge hydropower plant in a remote and pristine part of the country's north-east. 4,000 hectares of forest will be cleared in an area rich in biodiversity. The huge Dibang plant is one of hundreds of projects initially rejected in the past but now approved since the new government came to office. "The floodgates are open," warned an environmental researcher from Delhi. And then there was the 'Coalgate' corruption scandal. After it was discovered that every coal mining license allocated by the government between 1993 and 2009 had been granted in an "illegal and arbitrary" manner, the Modi government wants 46 of these mines to continue. Despite an estimated loss to the country of some $31 billion, development needs override all other considerations it seems.

And there are other worries. There are more than 17,000 glaciers in the Indus basin, that north-western area shared between Pakistan and India. 8,000 of these glaciers are in India, Jammu and Kashmir alone. The glaciers provide a natural reservoir for freshwater supplies to the Indus and its tributaries. The rich and fertile region – shaped by the Indus, Jhelum, Chenab, Beas, Ravi and Sutlej rivers – relies on melt water yet 'water stress' is increasingly a problem. Climate change "if the trend continues" will result "in an acute water shortage in the Indus basin in the coming decades," argue researchers monitoring the changes. The Indus Waters Treaty, agreed by Pakistan and India in 1960, today looks under threat as Prime Minister Modi claims that, "the waters in these rivers belong to India and our farmers." Climate change and water shortages provide a convenient basis for nationalist demands.

Massive water restructuring is not only a north-western concern. The country has begun work in 2016 on a huge river diversion programme that will channel water away from the north and west to drought-prone areas in the east and south. The project requires rerouting water from major rivers such as the Ganges and Brahmaputra and creating canals links to rivers in the south and east. This plan, argue environmentalists, could be a disaster for the local ecology. In addition, 100 million Bangladeshi people who live downstream of the rivers and rely on the rivers for their livelihoods are worried.

India is key to the future of global climate change. Together with China and the United States, the three countries are responsible for some 40% of global carbon emissions. Agreements and actions already made suggest some progress. India as the world's third largest emitter is again at one of those pivotal historical moments which will not only shape its own future but also our own.

Shit everywhere

When I was interviewing my group of 'frequent travellers' to

India regarding their views and experiences about everyday life in India in their travels around the country as tourists, they often raised interrelated issues that suggested they had quite a broad and wide understanding of the problems. 'Being poor' for example, was about more than so many dollars a day, important though that was. It was also a cultural identity – caste – religious thing. Food and being able to eat was obviously the bottom line; everything starts from this fact of life. But there were other concerns too. As Sany put it colourfully, "What shocks me the most is pretending to be animists and then there is this shit everywhere. It's a big paradox in India. It's OK for people to see shit and plastic bags everywhere and it doesn't shock them. They spend their time watching television and they don't see it is clean everywhere – soap operas, Bollywood movies? Don't they see it is clean?"

Jeff too highlights the rubbish. "It does wind me up a little. There seems to be a lack of concern about the environment. The plastic bag only came to India around 1994. I think before that everything must have been recycled bags. I was on the Rajasthani Express and I gave the young attendant some rubbish. I asked him if he could get rid of it as there were no bins on the train. And he just opened the train door and threw it outside." Things were not getting better, continued Jeff. "The smog in the cities is getting worse. In Bangalore, it is really bad."

Open defecating is but one dramatic, visible and measurable feature of the life in India. It is a complex issue that touches on issues of gender, well-being, poverty, the environment, and also health and hygiene. In a way it epitomises the 'new' and 'old' India, the differences between the rich and the poor and the caste inequalities that ravage the country.

Many things are invisible to us tourists. Other things are very visible and we wish they weren't. It is rare for example to be on a train leaving a city especially in the early morning and not see the hundreds of people defecating alongside the rail lines.

It is easy to imagine the humiliation and vulnerability of those forced into such behaviour. A staggering 70% of Indians living in villages – or some 550 million people – defecate in the open. This is also true for 13% of urban households. As the filmmaker Prahlad Kakkar put it graphically a few years ago, in Bombay "half the population doesn't have a toilet to shit in, so they shit outside. That's five million people. If they shit half a kilo each, that's two and half million kilos of shit each morning."

Nearly one in two people in other words defecate in the open in India. And yet, more people in India have access to or own a mobile phone connected to the mobile network. Despite having the highest numbers of people without access to toilets in the world, a United Nations report in 2014 also indicates that India is doing little to nothing to remedy the problem. As Gouri Choudhury from the NGO Action India wrote, "It's a question of belief in humanity [and] dignity, which somewhere along the line we seem to have lost." India's Southeast Asian neighbours such as Bangladesh and Vietnam have reduced open defecation to single percentages. Progress and big progress is possible. The report also notes that the countries with the highest open defecation figures have the highest number of deaths of children under the age of five, as well as high levels of undernutrition, high levels of poverty and large disparities between the rich and poor. Evidence again of Dréze and Sen's "interlocking and reinforcing levels of inequality and disempowerment." The absence of toilet facilities throughout the country, however, appears to be moving into mainstream policy agendas from its embarrassed invisibility. One of the reasons was the outcry over the horrific gang-rape and hanging from a tree of two young girls in a remote village in Uttar Pradesh in early 2014. Inter-caste tensions, patriarchal and misogynist attitudes underpinned the atrocity. The NPR website reported that lacking a toilet at home "on the night they were killed, the two teens did what hundreds of millions of women do across India each day. Under the cloak of darkness before sunrise or after sunset, they set out for an open field to relieve themselves." Women usually go out in pairs to avoid harassment. Guddo Devi a cousin of the two murdered girls said, "When we step out of the house we are scared. And we have to go in the mornings, in the evenings, and when we cannot stop ourselves, at times we go out in the afternoons as well... And there are no bathrooms. We don't have any sort of facility. We have to go out." Unfortunately, this horrific case is not unusual but the Uttar Pradesh incident provoked national anger.

Low cost, two pit designed toilets on a raised platform with swing doors, however, are available. Using very little water, these toilets biodegrade the waste for use as a fertiliser. Some entrepreneurs have paid to introduce these toilets to a number of villages but not in the numbers that seriously address the problems. Studies have found that there are cultural problems associated with using a toilet – linked to complex assumptions around purity and pollution. Learning needs to go hand in hand with new facilities.

A second reason for optimism is the recent pledge by Prime Minister Modi, as "one of the keystone efforts of his government", to expand sanitation in India and end open defecation. For Modi, elevating sanitation standards is part of the formula for tackling poverty and promoting outside investment. Open defecation is not good for business. By 2019, Modi plans to have a toilet in every household and school. The 'World Toilet Day' celebrations in November 2014 with its 700-kilogram cake shaped like a toilet, charity walks and pledges marked an encouraging start to eradicating a problem that, says the World Bank, could be costing India some $54 billion in health and medical costs.

Rubbish and environmental issues in India are issues that figure as media concerns when judged by newspaper and television coverage. Defecation is generally not one of them. However, deforestation together with noise, air and water pollution stories can be found in the press. For most tourists, however, it is solid waste pollution – plain old rubbish – that is usually commented upon, with good reason. It is not uncommon to monitor kilometre after kilometre trails of plastic debris along the rail lines, the denser the closer you are to urban centres. Thousands of torn plastic bags snagged in the thorn bushes provide an unwanted form of rural graffiti visible from speeding trains. In the towns and cities, large black crows squabble over rubbish piles often seen on the streets and pavements. Rivers and canals appear to be unofficial rubbish dumps. Given the fast-growing population densities of Indian cities, solid waste disposal is a massive problem. It is estimated that Indian cities generate around 100 million tonnes of solid waste a year. New Delhi alone throws away 10,000 tons a day and it is predicted to double in ten years. The municipal authorities are responsible for managing this rubbish, and modern rubbish trucks are not an uncommon site around cities. Since 2000 it has been a legal requirement for local authorities to have waste management programmes, recycling programmes and composting plans. Similar to many other countries, however, the problem is not plans, programmes or intentions. Rather it is a problem of implementation. The Organisation for Economic Co-operation and Development (OECD) estimates that up to 40% of municipal waste in India is simply not collected. There are new initiatives underway to deal with these problems. A few Indian cities, New Delhi for example, are establishing waste-to-energy projects, hoping to generate electricity from the collected rubbish. Privatisation of local solid waste programmes and of the employees have begun in a number of cities – always a sign of panic and absence of strategic solutions. Small, incremental signs of improvement though are visible. Rail stations in the big cities today are much cleaner than a few years ago with a noticeable absence of plastic bottles. Overall though I get the impression that solid waste pollution is a problem that threatens not only to grow rapidly throughout the country in the near future, but also to overwhelm local capacities and initiatives to deal with it.

It's not just tourists in the country that focus on the rubbish. Unfortunately, reports from around the world comment on the problem. Under the heading "'Incredible India' is getting incredibly trashed", there is an article from December 2013 in British daily newspaper the *Independent* which does nothing for the India tourist industry. "I was taking a photograph in a side street in the French quarter of Pondicherry," begins the article. "Elegant walls, balustrades, blue sky, all the colonial charm you've heard about. Snap. Then I moved the lens down a bit and to the left. Piles of debris. Newspapers, plastic bags, indeterminable food remains, rags, two stray dogs. The camera went snap – back in the bag." Most damaging of all is the conclusion: "After 10 or 12 visits to what the tourist board calls – and which often is – Incredible India, I am, for the first time, getting discouraged from going again."

'So, how is India?'

'How is India?' is a question often asked by North American friends to Professor Ananya Mukherjee. In short, her answer is, that "by and large, people continue to struggle, negotiate and survive as best they can, often winning victories that defy textbook understandings of agency and politics." Underlying any dominant narrative about 'India today' is "a deeply exclusionary and unequal material reality. Some 200 million are chronically hungry," she continues, "90% of the workforce have no option but informal work with abysmal wages and no security; 80% live under $2 a day; 70% depend on agriculture for their livelihood; 182,936 farmers have committed suicide and so on."

In August 2017, Indians celebrated their 70th year of Independence. Amidst the celebratory discussions was the enormous pride attached to the country's economic prowess. In terms of purchasing power, India is today the third largest economy, overtaking Japan. It is closing the gap on China, but perhaps more importantly for local consumption is eight times larger than that of Pakistan. It is looked upon enviously by most other countries from around the world given its very favourable demographic profile (lots of young people), a valuable technology-related services sector, plentiful natural resources, an open information economy and a desire for trade partnerships from around the world. A number of international agencies and commentaries expect the economic successes to continue in the decades ahead. Moreover, the large and wealthy international diaspora of around 25–30 million Indians not only seem to be enthusiastically Modi BJP supporters but, more importantly, are responsible for considerable remittances each year – around $70 billion per year. Rapid urbanisation coupled with uninterrupted democracy and peaceful transitions of power add to this optimism. Few other countries can rival this combination of assets and circumstances. No world leader worth his or her salt has not been seen beating a pathway to Modi's India. Although there has been no economic 'big bang' moment under Modi, the global consensus seems to be that his first few years have been sensible, well-planned infrastructural reforms aimed at building the economy. These same commentators together with majority opinion in India itself are listing their priorities for the next few years and they include the usual suspects. First, further bouts of privatisation, especially in public service provision such as education which remains restricted to private investment. Second, cut back strongly on the subsidies for food, fertilisers and fuels. 'Very inefficient' and a drain on fiscal resources, it is argued. Third, sort out the Employment Guarantee Scheme. Fourth, increase foreign investment. Fifth, sort out the country's archaic, inflexible labour laws. In sum, "India has the strong fundamentals necessary for continued macroeconomic success" if it tackles some of these "structural blockages." The creation of special economic zones is seen as a good way forward where the bureaucracy can be bypassed, and new laws and rules implemented that illustrate the irresistibility of change. Another dose of the neoliberal medicine, in other words.

Poverty is an embarrassment for any country keen on projecting itself as a global superpower in waiting. What is not usually mentioned in the dominant narratives and perspectives relating to India's economic success story is this issue of poverty and inequality. The list of reforms suggested for the Modi government mentioned above will do little to alleviate these problems. It might be argued that increased economic success will trickle down to wider groups, or that increased profits lead to more productive investments or that booming companies result in the growth of more jobs and growth of incomes, or that failure to attract large capital results in them going elsewhere. Empirically these fairy tales don't add up as the International Labour Office and, even recently, the International Monetary Fund have argued. Instead we have the growth of crazy bonuses, increased dividends to shareholders and 'jobless growth'. Poverty and inequality is a political problem, not an economic one. The only group to benefit from low-distribution policies are the super-rich. From a global perspective there has been astonishing growth in the developing world. Almost 30 countries have officially gained middle-income status over the last couple of decades – countries which include India, Zambia and Ghana. And yet India remains home to one-third of the world's poorest people. The combined net worth of the 46 Indian billionaires in 2012 is roughly equivalent to 10% of the country's GDP – equivalent to 424 billionaires in the US. For the majority of India's poor, they are caught in a hereditary problem. In a number of studies over the last thirty years, the *Chronic Poverty Research Centre* (CPRC) have concluded that over 50% of Indians are the 'chronic poor' – that is, those that remain poor throughout their lifetime. Moreover, there is a geographical pattern to this chronic poverty. There are 15 regions across six states where poverty is being concentrated and chronic. And the people in the tribal and forested or degraded forested regions are more likely to remain poor forever.

For a small number of commentators, the shame of India's poor is not accidental. As John Pilger for example notes, "India has become a model of the imperial cult of neoliberalism – almost everything must be privatised, sold off... (which) has produced in India a dystopia of extremes that is a spectre for all of us." Of course, India is not striking out on some new innovative path. It is following the new economic mantras that shape most of the Western economies today. In the sixth richest country in the world – Britain – we have an advanced model of what India is about to introduce. As mentioned earlier, Oxfam, the charity campaigning around development issues, has released a report entitled "A Tale of Two Britains" which maps out the gross and widening inequality driven by British governments over the last few decades. The extent and increasing nature of this inequality is illustrated by the variety of political measures introduced to protect the already wealthy at the expense of the majority of the population. The current $18 billion cuts to the British public welfare bill indicate that the most vulnerable will bear the costs of the restructuring. Meanwhile Britain is at the centre of a global tax system designed to evade payment of any tax. One-third of all global tax dodging is held in UK territories and dependencies amounting to at least $7.18 trillion. All this against a background of some 800,000 falling into absolute poverty. As the current British government is demonstrating, this is not all about economics. As in Modi's India, neoliberalism is ultimately about the creation of a new political settlement, about the building of a new 'common sense' which explains how things work, what things are important and what needs to be prioritised in the future.

'How is India doing?' Maybe Dréze and Sen can have the final word. There has been, they demonstrate, "an extraordinary tolerance of inequalities, stratification and caste divisions – accepted as allegedly necessary parts of social order." Any Government in India needs to have this conclusion emblazoned upon the entrance to its workplace.

Chapter 9

The "good days are ahead"

The great experiment

I have visited India a number of times since our first visit in 2003, travelling to different parts of the country and meeting many friendly local people who have always been happy to share with me their local stories, worries and hopes for the future. Our discussions and the places I visited, as usual, raised more questions than answers – one of the great attractions of being a tourist. Increasingly though, it seemed to me that India, and South Asia more generally, hasn't received in the West the attention its history and position today merits. In the West, India struggles to escape from contrasts with and the shadow from China. This Western media focus reflects largely the narrow economic and military agendas driving our domestic and global interests. We either wanted trade deals or to sell to India the newest military hardware. Occasionally, headlines will make the front pages of our newspapers; in the main, they play to a small number of stereotypes. Absent from most media attention are the surprises, bewilderment, joys, puzzlement and exhilaration that confront any half-nosy overseas tourist to the country. The absence of a serious and continuing media attention today is even more surprising given the case that the region must be one of, if not the, most crisis-prone part of the world. Wars, nuclear weapons and historically hostile neighbourly relations of suspicion and distrust characterise the region. Political developments and actions by the largest of the regional players – India – matter to everyone. And yet events in this part of the world are not characterised by their shared aspirations and interests but by their divisions and hatred. The continuing human costs have been great. The recent thirty-year civil war in Sri Lanka is only the most recent example of the murderous nature and brutal character of these communal hatreds. A by-product of this historical legacy is the twenty million strong diaspora residing outside of the region. Their returning cash remittances have continued to keep economies afloat but also to fund and sustain these communal divisions and conflicts. The lot of the "midnight's descendants", as John Keay describes them in his recent study, is a precarious and volatile one but one that could affect everyone. Politics do matter.

Alongside the burgeoning Indian economy, most visitors are aware of the country being the 'world's biggest democracy'. If they didn't know, it will be mentioned in all likelihood somewhere in their tourist discussions and reading. Indians justifiably are very proud of this fact. Together with its claims of secularism and harmonious territorial integrity, India's democratic nature is commonly seen as one of its great defining attributes. Elections are fair and regular, a vigorous press and independent judiciary and a linguistic diversity that is symbolic of integrating democracy with diversity are well documented. As Ramachandra Guha notes, India "is the world's most unnatural nation and its least likely democracy. Never before had a single political unit been created out of so many diverse parts. Never before had the franchise been granted to a desperately poor and largely illiterate population." Winston Churchill's response to the 1930s claims for political independence was both typical and predictable. If the British were to leave he argued, "India will fall back quite rapidly through the centuries into barbarism and privations of the Middle Ages." It wasn't only the colonial dinosaurs that forecast political catastrophes ahead; in 1967 the Delhi correspondent of *The Times* (of London) wrote that: "the great experiment of developing India within a democratic experiment has failed." Many others too felt that the massive problems of population numbers, poverty, literacy, cultural and linguistic diversity, religion, caste, gender and ethnic difference provided insurmountable obstacles. "When Nehru goes, the government will become a military dictatorship," wrote Aldous Huxley.

Sixteen general elections later India seems to be doing OK. At one level, it is an uplifting story. While most of the country's neighbours vote into office military generals, India ploughs on with "its great experiment". There hasn't been a process of military rule or Balkanisation. Instead, in the 2014 general election, some 814 million people were eligible to vote with around 150 million being first-time voters. As *The New York Times* put it, "the sheer size of the electorate makes this election the largest in the world and an inspiring celebration of universal adult suffrage." Five million people were required to administer the election with a similar number of police involved in the six weeks covering the nine phases of voting in the various states and regions. 930,000 polling stations were ready for this 16th general election since Independence with just under 1.5 million electronic voting machines. 543 seats were up for election to the Lok Sabha (Parliament). The statistics all involved huge numbers and were reported throughout the world's media during the elections. Apart from the political issues and likely results of the election there was this fascination from around the world with the logistics and bewildering complexities of 'democracy in action'. And as was reported excitedly in most countries, the National Democratic Alliance led by the Bharatiya Janata Party (BJP) won a sweeping victory with 336 seats (of which the BJP itself won 282 seats). The previous government of the United Progressive Alliance led by the Indian Congress Party took a miserable 58 seats (of which 44 were won by the Congress). The crushing victory of the BJP resulted in it being the first party since the 1984 general election to govern without the support of other parties. Once again and for a short while, India was the focus of the world's media. As Narendra Modi tweeted, the "good days are ahead." The tweet became India's most retweeted post after the 2014 election.

I was in India for the last two general elections, in 2009 and 2014. Not surprisingly the closer to the election date, the more the national and local newspapers were filled with election news. Because of the importance of political alliances between the national parties with those that are regionally based, the news for me as a tourist was difficult to follow. Just over 50 parties (registered with the Election Commission) were involved in the election. The personalities and the often family dynastic-based nature of the state parties resulted in a marginalisation of issues. Mention of individuals seemed to be a proxy means of summarising substantive issues – difficult to follow if you are a visitor to the country but more intelligible to local participants. In 2014 there was a noticeable edge of excitement and anticipation to the election given the consistent high opinion poll ratings for the BJP and the poor showing of the Congress Party over the last few years. I remember that in the previous election of 2009 there was surprise that the Congress Party had managed to win. This time there was little surprise. Perhaps the only surprise was the extent of the BJP's victory. The controversial nature of the BJP and its leader together with its huge number of seats led to much speculation about the future of India – economically, socially and religiously – in the post-election period.

In February 2014, I was travelling around Tamil Nadu in south-east India having arrived in Bangalore by plane from Europe. Here the particularities and complexities of Indian politics became apparent. This is 'the south', a shorthand for a distinctive history and people different to the more northern states. As mentioned earlier, the southern states suffered less historically from conquering people that periodically overran northern India. The three great dynasties that ruled and shaped the south over a period of a thousand years – the Cholas, the Pallavas and the Pandyans – developed their own distinct cultural and religious traditions. Tamil, one of the more popular

Dravidian languages spoken in southern India, has provided a strong and distinctive continuing link to ancient customs, devotional practices and classical culture. This distinctiveness has also shaped the politics of Tamil Nadu. A strong nationalist movement has characterised politics in the state over the last sixty years. A more anti-Brahmin, anti-Hindi, pro-poor outlook has been the defining quality of the political campaigns. The All India Anna Dravida Munnetra Kazhagam (AIADMK) under the popular but firm grip of the state's Chief Minister Jayaram Jayalalithaa (fondly referred to as Amma) won 37 out of the 39 parliamentary seats available in the state. Clearly there was no Modi-mania in Tamil Nadu. A previous film star, a Dalit and with numerous run-ins with the courts over charges of fraud and corruption, Jayalalithaa was a dominant political figure with a national profile. It's ironical, given the strong patriarchal culture of India, that three regional women Chief Ministers were seen as possible 'kingmakers' in the 2014 election. There was of course Jayalalithaa in Tamil Nadu, Mamata Banerjee in West Bengal and, finally, Mayawati Kumari in Uttar Pradesh. All three women came from poor backgrounds (although Mayawati is far from poor!) and, through a variety of ploys, contested and outfought opponents in the brutal, murky and male-dominated world of Indian politics. All three shared a mixture of populism and welfare provision underpinned by a strong display of personality cultishness.

This personality business was evident as I wandered around Chennai. Huge posters of Amma were evident everywhere and helped distract from the heat and humidity. In the main, they tended to be large rectangular posters depicting a face or full portrayal. Authority and control with a touch of intimacy and friendliness seemed to be the message behind the poses. In contrast to these 2014 election posters, there are the earlier more famous flamboyant designs promoting Amma. There is this famous photograph of a gigantic hoarding of Amma on the

Marina promenade that captures the populist and personality-centred nature of the state's politics. Other posters said to be have been paid for and promoted by 'grateful citizens' have Jayalalithaa centre stage, being applauded by a plethora of world leaders including those from North America, Japan, North Korea and Russia. There are other posters with this theme repeated. Then there is this roadside poster showing Jayalalithaa on the left, and in huge lettering, the message, "You are the unbeaten king. You always make the right move. You are our champion." on the right of the poster. And these are big posters, far bigger than would be allowed in Europe – perhaps eight by ten metres and usually supported by bamboo poles. Maybe this is not too surprising given the incestuous relationship between the powerful Tamil film industry and political parties – Jayalalitha came to prominence as an actress in Tamil cinema in the 1960s. The politicisation of the film industry provided a rich source of stories depicting Dalit-inspired victories against high caste baddies. Or again, the poster well-wishers might be reflecting the autocratic, hierarchical and dynastic features that characterise much of Indian politics. Whatever the reasons it is clear from the 2014 election results that something is working for the AIADMK party under Jayalalithaa. In December 2016, Jayalalitha, Chief Minister for some fourteen years, died.

Modi and the India of 2014

The results of the general election were stunning and, for a brief time, the issues of Indian politics were a major focus of the world's media. I had returned home from India by the time of polling but followed events closely. Perhaps in anticipation of surprises, newspapers and television channels in Europe and I'm sure elsewhere outlined some of the issues and personalities involved. Much analysis and reporting struggled to make sense of this post-election India.

At one level, the results were not a surprise. The BJP under

Narendra Modi was expected to win although the number of seats won (282 by the BJP alone from a total of 543 seats) was a surprise. This majority gives Modi the ability to govern alone unfettered by the constraints of alliance partners. Amongst the reasons given for this landslide was the economy. Under the last Congress government economic growth had slowed from around 8–9% to less than 5%. Not since the introduction of neo-liberal policies in the 1990s has India experienced such a wobble. The rupee was down strongly against world currencies – dropping by 20% – and a looming balance of payments was apparent. Price increases for food staples such as vegetables were rocketing. For the growing middle class these were worrying times.

However, it was not only a deteriorating economy that worried voters. Corruption in everyday life has traditionally been a feature of 'getting through' but had reached new heights of despair in the last four or five years. It encouraged a culture of patronage and favouritism which allowed senior politicians in particular to hand out business contracts and licenses. The corrosion of public institutions remains a particular source of anger. The lack of trust in the police and in local and national government officials is endemic as reported by the organisation, Transparency International: the global coalition against corruption. Connection to energy utilities or entrance to schools requires the traditional backhander. As mentioned earlier, a number of national scandals such as those surrounding the 2010 Commonwealth Games continued to be a major embarrassment to India on the world stage and a deep source of anger to its people. Then there were the 40 billion dollars stolen from the Treasury by the Communications Minister through selling the broadband spectrum at massively undervalued prices. The popular but short-lived anti-corruption protests and rallies under the social activist Kisan Baburao Hazare seemed to indicate for a moment anyway that people and the middle class in particular had had enough of these scams. The spectacular success of the new anti-corruption Aam Aadmi Party – the Common Man Party – in Delhi in recent years was evidence of this revolt against corruption.

Another factor accounting for the Modi landslide was the woeful campaign of the Congress Party. Most of the commentary in the British and, to a lesser extent, the Indian press mentioned the poor and unexciting campaign performances of Rahul Gandhi, leader of the Party and the latest incumbent of a well-known family! Lacklustre in front of the television cameras and unexciting when addressing campaign rallies, the historical allure of the Gandhi-Nehru brand fast disappeared. But it was not only a case of an absence of charismatic leadership in the Congress campaign, important as this is in India's increasingly 'presidential' style elections. More importantly, the election possibly heralded the end of the dynastic family Congress Party and possibly even the Party itself that emerged in the split in 1969, engineered by Rahul's grandmother Indira Gandhi. As Rahul himself remarked in 2013, "I am not afraid to say that the Congress has become moribund. It has scarcely a single leader with a modern mind... Congress has never succeeded into evolving into a modern political party," as was reported by Hartosh Singh Bal in *The Caravan*, January 2013. Increasingly dependent on the Gandhi brand and masked by the surprising 2009 general election success, the Congress Party had been shown to be in the main at least an empty political shell devoid of the basic organisational requirements especially at the local level necessary to win elections. Irrespective of one's views on the BJP, this was not the case in the BJP's organisation. They had recruited the local activists, they had built the local branch organisation, they organised the training of the cadre and they successfully mobilised their 'base' at opportune moments. Given the difficulty of addressing 'one' electorate in a country so vast and different at state and national level, the BJP professionally and slickly presented one man as the leader and national focus.

Newspapers reported that Modi had flown 300,000 kilometres and addressed 457 rallies during the campaign. These efforts were greatly and gratefully helped by an election war chest of an estimated 500 million pounds on the individual campaign of Modi. There is no limit on the spending by political parties as opposed to individual candidates. Much of this treasure chest came from eager corporate sponsors. They will be expecting a payback. The Congress Party by contrast, in their third period of office from 2009–2014, failed to get the 'faithful' out, failed to deal with the corruption, patronage and mismanagement charges of the last five years and failed to outline a convincing narrative and strategy for the country. They looked exhausted. The 2014 elections seemed to confirm the withering away of the Party. It could be argued that there is nothing left for Rahul to reform; the increasing importance of patronage and sycophantic adherents has resulted in a much reduced and weakened entity. In Delhi, the Congress lost in every seat. A party which had been in power for all but 18 of the last 67 years had been reduced to a historic humbling. William Dalrymple in an excellent article on the Indian election in the British journal *New Statesman* argued that the last few years of Congress government under the leadership of Dr Manmohan Singh had: "retreated into a vast programme of rural benefits and agriculture welfarism." This he argues could not be afforded and was typical of initiatives that have "hobbled the Indian economy for much of its post-independence history and which Singh (Finance Minister and later Prime Minister) initially won so many plaudits for reversing at the beginning of his ministerial career." As discussed in an earlier chapter, this is not a view that I share. If one is looking for plaudits resulting from 'freeing' the economy from its 'over-regulated', 'anti-private sector', welfare-heavy direction, then it seems to me that Mr Modi is going to massively outdo Mr Singh in the plaudit stakes.

Also mentioned in an earlier chapter, an important part of

Modi's appeal and of the BJP's campaign was his proclaimed 'success' in the management of the state of Gujarat which he has run since 2001. The 2014 campaign slogan based on his time in Gujarat was "Development For All". Modi appears to like slogans and his "Vibrant Gujarat" branding was to publicise the big business friendly, economically dynamic and politically stable state under his leadership. Some other commentators were more critical. According to Aditya Chakrabortty writing in 2014, "running Gujarat was based on handing cut-price land and soft loans to big business, who in turn flew him around in private jets. This brought cash into the state, but very little of it has been shared out beyond big cities such as Ahmedabad." Under Modi the Gujarat economy has tripled in size. His reforms of the electricity industry in the state (a source of grumbles and anger throughout India) resulted in Gujarat having one of the best and most reliable industries in the country; judges were required to work extra hours to clear the backlog of cases, and annual industry 'summits' provided publicity and investment pledges of significant sums. In 2008, Tata Motors moved its car plant from Communist-run West Bengal to Gujarat, an issue of major economic and political significance in India. According to the website, *openDemocracy*, this investment by Tata received a state subsidy that was at least 3–4 times greater and at a 0.1% interest rate that did not need to begin to be repaid for 20 years. "This was in addition to getting land at throwaway prices, free electricity and tax breaks." In 2011 Ford motorcars invested $1 billion in another new car plant. Gujarat was seen to be a state on the move and Mr Modi was seen as its driving force. As an article in the *Outlook* put it after the results of the 2014 election had been declared, "The stock market and the business community can hardly contain their jubilation. India's messiah with the magic wand has arrived." As discussed in an earlier chapter, less often mentioned was Gujarat's poor record on infant mortality, poverty and literacy rates.

Of course, the charges of aggressive corporate campaigning and funding for 'their' candidate together with issues of corruption and a sycophantic media are not particular to Indian politics or elections. Indeed, India and even the BJP under Modi has a lot to learn on these issues from politics and elections from the US and from the 'home' of parliamentary democracy, Britain. Speaking in 2016 for example, the noted anti-mafia journalist Roberto Saviano identified as the most corrupt country in the world not Afghanistan, Nigeria or India but Britain – or more particularly, London. The capital's banking institutions were key components, he argued, of 'criminal capitalism' which laundered drug money through offshore networks. Drug trafficking revenues are greater than that from the oil companies – cocaine alone is a £300 billion a year business. Furthermore, it is through Britain that 90% of the owners of capital in London have their headquarters offshore. The Anti-Corruption International Summit in London in 2016 came and went with little notice or expected impact. Maybe Francis Fukuyama is right when he suggests, first, that corruption has become the defining issue of the present century, and second, that the main reason for this is the weakening and fragile modern state. While there may be some truth in this, it is not the whole story. The leaked Panama Papers with the Fonseca law firm at the centre of the scandal provided a glimpse and only a glimpse of systematic tax evasion totalling to date around $2 billion perpetuated by companies and wealthy individuals. Kept under protective cover by British governments of various political persuasions, these offshore havens such as the British Virgin Islands have been used by those with wealth to hide from around the globe. Governments throughout the rich Western economies are complicit as "enablers of economic crime", as the anti-corruption organisation Global Witness puts it. Fragile states are part of the problem but the real culprits are the politicians from the 1980s onwards who have promoted the need for 'austerity' – shorthand for transferring wealth from the poorest to the richest. And commentators were surprised by the election of Donald Trump in America?

For us in the West, corruption is something that happens elsewhere, usually in emerging economies. The use of an extremely narrow definition of 'corruption' is a feature of a long tradition that portrays corruption as something limited to poor countries – that is, primarily something about bribes. Absent is a concern with systemic tax evasion, political funding patterns that buy influence and prestige, the channelling of public funding into private corporations through 'reforms' such as Public Finance Initiative and privatisation activities, massive defrauding and mis-selling of the public by financial institutions and the easy interchange between political and corporation offices. We tend to forget the fines of $123 million on Ernst and Young over its sale of tax avoidance schemes, or the earlier fine of $456 million on KPMG after it admitted to a fraud that generated at least $11 billion in fraudulent tax avoidance schemes. The fines of $2.6 billion for Credit Suisse, $780 million for UBS and the $554 million for Deutsche Bank can be added to the hall of fame tax avoidance stars. We could also try and explain to a visitor to Britain about the relationship between donations to political parties and ending up in the House of Lords, but they wouldn't believe it. India has indeed much to learn from Western economies. We might not bribe in an everyday way, but corruption is rife and 'crony capitalism' under recent British governments showed how hollowed out had become 'the home of parliamentary democracy'. In the US, the situation is no better with the domination of politics by big money being a widely-accepted feature of American democracy over the last 60–70 years. The latest examples in 2016 of this relationship between money and political influence were the John Doe files detailing over 1,500 pages of how millions of dollars are secretly donated by major corporations and very rich individuals to third party groups to sway elections. The list of culprits reads like a who's who of large corporations, Republican Party politicians as well as one Donald Trump.

And as a footnote, perhaps it would be useful to have a little more history and accountability about the role of looting and stolen assets by Western powers in countries for example such as Nigeria, Sri Lanka, Tunisia and India.

In the post-election analysis, the scale of the BJP's victory did throw up some interesting features. Young people were seen as a major force behind, and beneficiary from, the results. Around 100 million voters cast a vote for the first time and some pollsters estimated that up to 90% of 18–25 year olds voted for Modi. Furthermore the party appears surprisingly to have picked up significant votes in rural areas with some suggesting this reflected increased economic activity in the villages and smaller towns. And it is worth remembering that the undisputed winner of the election is a son of tea stall owner and is seen as an outsider of the political circles concentrated in Delhi. There was, however, a building inevitability, a Modi bandwagon visible as the elections approached. Media focus was seven times greater than on Rahul and, from my perusal of the daily press leading up to the election, reflected an increasingly pro-Modi perspective. A number of well-known authors, celebrities and commentators switched allegiance and came out enthusiastically endorsing Modi. Modi was now, it was suggested, a moderate developmentalist. And then in April, *Time* magazine of India headlined "Modi Gets a Bollywood Boost". Two well-known Bollywood Muslim stars endorsed Modi and launched a version of Modi's official website in Urdu. Urdu is the mother tongue of many of India's Muslims. As William Dalrymple summed up in his article written just before the election, the election "represents the whole world of contestations: left against right, insider against outsider, secular Nehruvian vs. sectarian nationalist, Brahminical dynastic princeling vs. lower-caste, working-class self-made man." It is little wonder that much of the world's media were fascinated for a brief time anyway by the 2014 contest.

However, all was not plain sailing. It was this issue of "sectarian nationalist" as Dalrymple put it, and in particular the March 2002 pogrom in Gujarat under Modi's leadership that was also of interest and comment in the international press. Within six months of Modi becoming First Minister of Gujarat, around 2,000 mostly Muslims were killed and about 200,000 people made homeless in an intercommunal bloodbath characterised by its planned, coordinated nature and by its savagery. The trigger for this outbreak of violence was an attack on a train carrying Hindu activists and pilgrims back from a ceremony in Ayodhya. Ten years earlier, a mosque – the Babri Mosque – said to have been built on the birthplace of one of the Hindu gods, Lord Ram, had been destroyed by Hindu activists in Ayodhya. This destruction of the mosque led to one of the worst episodes of communal violence in India since Independence. Modi has always denied his involvement in the riots, has never apologised for his government's lack of protection of the minorities and never shown remorse, although some of his political associates have been charged and imprisoned. The British and US governments made clear at this time that Modi was not welcome in their countries. His election as leader of the BJP government in 2014 hastily led to a reversal of this position and he was soon welcomed to both countries.

Modi's only reported expression of regret for the pogroms in 2002 compared them to a car running over a puppy while calling Muslim relief camps "baby making factories". He refuses to take questions on the issue, instead walking out of interviews. A report by Human Rights Watch, writes Dalrymple, asserted that his administration was complicit in the massacres and that there was extensive participation of the police and state government officials. Several formal investigations through the courts, however, have failed to convict Modi while at the same time not exonerating him from involvement.

Interwoven with the 2002 killings is the association of the BJP and Modi in particular with the notion of 'Hindutva' (Hinduness) and organisationally with, as Amit Chaudhuri writes, "disciplinarian, quasi-militant, extreme right-wing outfit, the Rashtriya Swayamsevak Sangh [RSS]," also known as the Sangh. Modi has been a lifelong member of the RSS which, as Pankaj Mishra notes, is "a paramilitary Hindu nationalist organisation inspired by the fascist movements of Europe, whose founders believed that Nazi Germany had manifested 'race pride at its highest' by purging the Jews." It was a former member of the RSS who murdered Gandhi in 1948 for being too soft on Muslims. "I got inspiration to live for the nation from the RSS. I learned to live for others, and not myself. I owe it all to the RSS," said Modi. Seeing the last Congress government under Mohammed Singh as only "working for the Muslims", sexual violence towards women as being the result of "Western ideas" and today's India being a colonial stunted creation and mere shadow of the "greater Bharat" stretching from Afghanistan to Indonesia, the RSS remains a formidable and organisational, influential political and religious presence. Present at most Modi political rallies were young men from the Bajrang Dal, a right-wing, hardline youth organisation dedicated to a muscular and revivalist version of Hinduism. Many are armed with ceremonial swords, others with combat knives and big-bladed hatchets. Throughout Indian cities especially in the poorest sections, thousands of RSS and Bajrang Dal groups meet daily at first light, sing and pray to 'Mother India', complete their drill sessions and then head off to get the voters out.

Quite how close and involved the RSS will be in the Modi government is at the moment not known. The influential but publicity-shy RSS is at the apex of a loose confederation of Hindu nationalist organisations, of which the BJP is the political wing. As Andrew Whitehead reports when reviewing Rajdeep Sardesai's book, *2014: The Election That Changed India*, the RSS is at the end of the day the final word within the Saffron 'family'. At the heart of this family and of the RSS is Hindutva – the belief that India's billion strong Hindus are burdened by the weight of centuries of Muslim and colonial rule. The secular tradition and trappings of public and political life, they argue, are too forgiving to religious minorities and not sufficiently respectful to Hindu values and traditions.

Modi has already demonstrated that he is prepared to reject key aspects of the RSS agenda, such as building a temple on the disputed site at Ayodhya. As Jason Burke who covered the elections for *The Guardian* asks, how much of the RSS agenda will be incorporated into government policy and could Modi restrain their campaigns if he so chooses? While Modi at the moment anyway is keeping some distance from the RSS, some of his more enthusiastic followers are less restrained. Kashmir is often mentioned and there is talk and activities of 'reconversion' to Hinduism or 'Ghar Wapsi' – the Hindutva belief that all Indians are really Hindus but have simply strayed from the true path. There are also complaints about intercommunal marriages and isolated acts of violence against non-Hindu individuals and villages.

There has been, however, some critical discussion of the Modi victory in the Indian press. An example is the commentary in the daily paper *The Hindu* by Nissim Mannathukkaren in March 2014. He discusses the various processes whereby the "banalisation of evil" takes place. As he puts it, "a terrifyingly fascinating (example of this process) is now underway in the election campaign (in) the trivialisation and normalisation of the Gujarat pogrom, to pave the way for the crowning of the emperor." He continues further on in the article with an even stronger line. "Fascism is in the making," he writes, "when economics and development are amputated from ethics and an overriding conception of human good, and violence against minorities becomes banal... And if India actually believes this election to be a moral dilemma, then the conscience of the land of Buddha and Gandhi is on the verge of imploding."

I have come across this coupling of 'fascism' with 'Modi' a few times in the media. In an Opinion piece for example in the *Times of India* in March 2014, Kanti Bajpai notes that, "There is every danger that a Modi-led India will be an India marked by soft fascism. At its core, fascism stands for state authoritarianism, intimidation by conservative-minded extra-legal groups, national chauvinism, submission of individuals and groups to a larger-than-life leader, and a Darwinian view of social life (the strong must prevail)." Kanti continues to argue "at least in the first instance" fascism will feature as the soft variety rather than hard fascism. Then there is an article on the *Kafila* website that talks of confronting "communal fascism". However, most thinkers and political analyses, I think, would not see the BJP or Modi as fascist; although right-wing, pro-capital, religiously extreme and politically authoritarian, there are not the context and political characteristics that defined the fascist parties of Europe. Additionally, there are the complexities of Hindutva which muddies the association of fascism with the BJP.

However, as perhaps was expected, critical comment on Modi is not encouraged. As Surjit S. Bhalla wrote in the daily *The Indian Express* shortly after the election, "to the best of my knowledge no individual in India or world history has been unjustly vilified as much as Modi has been. This vilification continues today, especially by the 'sickular' parties and their left-intellectual stormtroopers." Watch out, all you 'stormtroopers' – there is likely to be much more of this generous and tolerant view to discussion and disagreement in the years ahead! As Arundhati Roy remarked after the election, "Now we have a democratically elected totalitarian government."

India's democratic 'top dressing'

In a way, the Indian 2014 general election and landslide by the

BJP brought to a head a number of larger issues which have been rumbling away for some time – indeed, ever since Independence. Two of these issues are big, big issues – namely, the nature of democracy in India, and secondly, its claims to be a secular society. Maybe it was the shock of the Modi victory, the baggage that accompanies the BJP or the encroaching Hindu militancy and intimidation on everyday life unleashed by the victory that returned commentary and interest to these topics. Maybe they never disappeared, but instead, were resting for a while. Whatever the reasons, the issues of democracy and secularism once again were the focus of increasing comment and debate.

The post 2014 Lok Sabha (Parliament) has its lowest ever Muslim representation – 4% of a 14% population share. For the first time ever, India's largest state (200 million and the world's sixth most populous) – Uttar Pradesh – has no Muslim Member of Parliament despite constituting around a fifth of the population. And the first-past-the-post electoral system resulted in the country's fourth largest party the Dalit Bahujan Samaj Party (BSS) with 4% of the vote having no member in Parliament. Similarly the Congress Party which has historically benefited enormously from this electoral system was greatly disadvantaged this time around. India remains in many important ways "the greatest show of democracy in the world" as Ramachandra Guha wrote in 2012. Few people in 1947 gave India's proclamation to constitutional democracy much chance. But helpfully, Guha also drew attention to a number of worries and concerns around the greatest show – "pervasive faultlines," as he calls them.

Firstly, he identifies the threat to democracy of the territorial unity of the country. In three states – Nagaland, Manipur and of course, Kashmir – there are claims for independence backed by military activities. These situations are 'normalised' only through the presence of massive military strength by the central government. Secondly, Guha identifies the continuing struggles of the tribal communities aided by the 'Maoists' insurgency against mining companies and loss of lands in a number of states. Thirdly, there is the threat of religious fundamentalism from a number of sources that have often resulted in murderous pogroms. Fourthly, there is the problem of "the corrosion of public institutions". He mentions here the conversion of political parties into family firms, the politicisation of the police and bureaucracy, everyday corruption and huge scandals at the national level of government. The fifth threat to the democratic system is seen as the environmental degradation increasingly pervading the country. Examples given by Guha here are water pollution, chemical contamination of the soil and the continuing decimation of forests and biodiversity. The final threat given by Guha is the growing and gross economic inequalities. As he puts it, "The super rich exercise massive influence over politicians of all parties, with policies and laws framed or distorted to suit their interests."

This is a formidable list and charge sheet but Guha is not alone in his concerns about the nature and future of the country's political system. Andre Beteille, the doyen of Indian sociology, is another commentator who has discussed the understandings and practices of Indian democracy over a lengthy period of time and in popular outlets. One of his main points relates to the gap between the huge attention focused on the Constitution to the detriment of a focus on custom and culture. Irrespective of the claims and guarantees of equality in the Constitution, "everyday life is still governed substantially by hierarchical attitudes and sentiments carried over from the past," he writes. There is this gap or gulf, Beteille seems to be saying, between the formal, bureaucratised rituals of political parties and behaviour on the one hand, with existence and beliefs of many constituents especially the poor and those in rural areas on the other. Although he doesn't mention them, perhaps Beteille had in mind also the large number of Parliamentary members with criminal cases against them (around 30%), roughly the same percentage of members coming from "political families" and the widespread belief that politics is one of the quickest ways of becoming wealthy. A third of all Congress members in the previous administration inherited their seat through family connections and every one of them under the age of 35. It looks like the Lok Sabha (Parliament) increasingly is a club for the super-rich. Before the last elections one in five members were dollar millionaires; the total assets of all 543 members were estimated to be two billion dollars. And this is in a society where over half the population live on less than two dollars a day.

Today the gap between laws and customs and between the ruled and the rulers remains as wide today as it was at Independence. In a later 2012 article Beteille takes this concern with the malfunctioning democratic institutions in India a little further. Unlike other countries, India's democratic institutions did not evolve or renew themselves through conflict and turmoil. There was not this "churning", as Beteille puts it, in India. The argument for democracy emerged as part of the struggle against the British – a demand raised before the institutions were created and established on the ground around the country and reaching into everyday life. As Beteille reminds us, it was this structural weakness that led BR Ambedkar to argue, "that democracy in India is only a top-dressing on an Indian soil that is essentially democratic." Beteille's article finishes on a worrying note: "(W)e must recognise that the arguments about the virtues of democracy that served us well during the struggle for independence are not enough to bind us together now."

Journalist Simon Denyer, who has recently authored a book on democracy in India, agrees with Beteille. There is "this tension between Nehruvian ideals of a secular, democratic nation and India's dysfunctional parliament," he suggests. It is this dual nature of Indian democracy that is at the heart of understanding India. This reference back to Independence that Guha, Beteille and Denyer make when discussing democracy is not accidental or unusual. So too do Dréze and Sen in their study *An Uncertain Glory* that has been used in earlier chapters. There have been identifiable "flaws in India's practice of constitutional democracy" since the time of Nehru onwards. As examples of "lapses from democratic practice", the authors raise and discuss a number of examples which are not dissimilar to those raised by Guha. Top of their list is Kashmir which "is the most prominent case of infringement of democratic norms in India." Other cited examples similar to the Kashmir case are the separatist movements in the north-east where the "strategy of brutal suppression not only results in the violation of many basic human rights, but also it often ends up aggravating the situation." The Maoist rebellion in central India likewise has been met by state "violence that is completely out of tune with the norms of democratic India." The Armed Forces (Special Powers) Act of 1958 has similarly attracted much criticism with the parallels between the colonial powers and this 1958 legislation raising uncomfortable worries.

Common to most critical discussions on Indian politics though is the relationship between social and economic inequality and democratic practices and ideals. As was discussed in the previous chapters few countries in the world have to deal with such extreme inequalities and disparities in the economy and in caste, gender, sexuality and class. In a detailed discussion of these issues in their book, Dréze and Sen conclude that the political system's "achievement in removing inequality and injustice has nevertheless been quite limited." They ask in their book, published in 2014 before the general election, whether the country's democratic system is up to the task of remedying these hierarchies and answer, "mostly no." Later on they conclude, "What is really very special in India is the fact that the comparatively small group of the relatively privileged seem to have created a social universe of their own."

It is likely given the results of the 2014 election that the astounding inequalities and massive disparity between the privileged and the rest will increase. Although justly celebrated around the world, India's democratic system, argue Dréze and Sen, falls well short in terms of achievements. There is "strong incriminating evidence against taking Indian democracy to be adequately successful in consequential terms."

Yes, there are considerable achievements such as the democratic way of governance, multiparty elections, subordination of the military to the civilian government, independence of the judiciary and freedom of speech, but increasingly, there is a small growing focus on the weaknesses, failings and inadequacies of governance in India as practised and understood.

Secular India

The other great topic apart from the nature and characteristics of the political system, that has rumbled away ever since Independence but has now emerged from the shadows over the last decade or so, is secularism. Given that the country's constitution was seen as embodying three key ideas – socialism, democracy and secularism – it is not surprising that each of these is being re-examined in light of the Modi victory. For many people and commentators, it is this issue of secularism that has aroused the fiercest debates and worries with the victory of the BJP. Understandings of 'secularism' seem to vary. For some it is the separation of the state from religion; for others it is the equidistance that the state maintains between the different religions. In the case of the Congress Party especially in the struggle for independence, the legitimating ideology had always been seen as secular nationalism. Indeed one of Nehru's claims to historical greatness has traditionally been seen against all the odds as his commitment to secularism. His vision for the new India was enthusiastically endorsed by all, cutting across caste, geographical and religious divisions.

Lauded as a 'world statesman' largely because of what he suffered due to the struggle for independence and for being the country's first freely elected prime minister, Nehru's reputation today is more ambivalent, especially by those of a Hindutva persuasion.

The recent trend towards more polarised 'religious identities' together with the ever-simmering Kashmir situation has resulted in more critical appraisals of Nehru's secular settlement. Perry Anderson, for example, noted in his recent 2013 book *The Indian Ideology* that: "Congress failed to avert Partition because it could never bring itself honestly to confront its composition as an overwhelming Hindu party." It might have advocated a secular programme for all in the contest with the Raj, but in the years after Independence this was shown to be a lot more ambiguous. As Anderson puts it, "If the state was not truly secular... nor was it overtly confessional." It together with the Congress Party made much of its secular ideals but "both in composition and practice (Congress) is based squarely on the Hindu community... (party and state) both rested sociologically speaking, on Hindu caste society. The continued dominance of upper castes in public institutions – administration, police, courts, universities, media – belongs to the same matrix."

Maybe this underpinning of Hinduism to India from the beginning of its independence was and is of little significance. After all as some have argued, Hinduism is predominantly an extremely tolerant, peaceful collection of deities, beliefs and rituals that easily accommodates others, with or without faith. This might have been and maybe is still true today for some. However, this is not the brand of Hinduism espoused by the BJP. With their vision of Hindutva, they uphold secularism. How is this done? Because, "India is secular because it is Hindu."

It is the fear of increased communal violence that worries many people, inside and outside of India. As mentioned earlier, communalism is not a recent concern. It has rumbled away just below the surface since Independence, flaring up at different times in different circumstances. After all, and as was noted earlier, the Dalit and outstanding 'forgotten' activist at the time of the struggle for Indian independence, BR Ambedkar, converted to Buddhism in 1956 as a sign of his exasperation at the caste inequality and religious intolerance of Hinduism. These fears seem to have increased in recent decades and have proved stronger than Nehru's secularism, Gandhi's pacifism and Ambedkar's egalitarianism.

When tracing this rising tide of muscular Hinduism, it is worth noting that it was the Emergency of 1975 declared by Indira Gandhi that not only undermined the base of the Congress in the countryside (wealthy farmers leading the rebellion against the Emergency) but also breathed life into the BJP. This key episode still hotly debated today was declared by Indira Gandhi over a 21-month period between 1975–1977. Initially a very popular Prime Minister through her 'green revolution', her support for the creation of Bangladesh from East Pakistan and the military defeat of Pakistan, Indira Gandhi declared a state of emergency when she was convicted of political corruption by the High Court in 1975. An ensuing 'reign of terror' began with civil liberties suspended, the media censored, and the majority of the opposition and thousands of others imprisoned without trial. In March 1977 with the ending of the Emergency, new elections were called. Gandhi lost but was returned in fresh elections in 1980. She was assassinated in 1984 as a result of troops regaining by force the Golden Temple in Amritsar, the Holy Temple of the Sikhs.

Ironically one of the beneficiaries of the post Emergency situation was the BJP. As Anderson notes, the growing success of the BJP from around the 1980s onwards was that "they had the ability to articulate openly what had always been latent in the national movement, but neither candidly acknowledged, or consistently repudiated." Nehru was able to mask this "latent Hinduism" for the first decades of Independence through personal charisma and through a preference and focus on economic development rather than religion. He also had this mantle of legitimacy through his ties and links to Gandhi's religiosity which had been useful in the struggle against the British but were of little interest to Nehru in the New India. The Congress Party in the post-independent decades was the unchallenged party of the unchallenged ruling elite. Sixty years later things are very different.

In trying to situate secularism today and the Modi electoral landslide in 2014, Radhika Desai's writings have been useful in raising avenues which are not often explored in the popular press. The rise of the BJP and its associated groupings and organisations, she argues, need to be situated within a wider context. There are a variety of interrelated processes at work, namely the gradual shift in favour of an increasingly market-driven economy (slow at first and then turbo-charged from the 1990s onwards), the rise of regional parties from the 1980s onwards, and finally, the decline of the Congress Party. These changes, she argues, were working their way through the political system "like a slow earthquake". The first instance of BJP electoral success – a coalition government in 1998 under Vajpayee – witnessed, as Radhika Desai describes it, an "increasing 'saffronisation' of the state." The narrow, authoritarian and intolerant version of Hinduism that was encapsulated by Hindutva was increasingly embedded within the country's cultural, educational and civic society institutions. The five nuclear tests carried out by the government in 1998 against an anti-Pakistan backdrop together with the tension in Kashmir (the Kargil episode of 1999) increased political anxieties and further embellished the claims of Hindutva. The BJP and its brand of authoritarian Hindu nationalism, as Desai describes it, had managed to break out of its traditional Hindu bases in the northern states, its Gangetic heartland or 'cow belt'. Ironically, the BJP and subsequent regional political parties have been greatly helped in this political breakthrough through the desertion of the middle-caste supporters of Congress. These 'link-men' who traditionally delivered the rural vote tended to be propertied and saw the Congress' emphasis (rhetorically, at least) on the lower castes and the poor as too narrow for their economic and political aspirations. Their own economic and political situation was changing in the 1980s and 1990s with a focus that included investments in urban and industrial sectors. The growing importance of regional political parties provided a more sympathetic and possibly lucrative home. The 1984 general election won convincingly by Rajiv Gandhi on a wave of popular sympathy for his assassinated mother was as Desai put it, "a last hurrah of single party majority government." That was until 2014.

If a wider historical lens is used to examine the political and economic developments in India over the last decade or so, perhaps the emergence of the BJP is not that surprising. As Dréze and Sen document in painstaking detail, the sums of money provided for health, education, training and other services are pitiful when compared to other countries at a comparable stage of development. Redistribution of resources is urgently and massively required. In fact, their entire book *An Uncertain Glory: India and its Contradictions* is a powerful indictment of the Indian political order, the increasingly criminal nature of its political class, its priorities, its character and its democratic record. It is also a sustained and savage criticism of the numerous and triumphalist commentary around the current India growth rates and economic prowess. By contrast, their overwhelming focus on the need for redistribution and the ability of the poor to play a part in the new India – the 'capabilities' approach to development – places egalitarian agendas at the centre of their concerns.

But, but, but… Big questions remain – How are these vitally needed changes going to take place? How can you equate healthy economic growth rates with such widespread levels of poverty? How can a significant improvement in 'distributive outcomes' happen? The recent government claims for success in poverty reduction are confidently dismissed both on empirical and conceptual grounds. Changing how you define poverty does not amount to changing the circumstances of the poor. As Dréze and Sen remind us, "There has been extraordinary tolerance of inequalities, stratification and caste divisions – accepted as allegedly parts of the social order." So, yes – there must be a greater transparency in the State and regional institutions, as advocated by Dréze and Sen. Yes, there must be a greater participation by the poor themselves in decision-making channels and institutions, and it would help enormously if there was a public climate and discussion that was supportive of challenging social and economic inequalities. And yes, there must be a more vigorous prosecution of the guilty. The big answers to the big questions though, is as Vivek Chibber notes in a review of the book, lies in the political and economic contexts within which institutions are embedded. Reforms are likely to be curtailed or neutered because of structural characteristics rather than short fallings of individuals or weaknesses in the broader culture. At the end of the day, it is a question of power whether of a political, patriarchal or economic nature. As Chibber argues, "only a prior shift in power relations on the ground – that is, a greater capacity of ordinary citizens to exercise real power over the state, as a countervailing force against the power that flows from money or public office." Demands for greater accountability in public institutions will fail unless accompanied and supported by the organisational strength of working people. Reforms in the rural areas are meant well when addressing poverty in the countryside but unless the influence and power of the agrarian elites is confronted, many of the reforms will remain ineffectual.

A similar narrative is detectable in the urban centres. A rising clamour is heard almost daily, calling for reform of the country's trade unions. The general strike throughout India in September 2015 which brought millions of workers on to the streets was ignored outside the country but illustrated the anger and deep sense of injustice felt by many, including the BJP-affiliated trade unions. Websites such as *sanhati.com* detail the implications and results of these changes within particular states as well as on a national level. Increased workplace health and safety risks, regular flare-ups, reduced collective bargaining opportunities and increased use of temporary contracts are only some of the measures flowing from the Modi government's 'reforms' of industrial relations. As was suggested in a previous chapter, it is unlikely that these and similarly related economic 'reforms' will cease in the years ahead. The issue of redistribution and economic reforms, which Dréze and Sen's analysis focuses upon, is further complicated by the increasing fracturing of the political community. Despite its wonderful, uplifting, and unlikely story of 'being the world's largest democracy', the recent election demonstrated political voting patterns and complexities which are unlikely to smooth or improve in the future – all sorts of regional political groups doing all sort of deals, divided by caste, class, religion and geography. 'Redistribution', however a laudable goal of policy and economic reform, seems further away today than in earlier times.

As mentioned in the previous chapter, the emergence of neoliberalism as the dominant economic framework over the last three decades has resulted in a shift in the prevailing 'common sense'. Originally emerging from the English-speaking, Anglo-American economies as a response to the post-war downturn, neoliberalism today reigns dominant in most regions of the globe. The BRIC economies – Brazil, Russia, India and China – are seen by some as providing a challenge to the neoliberal dominance (especially with the promotion of their Development Bank), but I think this might be a little optimistic. Their criticisms of the International Monetary Fund (IMF) and of the World Bank are timely and shared by many but are unlikely to challenge the new common sense of gross economic inequality, consumerism and economic growth, at any cost.

Social democratic or welfare administrations attempting to negotiate a 'third way' alternative to neoliberal orthodoxy have failed and, instead, resulted in the return of right-wing parties. By the turn of the century, right-wing governments were back in charge in, for example, France, Austria, Spain, Italy and in India. The political "moving rightwards show" over the last decade or so has freed up political space further to the 'new' (right-wing) mainstream. In Europe, a number of politically ugly, racist and nationalist new parties have emerged into the 'respectable' normal, as in Poland, Austria, Greece, France and Italy.

And of course when it comes to democracy, there is little for India to learn or take from its old colonial power. The stunted and partial nature of the democratic practices and institutions in Britain's 'constitutional monarchy' has long been recognised. A deeply class-riven society, presided over by a deeply conservative Conservative Party and embedded aristocracy meanders into a greater irrelevancy in the early decades of the 21st century. In the case of India, however, a Nehruvian secularism expected a degree of 'generosity' by the majority towards the minorities. The growing intolerance and rise of ultra-nationalist Hindutva sentiments (and brutalities) increasingly exposes the fragility of this historic generosity. The current stresses and strains on democracy within the country are, concludes Pankaj Mishra, "its most sinister phase since independence." For all those inside and outside India who cherish the peoples, histories and cultures of this great country, these are indeed worrying times.

Chapter 10

Of Tigers and Elephants

The Sri Lanka nightmare

When thinking about it, I seem to have spent a lot of my time down in South India. Geographically, it's that part of the country that is triangle shaped. South India, sometimes referred to as Peninsular India, encompasses states such as Andhra Pradesh, Karnataka, Kerala, Tamil Nadu and the new kid on the block, Telangana. Kerala aside, it's not the most favoured of destinations for oversea visitors which is a bit of a surprise – it seems to offer a bit of everything. As mentioned in earlier chapters, I have spent very pleasant stays in some of the bigger cities in the region such as Madras, Bangalore, Cochin, Pondicherry and Madurai and ogled at some of the stone carvings, ornate Dravidian-style Hindu temples with their monumental towers and munched many a spicy coconut rice dish off fresh banana leaves. It was my visit to Sri Lanka in 2017 that sparked my thoughts and recollections about my travels in southern India. I didn't go to India that year. Instead I went for the first time to Sri Lanka and spent an enjoyable month wondering around the island. My route was probably very similar to that taken by most tourists – down south from Colombo (the capital), along the west coast on the train to Galle, east along the southern coast and then inland, going north up to Kandy. I based myself at Dambulla for about a week before returning to Colombo via Anuradhapura. I didn't make it to the Vanni, the northern region or to its capital, Jaffna: I ran out of time. In fact, I didn't even manage to get to visit the famous ancient Banyan tree in Anuradhapura. Commonly referred to as a Bodhi or the Bo tree or to give it its formal name, Jaya Sri Maha Bodhi, this particular tree is seen as one of the most sacred sites of the Buddhists in the country and is revered by Buddhists throughout the world. It is said to be the world's oldest documented tree. Received wisdom states that this tree originated from the right branch of the Banyan tree under which Buddha attained enlightenment in North India. Brought to Sri Lanka in 288 BCE, the Bodhi tree was the most important symbol of royal political power until the arrival of the Sacred Tooth Relic from Buddha in the fourth century and now housed – under heavy guard – in the temple at Kandy. The tree's significance became greatly enhanced after the destruction of the original Banyan tree at Buddhagaya in North India. It is said that many if not most of the Banyan trees growing throughout Southeast Asia originate from this Sri Lankan tree. I much regret not getting to visit, or at least touching or hugging, the allegedly 2,239-year-old tree. My excuse was that there were other more recent things that I was thinking about.

After the defeat of the Tamil Tigers in May 2009 in a bitter and bloody civil war that had lasted some three to four decades everyone was naturally trying to persuade me and other tourists that 'things were returning to normal'. The destructive tsunami of December 2004 had passed but was not forgotten. Everyone had these amazing heroic stories of exactly where they were, what they had done and how (with no government support) they were slowly putting their lives back together again since that fateful December. And the victorious but scary, vicious, dictatorial President Mahinda Rajapaksa had gone – surprisingly defeated in the 2015 general election by Maithripala Sirisena. Things have for many people got better, but I couldn't help feeling a little apprehensive. Communal disputes (and worse) promoted by militant, nationalist Buddhist monks and their followers against, in the main, Muslim communities continue. Little progress has been made over the widespread allegations of war crimes perpetrated, primarily, by government troops especially in the last months of the civil war. Press censorship has been lifted but the issue of the numerous disappeared journalists of the last decade has yet to be addressed. The great aristocratic families that have dominated Sri Lankan politics and the economy since Independence from the British in 1948 continue their dominance. Above all though, it is the humiliation and 'occupation' of the Tamils in the north of the country that is most worrying. The political and cultural marginalisation of the Tamils in the north by zealous forces of the military and police are to ensure once and for all that the Tamil problem will be no more. Buddhist statues, Sinhalese scripts instead of Tamil, road checks, a discriminatory education system, some 85,000 soldiers and a collapsed economy characterise the Hindu north. Sinhalese are being encouraged to move north so as to dilute the Tamil influence. Yes – the iconic A9 road into the north is open once again as are the train services from Jaffna to Colombo and tourist developments are afoot. However, banking everything on the humiliation and occupation of the Tamil north is not a proven way forward in Sri Lanka or elsewhere. It is, in fact, the opposite.

For me as for many around the world, the recent civil war was a continuing concern over the decades. As a recent visitor to the country it remained an overwhelming presence – something that was always there. Nearly everywhere that I went throughout the island had witnessed or knew intimate details of some atrocity or episode of the civil war. It was difficult to disconnect or disassociate my travels with this traumatising and engulfing episode. Things *are* improving but many issues will remain, perhaps understandably, a silent or blanked-out subject for most Sri Lankans in the decades ahead. As mentioned in the opening to this chapter, it was not perhaps surprising then that I often found myself reflecting back while in Sri Lanka on my times down Tamil southern India. Although only a few miles north, how had the people of southern India coped and managed with this onslaught just across the water from themselves? There are accounts of bungled Indian initiatives such as The Indian Peace

Keeping Force at the end of the 1980s. Prior to 2009, small pieces about the war appeared in the India media, but overall, there was a war-weary edge to the reports. However, the full story of the efforts and activities of India's Tamil people in support of the Tigers' (Liberation Tigers of Tamil Eelam) struggle for an independent Tamil state in Sri Lanka remains largely unexplored and undocumented.

An overbusy military

The other thing that kept occurring to me on the trip to Sri Lanka was the prominence of military conflict and struggle since independence in both countries. Although different in origins, timing and causes, both countries have suffered considerably in outbreaks of violence involving state forces. Given the abrupt and panicked departure of the British from this part of the world coupled with their system of 'governance' (to be generous), it is perhaps surprising that there has not been greater strife. In the case of Sri Lanka, the Tamil Tigers conflict is the more obvious example and in general, I think it is fair to argue, India is not seen as a country of conflict. Instead it is rarely mentioned. In recent years it has not been uncommon at this or that international forum or summit for India to be portrayed as the 'light on the horizon' or 'beacon of hope'. After a few years when the economy seemed to be slowing, the country today is seen as having recovered its mojo; it's back on track. Impressive growth figures continue to rise while those of China move in the opposite direction. Western economies meanwhile continue to limp along showing very little progress since the financial crash of 2009. Admittedly, there haven't been too many good news stories in the last decade. In fact the world seems a decidedly more dangerous place today than only a couple of years ago. Risks of confrontations and worse, political bullying and the growing respectability of a crude, gangster form of nationalism seem to be the new political norm. Continuing waves of political crisis dominate our morning newspaper headlines. India though doesn't figure significantly in these new troubled narratives. In the main it bobs along below the horizon, quietly getting on with becoming an economic superpower. Its Republic Day parades in Delhi continue to be festivals of pride, cheerfulness and misplaced assumptions of military prowess and significance. Important foreign dignitaries dutifully attend hoping to attract some of the magical economic glitter. Global stereotypes are polished and replicated once again on our television channels. Instead of a focus on developments within the country, the focus tends to be on the country's role internationally. Lack of 'hard power' is a favourite description of the country's showing on the international stage.

Kashmir does occasionally feature in international news reports but for all the wrong reasons: the region is one of the world's most dangerous military hotspots. Two nuclear armed nations – India and Pakistan – confront each other. Despite a United Nations 1957 resolution stipulating that a plebiscite conducted by the UN should determine the future of the state, India has blocked any such initiative knowing which way the Muslim majority would vote. Instead we have around 700,000 military and paramilitary Indian personnel based in the Kashmiri region – one soldier for every 17 civilians. A Special Powers Act allows these military forces to act with almost total impunity, a law which the UN states has "no place in a democracy". Thousands of unmarked graves have been discovered with 'disappearances' and 'encounter deaths' a common feature for most of Kashmir's history since Independence. Most calculations of militants trained in Pakistan tend to put the number under 500. The historical absence and invisibility of Kashmir brutalities in the international media is matched by the unanimously uncritical and nationalistic tone of India's press. Worse – there seems to be an indifference in the media towards struggles to win self-determination by Kashmiris. Yet, it is, reports Pankaj

Mishra in *The Guardian*, "the biggest, bloodiest and also the most obscure military occupation in the world." Since 1989 more than 80,000 people have been killed in an anti-India insurgency, supported by Pakistan. "Today Kashmir is the most densely militarised zone in the world," bravely reported Arundhati Roy. The history of Kashmir is complex, but worryingly, there are also other 'invisible' examples in India which provide serious concerns and worries. Separatist movements in the north-east of the country occasionally flare up. The struggle in Assam has been rumbling away for two to three decades and has claimed some 10,000 lives. The Naga people together with the claims for an independent Tripura are continuing. Outside visits to these parts of India are difficult and sometimes prohibited. However, "the single biggest internal security ever faced by our country," said Prime Minister Manmohan Singh a few years ago, was not in Kashmir or the north-east but in the state of Chhattisgarh. Located with the centre east of the country, the heavily wooded state with its numerous temples is home to the four-decade Naxalite or Maoist rebellion. In 2013 the insurgents wiped out almost the entire leadership on the state-governing Congress Party. Supposedly based and supported by the Adivasis (indigenous Tribal Indians) and poor farmers, the Maoists seek a socialist-communist government through the overthrow of the Indian state. According to the Global Research website, the insurgency has spread to encompass 20 states. The seven most affected states are Chhattisgarh, Jharkhand, West Bengal, Maharashtra, Orissa, Bihar and Andhra Pradesh. About 10,000 people have been killed in the expanding civil war since the 1980s. Estimates of the insurgent numbers are about 20,000 fighters with some 50,000 supporters. These forces are matched by some 81,000 paramilitary troops. Central to the grievances of the farmers and Adivasis is the looting in these states of the land and mineral resources. The state of Jharkhand in eastern India with its weak, corrupt government is the main focus of the struggles. Extraction of coal and iron and steel by large national companies has decimated the forests – the livelihood of the Adivasis. Making up just over a quarter of Jharkhand's population, the mining licenses granted to the private sector companies amount to the "genocide of the Adivasis," argued the editor of a newspaper dedicated to the support of the anti-mining coalition. Saranda Forest where 19 mining licenses have already been granted (fraudulently apparently) has been described by the Indian journalist as "to eastern India what the Amazon rainforests are to the world." Resistance to these encroachments has resulted in Jharkhand being today a 'fully militarised zone' with over a hundred military bases.

Today there appears a certain weariness in the media reports to the situation of the Adivasis, the exploitative mining companies and the corrupt state governments. Short reports of the latest atrocity appear in the press but without the urgency and strategic analysis required of the situation. Prime Minister Modi meanwhile has pledged electricity to the 400 million Indians in the next five years. In the way are environmental protests, court battles and the rights of the Adivasis people.

Things are different in Southeast Asia. Yes, there are formidable battles and fights that require solutions, not least to alleviate the huge suffering of those caught in the middle. And yes, the obstacles and problems confronting the countries when finally winning their independence from the British were massive and could have been overwhelming. The tools and means available to resolve these huge problems were minimal. Despite these disadvantages, enormous progress has been achieved. But it is unlikely to be a journey or solutions similar to those in the West, irrespective of the views and assumptions of Western journalists. The solutions are likely to be homemade solutions, different to those already made and dissimilar to other parts of the world. They are, however, solutions.

Maybe Gurcharan Das has it right when in his much-acclaimed book *India Unbound: From Independence to the Global Information Age* he writes that: "India will never be a tiger. It is an elephant that has begun to lumber and move ahead." He goes on to suggest – and this is in 2002 – that the possibly "wise elephant" will have a more stable, peaceful and negotiated transition into the future and is more likely to preserve its way of life and its civilisation of diversity, tolerance and spirituality against the onslaught of the global culture. This could be true. Das is surely right too when he notes in 2007 that, "India is now poised at a great moment in its history." Today, however, things are more difficult, more contradictory, more communally violent. Aside from the longstanding conflicts of the Adivasi people, Kashmir and secessionist movements, there is the rise of a violent Hindutva – a conservative Hindu Right. Of course, the aggression and violence associated with Hindutva is very different to that accompanying the military conflicts mentioned earlier. It is rather an everyday sort of violence that uses intimidation and vilification in the streets, in intellectual life, in the arts and culture, in the courts, in the media and in the villages as its primary weapon. As mentioned in the previous chapter, victims of attacks and lynchings are usually Muslims, minorities or Dalit. Whipping up religious passions through condemnation of beef eaters and cow slaughter is an increasing occurrence. Of diminished significance is a view and practice of Hinduism as a pluralist, diverse and tolerant religion. Cultural varieties of Hinduism evident in most regions in the country are being squeezed through the promotion of a monolithic version of Hindu nationalism. Appropriating national symbols such as the national flag and merging them with Hinduism aggressively promotes the nation with the religion. Local Hindu gods are replaced by those promoted by the BJP, such as Ram and Vamana.

And yet despite these latest worries and those of a historically more militarised nature India can also be seen as an uplifting story. India's version of democracy remains strong – an incredible achievement. Pride in these achievements and in the country's economic strength is strong, and millions of people believe their lives are more comfortable than their parents'. Development has never been a linear or uniform process. Instead, from around the world, it is a puzzling, contradictory and bewildering process with the extent and depth of suffering experienced by the many undocumented and ignored.

Historically, the development of India could have taken many different directions. It could have been a much bigger unified country incorporating a number of now independent countries. It could have ended up as a much smaller country than today. It could also have resulted in a collection of small independent kingdoms or dependencies. As it turned out, things today are not too bad. It's not surprising though that there is this intense interest and literature within India on its past. It's a too tortured, recent and disputed historical record, where those records exist. Likewise, the growing optimism of today's India is encouraging some tentative discussion about the future. The agenda or shopping list on what should happen next is a familiar one. For example, as the January 2017 *Seminar* journal puts it, if India is to progress to becoming a "proper middle-income economy", it must "learn some new tricks, adopt new technologies and organise itself differently from the past." Despite the mega recent growth rates, when compared to China in 2005 (no misprint!), India lags far behind on a variety of societal measures – such as literacy levels, life expectancy rates, investment rates and workforce rates in manufacturing when compared to agriculture. Above all the dysfunctional education system and inadequate health provision provides a drag on future progress. The glowing growth rate (GDP) figures that currently preface any international comment on India may provide a warm feeling of pride, but in fact mask the problems facing the country in the decades ahead.

Despite India's emergence recently as a global economic

player of some clout as well as the ongoing conflicts around the country, we get little coverage in the West of developments unfolding in the country and subcontinent. Passing coverage was made of the 70th anniversary of Partition on the 14th August 2017 but things moved on quite quickly. Local intercommunity and interfaith celebrations happened around the country but got little national coverage. A number of galleries and museums staged special displays and there were a number of radio programmes examining Partition – especially the BBC World Service programme. There were some very moving stories of personal experiences from those involved and who now live in Britain. As Pankaj Mishra put it, "hands were dutifully wrung about the imperialist skulduggery and savage ethnic cleansing that founded the nation states of India and Pakistan, defined their self-images and condemned them to permanent internal and external conflict." Overall then, the monumental events and humanitarian crises that defined one of the seminal episodes of the last century quickly came and went. And, it was so recent.

There were a couple other issues, however, that brought me up short – memories of my last visit wandering around this or that city returned. First, brief reports in the international press towards the end of 2016 mentioned the financial shockwaves throughout India – especially in the countryside – resulting from the surprising and unforeseen government's announcement on the 8th November 2016. A television announcement by the Prime Minister declared that all 500 and 1,000 rupee notes (worth around £6 and £12 respectively) were to be illegal tender. From the 9th November, banks and cash machines were closed for two days; a new 2,000 rupee note was introduced on the 10th November and people could exchange their old currency until the end of December. The reason behind the ensuing chaos, panic, bankruptcies, lengthening queues and sheer bewilderment was apparently the government's desire to rid the country of so-called 'black money' – illegal or unaccounted monies. While most countries East and West are struggling with systemic activities by the wealthy and powerful of hidden wealth and tax evasion, few of these countries locate the problem residing in the cash circulating within the economy. Usually the problem is located within offshore accounts and hidden within the property or gold markets. India does have a problem – only 1–2% of people pay direct income tax, but I doubt the 'demonetisation' (as it is called) measures will seriously engage with these structural problems.

The other issue that caught my attention was the heavy monsoon flooding in August–September 2017 across India, Bangladesh and Nepal that resulted in at least 1,200 deaths and devastated the lives of some 40 million people. The worse areas affected seemed to be the north along the Himalayan foothills along the India-Nepal border and in the north-east of the region. However, other reports of streets in Bombay being turned into rivers, buildings collapsing, hospitals being closed, plastic garbage blocking drains and the airport disrupted showed that eastern parts of the country too were suffering. Getting news of the devastations in Southeast Asia was difficult as the media in the West was almost exclusively focussed on the hurricanes and tropical storms passing through the islands and mainland of south-east USA. Graphic images and detailed stories, however, were available online of the humanitarian crisis resulting from, says the Red Cross in India, the fourth significant flood this year.

When something as devastating, widespread and traumatic as the monsoon flooding happens, it is inevitable not to wonder how people and families that befriended you, that coffee bar on the corner or those street sellers that we met most days, survived the waters. No reports are of course that detailed or intimate, but still, you wonder and worry.

That background noise

As I mentioned in the opening chapter to this book, one of the striking features that struck me when talking with many of the other overseas visitors to India was their knowledge and intimacy with different parts of this vast country. For these 'frequent returners' as I labelled them, there was something about the country that kept bringing them back. They could have gone elsewhere, such as Sri Lanka or Peru or South Africa. Instead they kept returning to India and, over time, had acquired an enviable working knowledge and know-how about the country and made many lifelong friends. Through a number of discussions with a small group of these travellers, I reported on their experiences and 'tourist histories' briefly in Chapter 2 and subsequent chapters. Their favourite journeys and destinations were different, and the issues and topics that most interested them varied. I guess that I too am on my way towards reaching the exalted status as 'frequent traveller'. I have now visited South Asia some six times in recent years. There is even a small, tiny number of areas and experiences that I feel a certain degree of familiarity with when returning to them – such as eating places, parts of cities, particular train journeys and even some small areas of the Western Ghats. There are parts of the country, however, that I have on my to-visit-next-time list, but for one reason or another never make it. Being on this list means that I keep checking on how things are going while I am back home. Kashmir remains top of the list with me and also many other tourists.

But as pointed out in the opening chapter, it wasn't simply places and visits that primarily interested me on trips to India. These were important as I have sought to outline in various chapters. It was, however, as I put it the first chapter, the "contextual features", "the background noise" of everyday life and the seeming presence and weight of history everywhere that strongly interested me and influenced my choice of destinations, reading and discussions with local people. These concerns and interests in turn led to a certain reflexivity on my behalf and to a more considered interest in the nature and experience of 'being a tourist'. I'm not too sure that I got anywhere with these 'considerations' apart from appreciating how strong a grip neoliberal thinking has colonised the field with and how big a business is the global tourist industry – and increasingly dominated by a small number of Western multinational companies. This reflexivity to my own experiences as a tourist in India was situated against the ongoing debate among Indian scholars about how to understand and situate developments in India. I can't pretend that I was able to follow all the extensive intricacies and conceptualisations in these discussions about post-colonial analysis and, in particular, subaltern studies. I was quite excited, however, when realising that I was ploughing through some of these difficult issues and texts as a result of being a tourist in India. Without 'being a tourist', in other words, I would not be seeking out or trying to make sense of this or that. Including oneself as an object of one's observation – reflexivity – has resulted in the adoption of a more personal perspective in the text as well as an examination of those assumptions and categories that I have used in my travels. I am after all and as mentioned in earlier chapters a white, rich, English-speaking and privileged male which shapes and characterises my understandings and descriptions of the world and what I experienced in India. Or as the travel writer Colin Thubron put it, "you can't escape your own sensibilities." More recent interpretative and critical themes in tourist writing or 'tourismscapes' are attempts to minimise these limitations. Disappointment and frustration with dominant thinking and analysis within scholarly touristic studies has led to some heavy philosophical debates on realism and ontology which are beyond me. I note though that some commentators call for the dismissal of questions such as 'what is a tourist' and 'what does tourism mean'? They are it is suggested examples of 'bean counting' – they are probably correct. At the moment, however, more practical and immediate considerations seem to be dominating the headlines and discussions. Countries especially those in Europe are beginning to limit the numbers of tourists visiting particular sites. Unable to cope with the numbers and demands of the visitors, restrictions are planned. Venice bans huge cruise ships and the picturesque Cinque Terre fishing ports in north-west Italy are introducing a tourist ticket system to control and reduce the number of visitors. "For us it is a question of survival," reported a local inhabitant. 'Broadening your mind' in an age of mass tourism risks interactions with those people and places losing both intimacy and depth. Maybe it has always been the case but all that is left from our encounter is the commercial exchange. As Tobias Jones put it, "Tourism has become equivalent to a one-night stand with each side grabbing what they want: the tourist gets a selfie in front of an iconic building and the locals empty visitors' pockets as thoroughly as possible." Unfortunately or fortunately, this is not a problem facing the tourist industry in India. Despite the promotions of "India Shining" or "Incredible India", overseas tourists are visiting South and Southeast Asia but not India. Vietnam – the size of Madhya Pradesh – has many more tourists than all of India; seven Asian cities have more visitors annually than all of India. China has annually about 60 million foreign tourists, just behind the US and France. India has around 6 million. Growth is good at about 4–6% but other Southeast competitors (Cambodia and Laos) are growing at 20–25%.

It's an interesting issue – why does India not attract more overseas visitors? At the end of the day though, it is not the most important question for us regular returners. Instead and as mentioned in the opening chapter, what is paramount for us is "trying to better understand and engage with this country that fascinates most of us and which we return to periodically". We bumble through with some things clearer and other things becoming more confused. But, at least, the regular returners won't be amongst that majority (59%) that think that the Empire was a good thing and probably won't be amongst those visiting recent films in the UK such as *Victoria and Abdul* or *Viceroy's House*. Instead they will look out for *Monsoon* or *The Lunchbox*, or if very lucky due to its poor distribution, *The Darjeeling Limited*. Despite Shashi Tharoor's new book *Inglorious Empire: What the British Did to India* damning Britain's imperial exploitation of India, nostalgia for the old Empire remains strong in the motherland. In light of the Brexit vote, there is talk of a new Empire 2.0 – rediscovered trading agreements amongst former colonies, especially white ones and those that share similar institutions and cultures. Racist delusions continue to deeply shape the past and also, it appears, the future. Yes, the regular returners will always remain 'tourists' but visitors whose visits not only provided discoveries and a deeper historical awareness to their stays but also to those of their own country.

By way of a conclusion it is perhaps worth calling upon an old favourite of mine. EP Thompson, a British historian, provides an apt summary about this interest in India which most of us 'regular returners' would share. He was writing a book about his father Edward Thompson's time with the Bengali poet Rabindranath Tagore. "India," he wrote some time ago, in the early decades of the twentieth century, "is not an important country, but perhaps the most important country for the future of the world. Here is a country that merits no one's condescension. All the convergent influences of the world run through this society: Hindu, Moslem, Christian, secular; Stalinist, liberal, Maoist, democratic socialist, Gandhian. There is not a thought that is being thought in the West or East which is not active in some Indian mind."

Heady stuff and written all those years ago.

BOOKS

O-BOOKS

SPIRITUALITY

O is a symbol of the world, of oneness and unity; this eye represents knowledge and insight. We publish titles on general spirituality and living a spiritual life. We aim to inform and help you on your own journey in this life.

If you have enjoyed this book, why not tell other readers by posting a review on your preferred book site? Recent bestsellers from O-Books are:

Heart of Tantric Sex
Diana Richardson
Revealing Eastern secrets of deep love and intimacy to Western couples.
Paperback: 978-1-90381-637-0 ebook: 978-1-84694-637-0

Crystal Prescriptions
The A-Z guide to over 1,200 symptoms and their healing crystals
Judy Hall
The first in the popular series of six books, this handy little guide is packed as tight as a pill-bottle with crystal remedies for ailments.
Paperback: 978-1-90504-740-6 ebook: 978-1-84694-629-5

Take Me To Truth
Undoing the Ego
Nouk Sanchez, Tomas Vieira
The best-selling step-by-step book on shedding the Ego, using the teachings of *A Course In Miracles*.
Paperback: 978-1-84694-050-7 ebook: 978-1-84694-654-7

The 7 Myths about Love...Actually!
The journey from your HEAD to the HEART of your SOUL
Mike George
Smashes all the myths about LOVE.
Paperback: 978-1-84694-288-4 ebook: 978-1-84694-682-0

The Holy Spirit's Interpretation of the New Testament
A course in Understanding and Acceptance
Regina Dawn Akers
Following on from the strength of *A Course In Miracles*, NTI teaches us how to experience the love and oneness of God.
Paperback: 978-1-84694-085-9 ebook: 978-1-78099-083-5

The Message of A Course In Miracles
A translation of the text in plain language
Elizabeth A. Cronkhite
A translation of *A Course in Miracles* into plain, everyday language for anyone seeking inner peace. The companion volume, *Practicing A Course In Miracles*, offers practical lessons and mentoring.
Paperback: 978-1-84694-319-5 ebook: 978-1-84694-642-4

Rising in Love
My Wild and Crazy Ride to Here and Now, with Amma, the
Hugging Saint
Ram Das Batchelder
Rising in Love conveys an author's extraordinary journey of
spiritual awakening with the Guru, Amma.
Paperback: 978-1-78279-687-9 ebook: 978-1-78279-686-2

Thinker's Guide to God
Peter Vardy
An introduction to key issues in the philosophy of religion.
Paperback: 978-1-90381-622-6

Your Simple Path
Find happiness in every step
Ian Tucker
A guide to helping us reconnect with what is really important in
our lives.
Paperback: 978-1-78279-349-6 ebook: 978-1-78279-348-9

365 Days of Wisdom
Daily Messages To Inspire You Through The Year
Dadi Janki
Daily messages which cool the mind, warm the heart and guide
you along your journey.
Paperback: 978-1-84694-863-3 ebook: 978-1-84694-864-0

Body of Wisdom
Women's Spiritual Power and How it Serves
Hilary Hart
Bringing together the dreams and experiences of women across
the world with today's most visionary spiritual teachers.
Paperback: 978-1-78099-696-7 ebook: 978-1-78099-695-0

Dying to Be Free

From Enforced Secrecy to Near Death to True Transformation

Hannah Robinson

After an unexpected accident and near-death experience, Hannah Robinson found herself radically transforming her life, while a remarkable new insight altered her relationship with her father, a practising Catholic priest.

Paperback: 978-1-78535-254-6 ebook: 978-1-78535-255-3

The Ecology of the Soul

A Manual of Peace, Power and Personal Growth for Real People in the Real World

Aidan Walker

Balance your own inner Ecology of the Soul to regain your natural state of peace, power and wellbeing.

Paperback: 978-1-78279-850-7 ebook: 978-1-78279-849-1

Not I, Not other than I

The Life and Teachings of Russel Williams

Steve Taylor, Russel Williams

The miraculous life and inspiring teachings of one of the World's greatest living Sages.

Paperback: 978-1-78279-729-6 ebook: 978-1-78279-728-9

On the Other Side of Love

A Woman's Unconventional Journey Towards Wisdom

Muriel Maufroy

When life has lost all meaning, what do you do?

Paperback: 978-1-78535-281-2 ebook: 978-1-78535-282-9

Practicing A Course In Miracles
A Translation of the Workbook in Plain Language and With
Mentoring Notes
Elizabeth A. Cronkhite
The practical second and third volumes of The Plain-Language
A Course In Miracles.
Paperback: 978-1-84694-403-1 ebook: 978-1-78099-072-9

Quantum Bliss
The Quantum Mechanics of Happiness, Abundance, and Health
George S. Mentz
Quantum Bliss is the breakthrough summary of success and
spirituality secrets that customers have been waiting for.
Paperback: 978-1-78535-203-4 ebook: 978-1-78535-204-1

The Upside Down Mountain
Mags MacKean
A must-read for anyone weary of chasing success and happiness
– one woman's inspirational journey swapping the uphill slog for
the downhill slope.
Paperback: 978-1-78535-171-6 ebook: 978-1-78535-172-3

Readers of ebooks can buy or view any of these bestsellers by
clicking on the live link in the title. Most titles are published
in paperback and as an ebook. Paperbacks are available in
traditional bookshops. Both print and ebook formats are
available online.

Find more titles and sign up to our readers' newsletter at
http://www.johnhuntpublishing.com/mind-body-spirit

Follow us on Facebook at https://www.facebook.com/OBooks/
and Twitter at https://twitter.com/obooks